Lecture Notes in Artificial Intel

Edited by J. G. Carbonell and J. Siekmann

Subseries of Lecture Notes in Computer Science

Bamshad Mobasher Olfa Nasraoui
Bing Liu Brij Masand

Advances in Web Mining and Web Usage Analysis

6th International Workshop
on Knowledge Discovery on the Web, WebKDD 2004
Seattle, WA, USA, August 22-25, 2004
Revised Selected Papers

 Springer

Series Editors

Jaime G. Carbonell, Carnegie Mellon University, Pittsburgh, PA, USA
Jörg Siekmann, University of Saarland, Saarbrücken, Germany

Authors

Bamshad Mobasher
DePaul University
School of Computer Science
243 S. Wabash Ave., Chicago, IL 60604, USA
E-mail: mobasher@cs.depaul.edu

Olfa Nasraoui
University of Louisville
Computer Science and Computer Engineering
Louisville, KY 40292
E-mail: olfa.nasraoui@louisville.edu

Bing Liu
University of Illinois at Chicago
851 South Morgan Street, Chicago, IL 60607-7053, USA
E-mail: liub@cs.uic.edu

Brij Masand
Data Miners Inc.
77 North Washington Street, Boston, MA 02114, USA
E-mail: brij@data-miners.com

Library of Congress Control Number: 2006934110

CR Subject Classification (1998): I.2, H.2.8, H.3-5, K.4, C.2

LNCS Sublibrary: SL 7 – Artificial Intelligence

ISSN	0302-9743
ISBN-10	3-540-47127-8 Springer Berlin Heidelberg New York
ISBN-13	978-3-540-47127-1 Springer Berlin Heidelberg New York

Springer is a part of Springer Science+Business Media

springer.com

© Springer-Verlag Berlin Heidelberg 2006

Typesetting: Camera-ready by author, data conversion by Scientific Publishing Services, Chennai, India
Printed on acid-free paper   SPIN: 11899402   06/3142   5 4 3 2 1 0

Preface

The Web is a live environment that manages and drives a wide spectrum of applications in which a user may interact with a company, a governmental authority, a non-governmental organization or other non-profit institution or other users. User preferences and expectations, together with usage patterns, form the basis for personalized, user-friendly and business-optimal services. Key Web business metrics enabled by proper data capture and processing are essential to run an effective business or service. Enabling technologies include data mining, scalable warehousing and preprocessing, sequence discovery, real time processing, document classification, user modeling and quality evaluation models for them. Recipient technologies required for user profiling and usage patterns include recommendation systems, Web analytics applications, and application servers, coupled with content management systems and fraud detectors.

Furthermore, the inherent and increasing heterogeneity of the Web has required Web-based applications to more effectively integrate a variety of types of data across multiple channels and from different sources. The development and application of Web mining techniques in the context of Web content, Web usage, and Web structure data has already resulted in dramatic improvements in a variety of Web applications, from search engines, Web agents, and content management systems, to Web analytics and personalization services. A focus on techniques and architectures for more effective integration and mining of content, usage, and structure data from different sources is likely to lead to the next generation of more useful and more intelligent applications.

This volume is comprised of revised and extended chapters based on WebKDD 2004, the sixth of a successful series of workshops on Knowledge Discovery on the Web. The WebKDD 2004 workshop was held in conjunction with the 10th ACM SIGKDD International Conference on Knowledge Discovery and Data Mining (KDD 2004), August 22-25, 2004, in Seattle, Washington. As in the five preceding years, the WebKDD 2004 workshop continued its tradition of serving as a bridge between academia and industry by bringing together practitioners and researchers from both areas in order to foster the exchange of ideas and the dissemination of emerging solutions for intelligent Web-based applications using Web usage, structure and content mining. In addition to participants from academia, the workshop attracted many participants from industry including Microsoft, Amazon, AT&T, Google, SAS, DaimlerChrysler, Accenture, buy.com, shopping.com, and others.

WebKDD 2004 included a joint session (comprised of three papers) with a new workshop, the KDD Workshop on Mining for and from the Semantic Web (MSW04). The *Semantic Web Mining* portion of this book includes selected papers from both workshops.

About This Volume

Together the chapters span four complementary areas related to Web mining:

1. Web Usage Analysis and User Modeling
2. Web Personalization and Recommender Systems
3. Search Personalization
4. Semantic Web Mining

Web Usage Analysis and User Modeling. The first two chapters deal with Web Usage Analysis and User Modeling. In "Mining Temporally Changing Web Usage Graphs", Desikan and Srivastava address the limited "data-centric" point of view of most previous Web mining research by examining another dimension of Web mining, namely the temporal dimension. They highlight the significance of studying the evolving nature of Web graphs, and classify the approach to such problems at three levels of analysis: single node, sub-graphs and whole graphs. They provide a framework to approach problems in this kind of analysis and identify interesting problems at each level. In "Improving the Web Usage Analysis Process: A UML Model of the ETL Process", Maier addresses the laborious and time-consuming task of populating a data warehouse, to be used for sophisticated analysis of the Web channel in a multi-channel environment of an organization. To this end, a logical object-oriented relational data storage model is proposed, which simplifies modeling the ETL process and supports direct deployment within a WUSAN (Web USage ANalyis) system.

Web Personalization and Recommender Systems. Three chapters focus on Web Personalization and Recommender Systems. In "Mission-Based Navigational Behavior Modeling for Web Recommender Systems", Zaiane, Li, and Hayward advocate the use of additional information channels such as the content of visited pages and the connectivity between Web pages, as an alternative to using only one information channel, namely the Web access history. They propose the concept of "missions", which are identified by different channels, to help in better modeling users concurrent information needs. The combination of three channels is shown to improve the quality of the recommendations. In "Complete this Puzzle: A Connectionist Approach to Accurate Web Recommendations based on a Committee of Predictors", Nasraoui and Pavuluri present a Context Ultra-Sensitive Approach to personalization based on two-step Recommender systems (CUSA-2-step-Rec). The approach relies on a committee of profile-specific neural networks. Similar to the task of completing the missing pieces of a puzzle, each neural network is trained to predict the missing URLs of several complete ground-truth sessions from a given profile. The approach outperforms nearest profile and K-Nearest Neighbors based collaborative filtering. In "Collaborative Quality Filtering: Establishing Consensus or Recovering Ground Truth?", Traupman and Wilensky present an algorithm based on factor analysis for performing Collaborative Quality Filtering (CQF). Unlike previous approaches to CQF, which estimate the consensus opinion of a group of reviewers, their algorithm uses a generative model of the review process to estimate the latent intrinsic quality of the items under review. The results of their tests suggest that asymptotic consensus, which purports to model peer review, is in fact not recovering the ground truth quality of reviewed items.

Search Personalization. Two chapters deal with Search Engine Personalization. In "Spying Out Accurate User Preferences for Search Engine Adaptation", Deng et al. propose a learning technique called "Spy Naive Bayes" (SpyNB) to identify the user preference pairs generated from clickthrough data. They then employ a ranking SVM algorithm to build a metasearch engine optimizer. Their empirical results on a metasearch engine prototype, comprising MSNSearch, Wisenut and Overture, show that, compared with no learning, SpyNB can significantly improve the average ranks of users' clicks. In "Using Hyperlink Features to Personalize Web Search", Aktas, Nacar, and Menczer introduce a methodology for personalizing PageRank vectors based on hyperlink features such as anchor terms or URL tokens. Users specify interest profiles as binary feature vectors where a feature corresponds to a DNS tree node. Then, given a profile vector, a weighted PageRank can be computed, assigning a weight to each URL based on the match between the URL and the profile features. Preliminary results show that Personalized PageRank performed favorably compared with pure similarity based ranking and traditional PageRank.

Semantic Web Mining. Four chapters in the book relate to Semantic Web Mining. In "Discovering Links Between Lexical and Surface Features in Questions and Answers", Chakrabarti presents a data-driven approach, assisted by machine learning, to build question answering information retrieval systems that return short passages or direct answers to questions, rather than URLs pointing to whole pages. Learning is based on a simple log-linear model over a pair of feature vectors, one derived from the question and the other derived from a candidate passage. Using this model, candidate passages are filtered, and substantial improvements are obtained in the mean rank at which the first answer is found. The model parameters reveal linguistic artifacts coupling questions and their answers, which can be used for better annotation and indexing. Meo et al., in "Integrating Web Conceptual Modeling and Web Usage Mining", present a case study regarding the application of the inductive database approach to the analysis of Web logs to enable the rapid customization of the mining procedures following the Web developers' needs. They integrate the user request information with meta-data concerning the Web site structure into rich XML Web logs, called "conceptual logs", produced by Web applications specified with the WebML conceptual model. Then, they apply a data mining language (MINE RULE) to conceptual logs in order to identify different types of patterns, such as recurrent navigation paths, page contents most frequently visited, and anomalies. Bloehdorn and Hotho, in "Boosting for Text Classification with Semantic Features", propose an enhancement of the classical term stem based document representation through higher semantic concepts extracted from background knowledge. Boosting, a successful machine learning technique, is used for classification, and comparative experimental evaluations show consistent improvement of the results. In "Markov Blankets and Meta-Heuristics Search: Sentiment Extraction from Unstructured Texts", Airoldi, Bai, and Padman address the problem of extracting sentiments (positive versus negative comments) from unstructured text by proposing a two-stage Bayesian algorithm that can capture the dependencies among words, and find a vocabulary that is efficient for the purpose of extracting sentiments. Their work has potential to mine on-line opinions from the Internet and learn customers' preferences for economic or marketing research, or for leveraging a strategic advantage.

January 2006   Bamshad Mobasher
                                                       Olfa Nasraoui
                                                          Bing Liu
                                                       Brij Masand

Table of Contents

Mining Temporally Changing Web Usage Graphs

Prasanna Desikan and Jaideep Srivastava

Department of Computer Science
University of Minnesota, Minneapolis, MN 55414, USA
{desikan, srivastava}@cs.umn.edu

Abstract. Web mining has been explored to a vast degree and different techniques have been proposed for a variety of applications that include Web Search, Web Classification, Web Personalization etc. Most research on Web mining has been from a 'data-centric' point of view. The focus has been primarily on developing measures and applications based on data collected from content, structure and usage of Web until a particular time instance. In this project we examine another dimension of Web Mining, namely *temporal dimension*. Web data has been evolving over time, reflecting the ongoing trends. These changes in data in the temporal dimension reveal new kind of information. This information has not captured the attention of the Web mining research community to a large extent. In this paper, we highlight the significance of studying the evolving nature of the Web graphs. We have classified the approach to such problems at three levels of analysis: *single node, sub-graphs* and *whole graphs*. We provide a framework to approach problems in this kind of analysis and identify interesting problems at each level. Our experiments verify the significance of such an analysis and also point to future directions in this area. The approach we take is generic and can be applied to other domains, where data can be modeled as a graph, such as network intrusion detection or social networks.

1 Introduction

Web Mining, defined as the application of data mining techniques to extract information from the World Wide Web, has been classified into three sub-fields: Web Content Mining, Web Structure Mining and Web Usage Mining based on the kind of the data. The evolving structure of interlinked documents, such as the World Wide Web, and their usage over a period of time has evoked new interest to both researchers and industry. These sets of documents form a graph, with nodes representing documents and edges representing hyperlinks. Extracting information from the pure structure of such graphs and the usage of these documents, especially with respect to the World Wide Web, has been extensively studied [29]. The significance of mining information from the Web graph structure is evident from the success of Google, whose PageRank technology is based on the hyperlink structure of the Web. A survey on Hyperlink Analysis is provided by Desikan et al [7]. Usage aspects of graphs such as the Web and user navigation patterns have also received wide attention [13, 25, 28].

Most research has thus focused more recently on mining information from structure and usage of such graphs at a given time instance. This paper focuses on another

B. Mobasher et al. (Eds.): WebKDD 2004, LNAI 3932, pp. 1–17, 2006.

important dimension of Web Mining - the Temporal Evolution of the Web; as identified by our earlier work [8, 29]. The Web is changing fast over time and so is the user's interaction in the Web suggesting the need to study and develop models for the evolving Web Content, Web Structure and Web Usage. Changes in Web data occur either rapidly or slowly. In other domains where data can be modeled as graphs these changes may also occur suddenly representing anomalous behavior. A typical example of such graphs would be network flow connections. We have applied the techniques presented in this paper on that domain; where sudden changes may characterize network intrusions. The content of certain web sites, such as news channels, change very dynamically due to new and updated information that comes in frequently. On the contrary, there are other web sites, such as encyclopedias, that are very informative, but whose content does not change very rapidly. Similarly, the change in the web structure is also dependent on the web site in particular. Some web sites may change their structure more rapidly to address the user navigation issues. The structure of the whole Web graph has been found relatively stable [16]. It is observed that Web usage graphs, which are constructed from web server logs, will tend to vary more with time; as they reflect the user behavior and needs on daily basis. Due to the nature of different rate of changes in data, the properties that need to be measured and the techniques that need to be developed to capture the changing behavior will need to differ. Mining evolving web streams and web dynamics has been an focus of research in recent works [12, 18, 20]. The techniques developed will also depend on the scope of analysis. The temporal behavior of the Web graph can be analyzed at three levels:

Single Node: Studying the behavior of a single node across different time periods. Node properties such as total hits, hub and authority scores, indegree and outdegree, may vary across time.

Sub-graphs: Set of nodes that form sub-graph structures that occur in the Web graph. The frequency of their occurrence across time periods and also the sequences of subgraphs would require different techniques.

Whole graph: The variation of the basic and derived graph properties such as order, size, number of components, maximum indegree, maximum outdegree, average hub score, average authority score; will help in the profiling of the behavior of the graph.

The rest of the document is organized as follows: We talk about our motivation to study this problem in Section 2. In Section 3 we present the related work in this area and in the following section, we put forward the various kinds of analysis that can be carried out on temporally changing graphs. We also identify key issues and provide framework to address such problems. We present our approach to study these problems in Section 5. Section 6 discusses the experiments performed and the results. Finally in Section 7 we summarize our approach and provide pointers to future work.

2 Motivation

The dynamic nature of Web data has aroused interest in the Web research community to mine temporal patterns of the Web data. The study of change in the behavior of Web content, Web structure and Web usage over time and their effects on each other

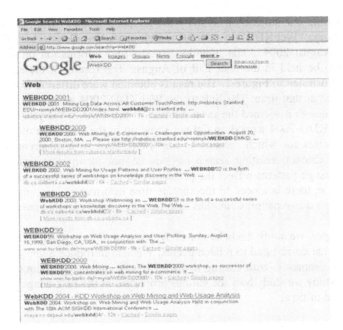

(a) Google Search results for 'WebKDD' in August 2004

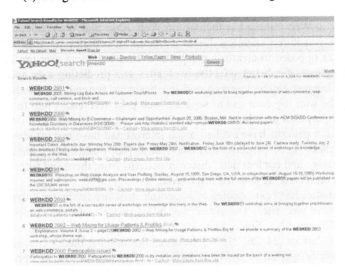

(b) Yahoo Search results for 'WebKDD' in August 2004

Fig. 1. Search Engine Results missing 'recency' of information

would help in understanding better, the way the Web is evolving and the necessary steps that can be taken to make it a better source of information. Incorporating the time dimension brings into perspective concepts such as 'recently popular' versus 'historically significant'.

We illustrate our motivation to study the temporal changes with an example. We issued a query, "WebKDD" to popular search engines – Google and Yahoo in the middle of August 2004. The intention was to find information on the WebKDD workshop to be held in the later half of August. The results of the example search query are illustrated in Figure 1. The results obtained were different from what a user would expect at that time. The link to the WebKDD 2004 workshop in Google was ranked 4th, though it seemed the most relevant at that time of the year. In Yahoo, the link to WebKDD 2004 workshop did not show up in the first page of results. Similarly for queries for which recency is important, such as a quadrennial event like World Cup Cricket, existing search engines do not incorporate time information. Also, Web usage patterns reflect the popularity of an event or topic for a given time period. Hence, there is a need to incorporate time information in mining Web Pages. Studying Web usage patterns can thus help in detecting events that are represented by these pages.

In this paper, we study the behavior of Web usage of individual Web pages to find similarities that correspond to related events. We also introduce a *time-aware* ranking metric and compare it with exiting *non-time aware* ranking techniques. In the final part of our study we study how the various properties of the Web usage graphs change over a period of time.

3 Related Work

Recent work in Web mining has focused on Web usage and Web structure data. Web usage data has captured attention due to its nature of bringing the user's perspective of the Web as opposed to creator's perspective. Understanding user profiles and user navigation patterns for better adaptive web sites and predicting user access patterns has evoked interest to the research and the business community. Methods for pre-processing the user log data and to separate web page references into those made for navigational purposes and those made for content purposes have been developed [6]. User navigation patterns have evoked much interest and have been studied by various other researchers [2, 5, 14, 25]. Srivastava et al [28] discuss the techniques to pre-process the usage and content data, discover patterns from them and filter out the non-relevant and uninteresting patterns discovered.

Usage statistics has been applied to hyperlink structure for better link prediction in field of adaptive web sites. The concept of adaptive web sites was proposed by Per-kowitz and Etzioni [24]. Since then, Markov models have been used extensively to predict user behavior [24, 26, 27, 31]. Information foraging theory concepts have also been successfully applied to the Web domain by Chi et al [4] to incorporate user behavior into the existing content and link structure. Clustering of user sessions and navigation paths with different underlying models can be used to capture similarity in the user behavior [3, 11, 19, 21, 30].

Research in Web structure mining has focused primarily on hyperlink analysis and has found its utility in a variety of applications [7]. There have been different hyper-link based methods that have been proposed to address various problems such as determining the importance of a page, topic classification and identification of Web communities. Among these techniques, PageRank[23], developed by Google founders, is the most popular metric for ranking hypertext documents according to their importance. Oztekin et al [22], proposed Usage Aware PageRank incorporating usage statistics into framework of PageRank model. We discuss these two metrics in more detail in Section 5.

The other popular metric is *hub* and *authority* scores. From a graph theoretic point of view, *hubs* and *authorities* can be interpreted as 'fans' and 'centers' in a bipartite core of a Web graph. The hub and authority scores computed for each Web page indicate the extent to which the Web page serves as a 'hub' pointing to good 'authority' pages or the extent to which the Web page serves as an 'authority' on a topic pointed to by good hubs. The hub and authority scores for a page are not based on a formula for a single page, but are computed for a set of pages related to a topic using an iterative procedure called HITS algorithm [15].

The Internet Archive [32] is one of the key data sources for studying the change in the web structure and content of different web sites. There are also tools available such as the AT&T Internet Difference Engine that detects the change in the existing html documents. However, these tools do not capture the temporal nature of the changing documents.

4 Analysis of Temporal Behavior of Graphs

As discussed in Section 1, the analysis of the temporal behavior can be classified at three levels that are discussed below in detail.

4.1 Single Node Analysis

The behavior of the Web data can be modeled at the level of a single node, monitoring the behavior of each node in the graph. For each single node that is labeled, we can compute properties based on its content, structure and usage. Over a period of time, the content of the page represented as a node can change, indicating a change in the topic addressed by the Web page. Also the structural significance of the node can be derived by computing properties that are purely structure based, such as indegree, outdegree, authority score, hub score or PageRank score. Such kind of behavior will also serve as a very useful feedback to the web site designer. Finally the usage data of a single node will reflect the *popularity* of the node during a given time period. Such popularity will reflect the current trend and may help in prediction of *popular* topics. A vector of a property (p), for set of nodes, as a function of time (t), is described in Equation 1:

$$SN(t)_{n,p} = \begin{bmatrix} s_1(t) & s_2(t) & s_3(t) ..... & s_n(t) \end{bmatrix} \tag{1}$$

Where $s_i(t)$ represents the score of the ith node at time t; n is the number of nodes in the graph and $SN(t)_{n,p}$ represents the vector of scores of a particular property, p, of each node at a given time t. Here, n is the number of nodes (assuming each node has a unique label that it retains across the time period) for the graph built over the time period. If a node doesn't exist at any time instance it would be assigned a score of zero for that particular time instance. This is a naïve model at this stage, but captures most significant properties we are interested in. These models could however be extended.

4.2 Sub-graph Analysis

The changing sub-graph patterns also evoke interest. These sub-graphs may represent different communities and abstract concepts that evolve over time. The idea of mining frequent sub-graphs has been applied with a large graph as an input or a set of small graphs as input [16]. However, with the temporal dimension coming to picture, we now look at an evolving graph, which may have different sets of sub-graphs at different time instances. Figure 2 illustrates an example of an evolving graph, and the sequential patterns that can be mined.

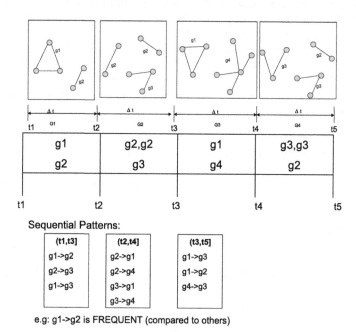

Fig. 2. Sequential Pattern Mining of Sub-graphs

It can be seen that mining of sequential patterns of sub-graphs might provide useful information in profiling the change behavior. Sequence mining may also help in predicting an upcoming trend or predict an abnormal behavior in the Web structure. These changes may occur due to change in the strategy of an organization or a launch of new product by an e-commerce site. While such changes provide interesting conceptual information, mining such patterns poses interesting challenges to the research community to develop efficient algorithms, due to the large size of the graphs and the number of such graphs that are needed to model the temporal behavior. Formally the set of such sequences can be captured using Equation 2.

$$G_{t,t+\Delta t}(\Delta t) = \left\{ g_i \rightarrow g_j \middle| g_i \in FSG(G_t); g_j \in FSG(G_{t+\Delta t}) \right\} \qquad (2)$$

where $G_{t,t+\Delta t}(\Delta t)$ represents the set of sequences of sub-graphs in a Δt time period; g_j represents a sub-graph and $FSG(G_t)$ represents all the frequent sub-graphs of the graph, G_t, where G_t represents the graph at a time instance t. Equation 2 provides the basis of information to mine the interesting sub-graph sequences.

4.3 Whole Graph Analysis

While the single node analysis and sub-graphs tend to give more specific information, the analysis at the level of the whole graph will reveal higher level concepts. The goal of such mining is to build a vector of the feature space consisting of *basic properties* and *derived properties* for each sequence of graphs, at different time instances. Figure 3 illustrates the concept of the graph evolution and how the different graph properties change with time. Modeling such a vector space and analyzing it over a time period poses interesting challenges.

The research directions involve identifying the key properties that model the behavior of change of the Web structure and any correlation between such properties. The features space can be divided into two different sets of properties of the whole graph:

- **Basic Properties:** These are basic properties of any graph such as the order, size, density, number of components. These can measured using basic graph algorithms.
- **Derived Properties:** Properties of graphs such as average or maximum hub score, average or maximum authority score.

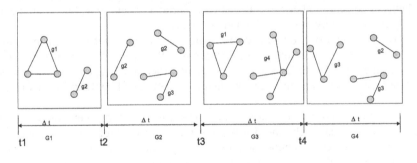

G 1	G 2	G 3	G 4
|v|=n(G1)=5	|v|=n(G2)=7	|v|=n(G3)=8	|v|=n(G4)=8
|E| =e(G)=4	|E| =e(G2)=4	|E| =e(G)=7	|E| =e(G4)=5
# of Cpts= 2	# of Cpts= 3	# of Cpts= 2	# of Cpts= 3

Fig. 3. Modeling features of graphs that evolve over a time period. (Note: the set of properties shown is just an illustration, it is not exhaustive)

Other interesting issues might be how the distribution of such scores varies over a period of time. Such variation in distributions may indicate the variation of the kind of graph such as scale-free graphs versus random graphs. The vector space of features as a function of time is formulated in Equation 3.

$$GF(t) = [BF_1(t) \quad BF_2(t) \quad ... \quad BF_m(t) \quad DF_1(t) \quad DF_2(t) \quad ... \quad DF_n(t)] \tag{3}$$

where $GF(t)$ represents the feature space of the basic features $(BF_i(t))$ and derived features $(DF_i(t))$ at a time instance t. Analyzing this feature space over a time period will reveal information about the temporal behavior of the whole graph.

5 Our Approach

We study the behavior of changing usage graphs at two levels of analysis- *Single Node Level* and *Whole Graph Level*. We first present a detailed discussion on analysis at single-node level and then present our initial approach to study the properties at whole graph level.

We follow a two-fold approach to study the significance of temporal behavior of a single node. The first part of the work involves the detection of events based on Web page accesses. In order to detect events, we assume during an event, all web pages related to event will be accessed in a similar pattern. To find similarity in web page access patterns, we modeled a feature vector of number of hits within a time granularity of a single day for a time period for each Web Page. Using cosine product as the similarity measure for these vectors, the Web pages with similar access patterns are clustered. This is useful in identifying Web pages that are related to each other in terms of access for a certain time period. The group of such similar Web pages helps in identifying events that have taken place during that particular time period, and that is not evident by looking only at content, structure or aggregate usage information. It also helps in detecting related events that co-occur at a certain time, but where the relation might not be obvious by the content or structure.

In the second part of the work, we compare 'time aware' metrics with 'non-time-aware' metrics for determining the importance of a Web page. We first discuss in detail 'non-time-aware' metrics such as PageRank (*PR*) and Usage Aware PageRank (*UPR*) and later present a 'time-aware' metric, 'PageUsage Popularity' as defined by this work.

PageRank is a metric based purely on the link structure of the Web graph. The key idea is that a page has high rank if it is pointed to by many highly ranked pages. So the rank of a page depends upon the ranks of the pages pointing to it. This process is done iteratively till the rank of all the pages is determined. The rank of a page p can thus be written as:

$$PR(p) = \frac{d}{N} + (1-d) * \sum_{(q,p) \in G} \frac{PR(q)}{Outdegree(q)} \tag{6}$$

Here, n is the number of nodes in the graph and *OutDegree(q)* is the number of hyperlinks on page q. Intuitively, the approach can be viewed as a stochastic analysis of a random walk on the Web graph. The first term in the right hand side of the equation corresponds to the probability that a random Web surfer arrives at a page p out of nowhere, i.e. (s)he could arrive at the page by typing the URL or from a bookmark, or may have a particular page as his/her homepage. d would then be the probability that a random surfer chooses a URL directly – i.e. typing it, using the bookmark list, or by default – rather than traversing a link . Finally, $1/n$ corresponds to the uniform probability that a person chooses the page p from the complete set of n pages on the Web. The second term in the right hand side of the equation corresponds to a factor contributed by arriving at a page by traversing a link. $(1- d)$ is the probability that a person arrives at the page p by traversing a link. The summation corresponds to the sum of the rank contributions made by all the pages that point to the page p. The rank contribution is the Page Rank of the page multiplied by the probability that a particular link on the page is traversed. So for any page q pointing to page p, the probability that the link pointing to page p is traversed would be $1/OutDegree(q)$, assuming all links on the page are chosen with uniform probability.

UPR is a modified version of the basic PageRank that incorporates aggregate usage information. Here weights are assigned to the links based on the number of traversals on the link, and thus modifying the probability that a user traverses a particular link in the basic PageRank from $1/OutDegree(q)$ to $W_l/OutTraversed(q)$, where W_l is the number of traversals on the link l and $OutTraversed(q)$ is the total number of traversals of all links from the page q. And also the probability to arrive at a page directly is computed using the usage statistics. Usage Aware PageRank can thus be defined as:

$$UPR(p) = \alpha \cdot \left(d/N + (1-d) \cdot \sum_{(q,p) \in G} UPR(q)/Out\deg ree(q) \right) + \tag{7}$$

$$(1-\alpha) \cdot \left(d \cdot W_{nl} + (1-d) \cdot \sum_{q \to p} UPR(q)/(W_l/OutTraversed(q)) \right)$$

where α is the emphasis factor that decides the weight to be given to the structure versus the usage information.

While PageRank is based on structure information and Usage Aware PageRank incorporates usage statistics into the basic PageRank model, both metrics are 'non-time-aware'. They do not take into account when a Web page was created or its usage statistics across a time period. This results in loss of information that is typically a consequence of aggregating information for a whole time period. The recency or frequency of usage is not captured. As a result , topics that are new and are popular lose their rank to topics that have been popular during an earlier time period. To overcome this problem , we introduce a 'time-aware-metric' called "Page-Usage-Popularity" which is defined as follows:

$$PageUsagePopularity(p) = \alpha \cdot \frac{Hits(T - r(T))}{T - r(T)} + (1-\alpha) \cdot \frac{Hits(r(T))}{r(T)} \tag{8}$$

Here, T is the total time period considered for ranking. $Hits(t)$ is the total number of hits in a time period, t. $r(t)$ is the time period that is considered 'recent'. The weight given for a recency of information is determined by the weighing factor α , which is the weight given to the 'past' time period. Thus α serves as a knob to determine if the results need to be "recently popular" versus "historically significant".

We now proceed to the level of an entire graph and to study its behavior over a period of time. We break our analysis into two levels. At first, we study the basic properties of the graphs such as order, size and number of components. We then proceed to study the behavior of graph in terms of computed or derived metrics such as pagerank, hubs, and authorities. Since these metrics are defined for a single node, we look into aggregated properties such as average score or maximum score of these metrics and study the variation of these scores with respect to time. We do this in order to be able to capture changes in the dynamics of graph that can enable us to detect events or patterns such as forming of new communities or connectivity of the graph.

6 Experiments and Results

We performed experiments at two different levels of analysis – single node level and the whole graph level. Our present analysis was focused on change in Web usage data, as the change in such usage graphs is more evident over a short period of time.

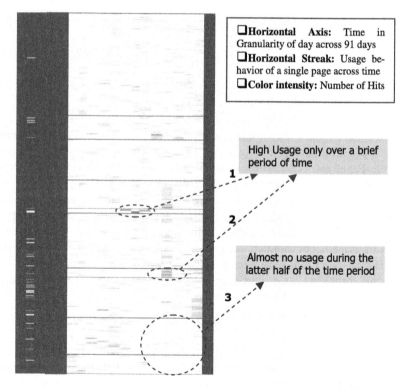

(a) Visualization of Cluster results using CLUTO

Fig. 4. Grouping Web pages with similar usage trends

Wedding Pictures from 'user1' that were accessed high for few days

1	www-users.cs.umn.edu/~user1/Wedding/speech.html www-users.cs.umn.edu/~user2/user3/re0.html www-users.cs.umn.edu/~user2/user3/wap.html www-users.cs.umn.edu/~user1/Wedding/photo2.html www-users.cs.umn.edu/~user1/Wedding/wedding.html

Webpages of a talk – accessed high for few days in and around the talk date

2	www.cs.umn.edu/event/spin/talks/presenter-jan-00/sld016.htm www.cs.umn.edu/crisys/spin/talks/presenter-jan-00/sld017.htm www.cs.umn.edu/Research/airvl/its/ www.cs.umn.edu/event/spin/talks/presenter-jan-00/sld055.htm www.cs.umn.edu/event/spin/talks/presenter-jan-00/sld056.htm

Class Web pages that were not frequently accessed after the end of semester

3	www-users.cs.umn.edu/~user4/hpdmtut/sld110.htm (Data Mining Tutorial slides) www-users.cs.umn.edu/~user4/hpdmtut/sld113.htm www-users.cs.umn.edu/~user4/hpdmtut/sld032.htm www.cs.umn.edu/classes/Spring-2002/csci5707/ www.cs.umn.edu/classes/Spring2002/csci5103/www_files/contents.htm

(b) Sample Results of Interesting Clusters

Fig. 4. (*Continued*)

6.1 Single Node Level Analysis of Web Usage Graph

The data considered was from April through June 2002. We clustered the Web pages access patterns over the three month period; with the granularity of day to count the number of accesses at a time instance. Results of the clustering output are shown in Figure 4(a). Some interesting patterns were observed. The sample of Web pages corresponding to these patterns is shown in Figure 4(b). One of the clusters belongs to the set of pages that were accessed a lot during a very short period of time. Most of them are wedding photos that were accessed a lot, suggesting some kind of a 'wedding' event that took place during that time. Similar behavior was observed in another cluster, and the set of pages belonged to talk slides of some event that took place during that period. The third cluster was the most interesting. It had mostly pages related to 'Data Mining' notes. These set of pages had high access during the first period of time, possibly the spring term and then their access died out; indicating the end of the semester. Interestingly enough, there was no Data Mining course offered during that term suggesting someone was studying 'data mining' during that semester, as a part of another course or due to other interests. Our observations suggest that clustering Web page access patterns over time helps in identifying a 'concept' that is 'popular' during a time period.

1. 0.01257895 www.cs.umn.edu/cisco/data/doc/cintrnet/ita.htm
2. 0.01246077 www.cs.umn.edu/cisco/home/home.htm
3. 0.01062634 www.cs.umn.edu/cisco/data/lib/copyrght.htm
4. 0.01062634 www.cs.umn.edu/cisco/data/doc/help.htm
5. 0.01062634 www.cs.umn.edu/cisco/home/search.htm
8. 0.00207191 www.cs.umn.edu/help/software/java/JGL-2.0.2-for-JDK-1.1/doc/api/packages.html
9. 0.00191835 www.cs.umn.edu/help/software/java/JGL-2.0.2-for-JDK-1.0/doc/api/packages.html
10. 0.00176296 www.cs.umn.edu/help/software/java/JGL-2.0.2-for-JDK-

e.g These Web pages do not figure in usage based rankings

(a) PageRank

1.	0.000723	www.cs.umn.edu/
2.	0.000145	www-users.cs.umn.edu/~mein/blender/
3.	0.000081	www-users.cs.umn.edu/~oper/linuc/allen/
4.	0.000053	www-users.cs.umn.edu/~xyz/hpdmtut/
5.	0.000051	www-users.cs.umn.edu/~1234/wiihist/
6.	0.000050	www-users.cs.umn.edu/grad.html
7.	0.000050	www.cs.umn.edu/faculty/faculty.html
8.	0.000046	www-users.cs.umn.edu/~oper/allen/200393/
9.	0.000044	www-users.cs.umn.edu/~self/links.html
10.	0.000042	www.cs.umn.edu/courses.html

(b) Page Usage Popularity

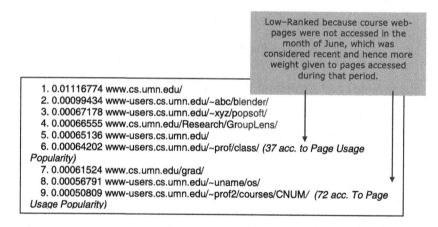

Low-Ranked because course web-pages were not accessed in the month of June, which was considered recent and hence more weight given to pages accessed during that period.

1. 0.01116774 www.cs.umn.edu/
2. 0.00099434 www-users.cs.umn.edu/~abc/blender/
3. 0.00067178 www-users.cs.umn.edu/~xyz/popsoft/
4. 0.00066555 www.cs.umn.edu/Research/GroupLens/
5. 0.00065136 www-users.cs.umn.edu/
6. 0.00064202 www-users.cs.umn.edu/~prof/class/ *(37 acc. to Page Usage Popularity)*
7. 0.00061524 www.cs.umn.edu/grad/
8. 0.00056791 www-users.cs.umn.edu/~uname/os/
9. 0.00050809 www-users.cs.umn.edu/~prof2/courses/CNUM/ *(72 acc. To Page Usage Popularity)*

(c) Usage Aware PageRank

Fig. 5. Comparison of 'non-time-aware' metrics with 'time-aware-metrics'

Our next set of experiments involved comparison of 'non-time-aware' metrics such as PageRank and UPR with 'time-aware' metrics such as Page Usage Popularity as defined earlier. The results are presented in Figure 5. It was observed that PageRanks (Figure 5(a)) tend to give more importance to structure; hence pages that are heavily linked may be ranked higher though not used. Usage Aware PageRank (Figure 5(c)) combines usage statistics (cumulative for the time period considered) with link information giving importance to both the creator and the actual user of a web page. Page Usage Popularity (Figure 5(b)) helps in ranking 'obsolete' items lower and boosting up the topics that are more 'popular' during that time period. Thus it signifies the importance of bringing the temporal dimension as opposed to analysis of a static graph.

6.2 Whole Graph Level Analysis of Web Usage Graph

Our next set of experiments involved analyzing the basic and derived features of Web usage graphs over a three month period. We have plotted these features against time period granularity of single day.

Our initial results suggested some seasonal patterns that were not observed for the new dataset. From these plots shown in Figure 6, there were some interesting observations. The first set of plots, in Figure 6(a), reflects variation of basic properties of the graph, such as order, size and the number of components. While order and size reveal the number of pages traversed and links traversed, the number of components will reflect how connected the graph is. We eliminated robot behavior collected in web server logs. Any robot like behavior would decrease the number of components sharply. In the network log data, the drop in number of components also helped us

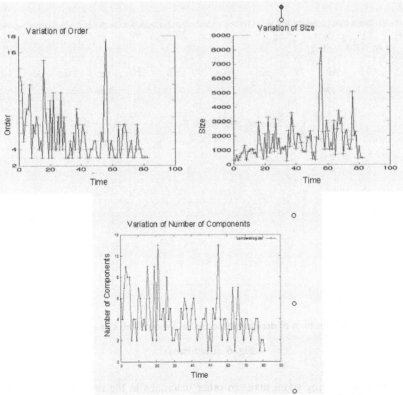

(a)   Variation of Basic Properties of Whole Web Usage Graph

Fig. 6. Analysis of variation of Whole Web Usage Graph across a time period

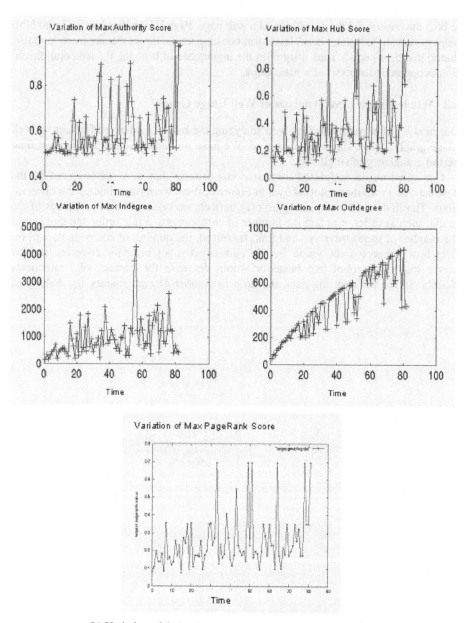

(b) Variation of derived properties of Whole Web Usage Graphs

Fig. 6. (*Continued*)

detect machines sending spam mails to other machines in the network. Those results are not presented due to lack of space and relevance to this context. The second set of plots, in Figure 6(b), reflects behavior of derived properties with time. Due to the normalization of hub, authority and PageRank scores; we can just judge that Web pages that were most relevant for that given time instance. The variation of Indegree and Outdegree scores reflect the number of connections as opposed to the pure relevance score. It is seen that that the maximum outdegree score of the graph seems to have an increasing trend.

These results suggest that the variation of different properties of these graphs need to be studied. The difference in the variation of related metrics, such as hub scores versus outdegree scores, suggests that the distribution of these scores change and studying the change in the distribution of the scores would be interesting. It would reflect the nature of evolving graphs.

7 Conclusions

We have presented in this paper the significance of introducing the dimension of time into Web mining research as identified by some of our earlier works. We have classified the scope of analysis into three levels namely; single node analysis, sub-graph analysis and whole graph analysis. At a single node level analysis, we observed, the usage based ranking metrics, boost up the ranks of the pages that are used as opposed to the pure hyperlink based metrics that rank pages that are used rarely high. In particular, we notice that the Page Usage Popularity ranks the pages that have been used more recently high and brings down the rank of the pages that have been used earlier but have had very low access during the recent period. At the level of the whole graph, we notice the trend and seasonal components in the behavior of the basic properties. The issues that need to be addressed at each level are discussed in detail.

The two primary tasks for research are to identify the appropriate set of properties that define the changing behavior at each level and to develop efficient algorithms that scale to the large data sets. We have also applied these generic techniques to other graph data such as Netflow connections, to help profile normal and anomalous behavior. We thus see a clear need to pursue research in the area of evolving graphs which hold significance in application domains like Web Analytics, Network Intrusion or Social Networks. Another engineering issue would be developing a grammar for querying interesting graph patterns.

Acknowledgements

The initial ideas presented were the result of discussions with Prof. Vipin Kumar and the Data Mining Research group at the Department of Computer Science. Uygar Oztekin provided the ranking results using PageRank and Usage Aware PageRank metrics. This work was partially supported by Army High Performance Computing Research Center contract number DAAD19-01-2-0014. The content of the work does not necessarily reflect the position or policy of the government and no official endorsement should be inferred. Access to computing facilities was provided by the AHPCRC and the Minnesota Supercomputing Institute.

References

1. S.Acharyya and J.Ghosh, "A Maximum Entropy Framework for Link Analysis on Directed Graphs", in LinkKDD2003, pp 3-13, Washington DC, USA, 2003
2. A. Buchner, M. Baumagarten, S. Anand, M.Mulvenna, and J.Hughes. Navigation pattern discovery from internet data. In Proc. of WEBKDD'99 , Workshop on Web Usage Analysis and User Profiling, Aug 1999.
3. I Cadez, D. Heckerman, C. Meek, P. Smyth, S. White, "'Visualization of Navigation Patterns on a Web Site Using Model Based Clustering", Proceedings of the KDD 2000
4. E.H. Chi, P. Pirolli, K. Chen, J. Pitkow. Using Information Scent to Model User Information Needs and Actions on the Web. In Proc. of ACM CHI 2001 Conference on Human Factors in Computing Systems, pp. 490--497. ACM Press, April 2001. Seattle, WA.
5. M. S. Chen, J.S. Park, and P.S. Yu. Data Mining for path traversal patterns in a web environment. In 16th International Conference on Distributed Computing Systems, 1996.
6. R. Cooley, B. Mobasher, and J.Srivastava. "Data Preparation for mining world wide web browsing patterns". Knowledge and Information systems, 1(!) 1999.
7. P. Desikan, J. Srivastava, V. Kumar, P.-N. Tan, "Hyperlink Analysis – Techniques & Applications", Army High Performance Computing Center Technical Report, 2002.
8. P. Desikan, J. Srivastava, "Temporal Behavior of Web Usage", AHPCRC technical report, August 2003
9. C. Ding, H. Zha, X. He, P. Husbands and H.D. Simon, "Link Analysis: Hubs and Authorities on the World Wide Web" May 2001. LBNL Tech Report 47847
10. F. Douglis, T. Ball, Y-F. Chen, E. Koutsofios, "The AT&T Internet Difference Engine: Tracking and Viewing Changes on the Web", World Wide Web, January 1998, pp. 27-44.
11. O. Etzioni, "The World Wide Web: Quagmire or Gold Mine", in Communications of the ACM, 39(11):65=68,1996.
12. F. Grandi, "Introducing an Annotated Bibliography on Temporal and Evolution Aspects in the World Wide Web", SIGMOD Record 33(2): 84-86 (2004).
13. J.Z Huang, M. Ng, W.K Ching, J. Ng, and D. Cheung, "A Cube model and cluster analysis for Web Access Sessions", In Proc. of WEBKDD'01, CA, USA, August 2001.
14. X.Jin, Y.Zhou and B. Mobasher, "Web Usage Mining Based on Probabilistic Latent Semantic Analysis". In Proceedings of KDD'04, Seattle, August 2004
15. J.M. Kleinberg, "Authoritative Sources in Hyperlinked Environment", 9th Annual ACM-SIAM Symposium on Discrete Algorithms, pages 668-667, 1998
16. J. Klienberg et al. "The web as a graph: measurement models & methods".Proc ICCC 1999.
17. M. Kuramochi and G. Karypis "Finding Frequent Patterns in a Large Sparse Graphs", SIAM Data Mining Conference, 2004.
18. M. Levene and A. Poulovassilis, "Web Dynamics: Adapting to Change in Content, Size, Topology and Use", 2004, XIII, 466 p., Hardcover ISBN: 3-540-40676-X.
19. B. Mobasher, H. Dai, T. Luo, Y. Sung, J. Zhu, Integrating Web Usage and Content Mining for More Effective Personalization, in Proc. of the International Conference on E-Commerce and Web Technologies (ECWeb2000), Greenwich, UK, 2000.
20. O. Nasraoui, C. Cardona, C. Rojas, and F. Gonzalez, "Mining Evolving User Profiles in Noisy Web Clickstream Data with a Scalable Immune System Clustering Algorithm", in Proc. of WebKDD 2003 – KDD Workshop on Web mining as a Premise to Effective and Intelligent Web Applications, Washington DC, August 2003, p. 71.

21. O. Nasraoui , A. Joshi, and R. Krishnapuram, "Relational Clustering Based on a New Robust Estimator with Application to Web Mining," Proc. Intl. Conf. North American Fuzzy Info. Proc. Society (NAFIPS 99), New York, June 1999.
22. B.U. Oztekin, L. Ertoz and V. Kumar, "Usage Aware PageRank", World Wide Web Conference, 2003.
23. L. Page, S. Brin, R. Motwani and T. Winograd "The PageRank Citation Ranking: Bringing Order to the Web" Stanford Digital Library Technologies, January 1998.
24. M. Perkowitz and O. Etzioni, "Adaptive Web sites: an AI challenge". IJCAI97
25. D. Pierrakos, G. Paliouras, C. Papatheodorou, and C. Spyropoulos, 'Web usage mining as a tool for personalization: A survey'. User Modeling and User-Adapted Interaction, 2003.
26. P. Pirolli, J. E. Pitkow, "Distribution of Surfer's Path Through the World Wide Web: Empirical Characterization." World Wide Web 1:1-17, 1999.
27. R.R. Sarukkai, "Link Prediction and Path Analysis using Markov Chains", In the Proc. of the 9th World Wide Web Conference , 1999.
28. J. Srivastava, R. Cooley, M. Deshpande and P-N. Tan. "Web Usage Mining: Discovery and Applications of usage patterns from Web Data", SIGKDD Explorations, 2000.
29. J. Srivastava, P. Desikan and V. Kumar, "Web Mining – Concepts, Applications and Research Directions", NGDM, MIT/AAAI Press.
30. T. Yan, M. Jacobsen, H. Garcia-Molina, and U. Dayal., "From user access patterns to dynamic hypertext linking", In Proceedings of the 5th International World Wide Web conference, Paris, France, 1996.
31. J. Zhu, J. Hong, and J.G. Hughes, Using Markov Chains for Link Prediction in Adaptive Web Sites. In Proc. of ACM SIGWEB Hypertext 2002.
32. Internet Archive, http://www.archive.org/

Improving the Web Usage Analysis Process: A UML Model of the ETL Process

Thilo Maier

Catholic University Eichstätt-Ingolstadt
Auf der Schanz 49
85049 Ingolstadt, Germany
thilo.maier@gmail.com

Abstract. Integrating OLAP and Web usage analysis in a data warehousing environment is a promising approach for sophisticated analysis of the Web channel in multi-channel environments of organizations. Populating the data warehouse is a laborious and time-consuming task (especially for small projects), which is – in practice – a big obstacle for concrete ECRM projects. Especially if Web usage analysis researchers need to conduct experiments with a Web warehouse, an intuitive and easy to deploy ETL component is essential. In this paper we propose a logical object-oriented relational data storage model in UML, which is based on a formal model. A concrete Java instance of our model simplifies modeling and automating the ETL process. The Java instance of our model has been integrated into our WUSAN (**W**eb **US**age **AN**alyis) system. Finally, we illustrate the usage of our model for Web usage analysis purposes, though the model is principally not restricted to this domain.

1   Introduction

Many customers interact with the marketing, sales, and customer service divisions of organizations via a number of different interaction channels, each of which has its specific characteristics (see fig. 1 on the facing page). For big organizations, which serve a mass customer base, it is difficult to understand the particular needs of individual customers and to maintain consistency across all channels. Due to the important role the World Wide Web plays in everyday life and its excellent possibilities to track track individual user behavior on Web sites [14], for many organizations, the Web channel will be the most important interaction channel to analyze and manage customer relationships.

In order to acquire a complete picture of the customer in a multi-channel environment, it is critical to collect data at all customer touch points, in order to achieve a complete, holistic, and integrated view of the customer [27]. This includes customer transactions, interactions, service history, characteristics and profiles, clickstream/browsing behavior, and demographics.

To respond to the challenge of integrating large volumes of data from various data sources, deploying a data warehouse within the ECRM process is proposed by [21]. Although many authors agree on the benefits of using a data warehouse

B. Mobasher et al. (Eds.): WebKDD 2004, LNAI 3932, pp. 18–36, 2006.

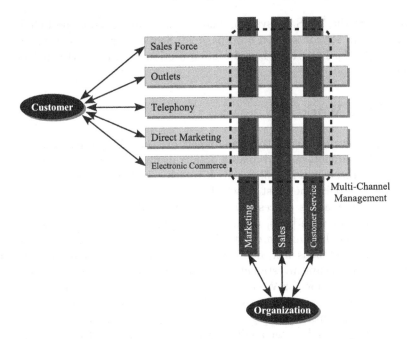

Fig. 1. Multi-channel environment, derived from [23,22]

(i) to combine data mining and OLAP analyses [7], (ii) to integrate various data sources and handle large volumes of data [12], and (iii) to improve and leverage Web usage analysis [10,25,34], little is stated about how to populate and update a data warehouse by deploying a systematic conceptual model for the *extraction, transformation, loading* (ETL) process, in order to reduce the time and costs needed for this task, which according to [11, introduction] account for up to 70% of the total data warehousing expenses.

Especially for data from the Web channel, which can be continuously collected in large volumes, the ETL process must be deployed in a way that automates this task and minimizes manual interactions. Furthermore ETL must be integrated into the *preprocessing phase* of the Web usage analysis process (see [3]), in order to reduce the amount of time and efforts required for both subtasks. Thus, it is necessary to provide a structured, practicable model of the ETL process, which (i) supports the integration of multiple data sources, (ii) is robust in view of changing data sources, (iii) supports flexible transformations, and (iv) can be easily deployed. In this paper, we propose a logical object-oriented relational data storage model (LOORDSM) to design the relational schemas and the corresponding ETL process, fulfilling above-mentioned four requirements. The LOORDSM has been implemented within our Web usage analysis system (WUSAN), which will be briefly outlined prior to going into the details of the LOORDSM.

The remainder of this chapter is organized as follows: in section section 2 on the next page we present related work. In section section 3 on page 21 we briefly outline the WUSAN system, which is the container for the LOORDSM – introduced in section section 4 on page 24. Section 5 provides an example of how to apply the LOORDSM, and section section 6 on page 34 concludes the paper.

2   Related Work

At first, the question arises to what extend existing Web usage analysis tools support data warehousing and related data transformations for Web usage analysis. For the recent study [15], we took a closer look at state of the art Web usage analysis tools, the most of which do not completely cover all phases of the Web usage analysis process. Only Blue Martini's integrated Web application server architecture [1,14] covers the complete Web usage analysis process (deployment included) and integrates a proprietary data warehousing solution. However, this system is intended for complex electronic commerce Web sites and requires significant investments in terms of money and technical knowledge and is hence no option for Web usage analysis projects with limited resources (especially academic research projects). Furthermore, the system accounts only for data stemming from its integrated Web application server.

Alternatively, a Web usage analysis system can be assembled from standardized components (if available). For this approach, the ETL component is of central importance. In order to manage the complex task of populating a data warehouse, there exist various specialized ETL or data integration software packages, which support the integration of heterogenous data sources. Due to the lack of an overall model that integrates all kinds of middle-ware required for data warehousing, ETL and data integration tools have contributed to the myriad of poorly integrated systems in a data warehousing environment [28].[1] The most prominent tasks of an ETL tool include [31]: (i) extraction of relevant information in data sources, (ii) integration of information coming from multiple sources into a common format, (iii) cleaning of the resulting data with regard to analysis purposes, and (iv) the propagation of data to the data warehouse.

The commercial market of ETL and data integration tools offers a wide spectrum of solutions, which primarily have the following things in common: (i) they work with a proprietary meta-data model and meta-data management, (ii) they implement a proprietary transformation model, (iii) their configuration and set-up is very complex, (iv) they have strong hardware requirements and are thus not practicable for small-sized and medium-sized projects, (v) they have no standardized API, (vi) they are autonomous and can only be combined with a restricted set of other systems in a data warehousing environment.

The most prominent tools are *Ascential DataStage* [2], which also handles data quality assurance, *ETI Solution* [5], which includes multiple complex packages, *Informatica PowerCenter* [9], and Microsoft's *Data Transformation Services*

---

[1] With the release of CWM 1.0 (Common Warehouse Meta-Model) [20] in 2001, this lack has been addressed at least in theory. It will take some time until the CWM will be supported on a broad basis (or at least some portions of it).

[17], which only integrate with Microsoft's own proprietary standards (ODBC, OLE DB), but which are nevertheless practicable for small projects.[2]

From the academic perspective there exists a sequence of papers [31,32,33] that describe the system *Arktos/Arktos II*, which is a tool that models and realizes the ETL process and ETL transformations. An ETL scenario can be modeled graphically by using a graphical specification language, based on a formal conceptual and logical model, which describe data sources, data targets and the transformations between the two. Although both Arktos projects cover the complete ETL process, their meta-models do not conform to emerging standards like the Common Warehouse Meta-Model (CWM) [20] and, similar to the commercial tools mentioned, makes it difficult to integrate the tool into existing heterogeneous data warehousing environments. Arktos' strength is its template collection that makes it possible to embed predefined ETL transformations into a new ETL scenario. The Arktos projects do not aim at Web usage analysis but at general data warehousing ETL requirements. To the best of our knowledge there exists no ETL tool, which specifically supports Web usage analysis.

3   A System for Effective Web Usage Analysis

According [13,8], there are two types of data transformations that need to take place during the preprocessing phase of the Web usage analysis process: (i) *ETL transformations* to populate a data warehouse with data from Web application servers[3], and (ii) business intelligence transformations to transform data in order to answer specific business questions with Web usage analysis. While the former transformations remain relatively constant unless the data collection mechanism for raw Web usage data is altered, the latter transformations account for a great portion of the overall time spent during the preprocessing phase.

In a Web usage analysis system, both transformation types should be configurable in a structured and straightforward matter, in order to automate them and minimize manual interactions. Albeit this is a common problem for data mining or business intelligence in general, it is notably a caustic problem for Web usage analysis, since this domain involves sheer amounts of data that make any manual interactions a tedious task. Furthermore, if one really strives for the goal of closing the loop in the Web usage analysis process, automating the preprocessing phase is compulsory.

A data warehouse architecture can be described as a system with four main components [4]: (i) *population tools*, which manage extraction, integration, transformation, and loading of operational data into the data warehouse, (ii) a *DBMS*, which stores the data and is materialized either by the multidimensional OLAP (MOLAP) or relational OLAP (ROLAP) approach, (iii) *meta-data repositories*, which handle meta-data interchange, (iv) *OLAP tools*, which provide a multidimensional view of the data warehouse data. All four components must be

---

[2] Many more commercial ETL tools are listed in [11, chapter 7].

[3] [14] plead for data collection with Web application servers, because this approach results in significantly less noise in raw Web usage data.

covered by our Web usage analysis system, either by integrating existing software packages, or implementing a component from scratch. In this section we briefly outline WUSAN, a system for effective Web usage analysis, which implements the LOORDSM that will be discussed in section 4 on page 24.

3.1 ROLAP Systems vs. MOLAP Systems

While ROLAP provides a straightforward mapping of the multi-dimensional logical data model to a relational DBMS (RDBMS) by using star schemas or related schemas [16], such a mapping to the underlying structures of a genuine multi-dimensional DBMS is more complex, because data is stored in multi-dimensional arrays (leading to a better performance compared to ROLAP). For WUSAN, we chose the ROLAP approach, for which off-the-shelf RDBMSs can be used. Our decision in favor of ROLAP is confirmed by the study [6], which concludes that after a considerable experience with OLAP, users prefer ROLAP systems because of their flexibility and ability to handle complex queries in a business environment, where analysis requirements change frequently.

The kernel of an ROLAP system is the *ROLAP engine*, which translates dynamically between the logical multi-dimensional data model and the relational model of a RDMS [4]. Each incoming multi-dimensional query is transformed into one or more relational queries, which are optimized and run against the RDBMS. The ROLAP engine is the bottleneck of a ROLAP system, since translated SQL queries generally contain a large number of joins on large volumes of data and hence must be optimized carefully, in order to minimize response times. For WUSAN we did not implement a critical component like the ROLAP engine from scratch, but integrated the open source ROLAP engine Mondrian [19], which uses Microsoft's multidimensional expressions language MDX [18] for multi-dimensional queries. This component could be replaced by any other commercial or non-commercial ROLAP engine.

3.2 Overall Architecture of the WUSAN System

Fig. 2 on the facing page depicts the overall architecture of WUSAN. Operational data and additional data sources can be accessed through streams (covered in section section 4.2 on page 26), which implement a cursor and deliver data to the population component record by record. Streams also provide meta-data about their attributes – a prerequisite for subsequent ETL transformations. The population component takes each record and performs a set of data transformations (for example extracting, combining, or splitting attributes), the results of which are written to relational schemas that are modeled in an object-oriented way. The population component includes caches that (i) collect single record database insertions for more efficient batch insertions, and (ii) buffer reading database accesses, in order to minimize response times for primary key lookups.

Once the RDBMS is populated, data can be accessed by streams (`Mining-QuerySqlStream` and `MiningQueryMdxStream`) using SQL or MDX queries to select data for data mining tasks. Since WUSAN provides data and meta-data

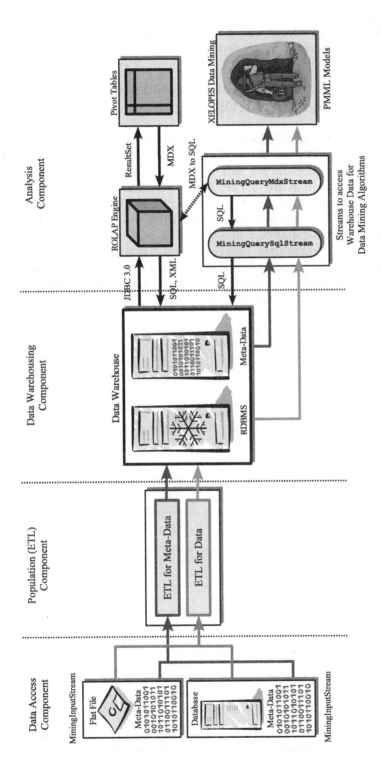

Fig. 2. Overall architecture of the Web usage analysis system (WUSAN)

whenever data is accessed, generally no further preprocessing is necessary before data mining algorithms can be applied.[4]

4   Towards a Logical Object-Oriented Relational Data Storage Model (LOORDSM)

Fig. 3 depicts how the LOORDSM can subsumed within WUSAN. As depicted in fig. 2 on the previous page, WUSAN's data warehouse is based on a RDBMS, which provides a vendor-specific data storage model that can be accessed in a uniform way through JDBC 3.0 or the CWM relational model. Because all major state of the art RDBMSs do not support the CWM yet, we use JDBC 3.0 to realize the mapping between our LOORDSM and the RDBMS's data storage model. The LOORDSM realizes the ETL process, which populates the data warehouse and shifts data into the underlying RDBMS. This process is realized independently from any logical multi-dimensional model. Once the data warehouse is populated, the logical multi-dimensional model for the ROLAP engine can be defined based on a concrete instance of the LOORDSM.

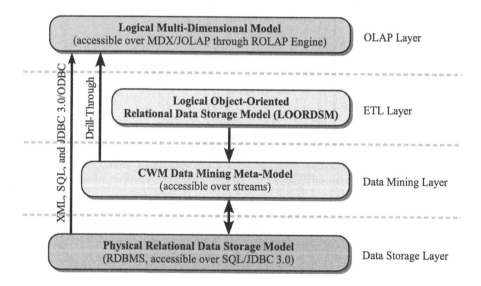

Fig. 3. Subsumption of the LOORDSM

4.1   Preliminary Notions and Definitions

W.l.o.g. an *attribute* A is a variable that takes values in its *coordinate-domain* $D(A) \cup \{\infty\}$, where $D(A) \subseteq \mathbb{R}$ is denoted as *domain*. $a \in D(A) \cup \{\infty\}$ denotes the attribute's current value. We use $\mathbb{R}$ as standard attribute domain and represent

---

[4] Provided that all relevant business information for a certain Web usage analysis business question are already contained in the data warehouse.

missing values by ∞. Hence, an attribute takes a value in its coordinate-domain at all times. Since all attributes take values in $\mathbb{R} \cup \{\infty\}$, it is necessary to add to each attribute meta-data, which bear semantic information, in order to model the semantics and types of an attribute. Any bijective mapping

$$\mu_A : D(A) \cup \{\infty\} \to \mu(A) \cup \{\infty\}$$

(where $\mu_A(\infty) = \infty$, and $\mu(A)$ denotes a user-defined semantic domain that is referred to as *meta-data* of A) is called *semantic basis* appendant to A. The tuple (A, μ_A) denotes a *mining attribute*. In summary it may be said that a mining attribute takes its values (or coordinates) in the coordinate-domain, whose meaning is explained by the assigned semantic basis.

We further classify a mining attribute according to its domain and semantic basis. If $\mu_A \equiv I_{D(A)}$, that is the identical mapping is chosen as semantic basis, $(A, I_{D(A)})$ is described as *numeric attribute*. If $D(A)$ is a countable subset of $\mathbb{R}$, (A, μ_A) is characterized as *discrete attribute*. If $D(A) = \{0, 1, \ldots, n\}$, $n \in \mathbb{N}$, and μ_A does not stand for the identical mapping, (A, μ_A) is referred to as *categorical attribute*. If, in addition, there exists a total order[5] on $\mu(A)$, (A, μ_A) is called *ordinal attribute*. In order to simplify notation throughout the remaining of this paper, we refer to a mining attribute (A, μ_A) as attribute A, but keep always in mind, that each attribute requires a semantic basis.

W.l.o.g let $(A_1, \ldots, A_m)$, $m \in \mathbb{N}$ be a permutation of a set of attributes $\{A_1, \ldots, A_m\}$,

$$\mathcal{D}(A_1, \ldots, A_m) := \big(D(A_1) \cup \{\infty\}\big) \times \cdots \times \big(D(A_m) \cup \{\infty\}\big),$$

and let

$$\mu(A_1, \ldots, A_m) := \big(\mu(A_1) \cup \{\infty\}\big) \times \cdots \times \big(\mu(A_1) \cup \{\infty\}\big).$$

Furthermore, let

$$\mu_{A_1, \ldots, A_m} : \mathcal{D}(A_1, \ldots, A_m) \to \mu(A_1, \ldots, A_m),$$

where $\mu_{A_1, \ldots, A_m}(\mathbf{a}) = \big(\mu_{A_1}(a_1), \ldots, \mu_{A_m}(a_m)\big)$, $\mathbf{a} := (a_1, \ldots, a_m)$. Then the tuple $(\mathbf{a}, \mu_{A_1, \ldots, A_m})$ denotes a *mining vector* with coordinates $\mathbf{a} \in \mathcal{D}(A_1, \ldots, A_m)$ relative to its *semantic basis* $\mu_{A_1, \ldots, A_m}$. Subsequently, we refer to a mining vector as *vector* only.

A sequence (that is an ordered multi-set) $\mathbf{A} := (\mathbf{a}^1, \ldots, \mathbf{a}^n)^\top$, $n \in \mathbb{N}$ is called *data matrix*. If there exists a total order $\big(\mu(A_\ell), \preceq \big)$, $\ell \in \{1, \ldots, m\}$ and if the rows of $\mathbf{A}$ are ordered ascending or descending according to $\big(\mu(A_\ell), \preceq \big)$, $\mathbf{A}$ is called *ordered data matrix*. $\mu_{\mathbf{A}} \equiv \mu_{A_1, \ldots, A_m}$ can also be regarded as semantic basis of $\mathbf{A}$. Finally, we define $\mu(\mathbf{A}) := \mu(A_1, \ldots, A_m)$ as *meta-data* of $\mathbf{A}$.

The notions and definitions, which have been introduced in this section, pick up the idea of strictly separating coordinates (representing current values) from

---

[5] A binary order relation R on a set fulfills reflexivity, anti-symmetry, and transitivity. R is a total order relation, if two arbitrary elements of the set are comparable.

their basis (representing the semantic meaning of coordinates) for mining attributes. This idea has been introduced implicitly by the CWM. As a consequence, the meaning of data accessed by streams can be described semantically by their semantic basis. This approach is crucial, when it comes to creating concrete ETL transformations with the LOORDSM.

In practice, we encounter a variety of instances of data matrices, for example flat files, that contain log data, database tables in a RDBMS, or multi-dimensional arrays in higher programming languages. Data matrices are the point of origin for all kinds of data preparation transformations and the application of data mining methods and algorithms, and thus represent the various data sources needed during the ETL process.

4.2 Streams to Access Data Matrices

Our LOORDSM is founded on two CWM packages, the *Data Mining* and *Transformation* packages. Both have been specified in UML and are described in detail in [24] and [20]. The first CWM package mentioned, the transformation package, contains classes and associations that represent common transformation meta-data used in data warehousing. It covers basic transformations among all types of data sources and targets. [29] regards CWM's transformation package as one of the biggest assets of the complete CWM standard. Although the package addresses a wider range of transformations than those of the data mining realm, we use it as means of modeling vector transformations within the ETL process. Speaking in terms of UML classes, the CWM transformation package provides a class `TransformationActivity`, which contains a sequence of `TransformationSteps`. Each `TransformationStep` can be regarded as a collection of interdependent relatively simple transformations, which are grouped together to build a more complex transformation.

The second package mentioned, the data mining package, contributes classes and associations, which lay the foundations for the application of data mining algorithms. The core contribution of the data mining package is the realization of the basic notions and definitions, which have been introduced in the previous section[6].

For our concrete modeling of the LOORDSM, we make use of the *Xelopes* Java data mining library [30]. According to its authors it is one of the first concrete implementations of the CWM transformation package, and the first implementation of the CWM data mining package. The library implements and extends both packages with regard to the application of data mining algorithms, preserving compatibility to the CWM's core meta-model.

Xelopes' central extension is the abstract class `MiningInputStream`, which provides flexible access mechanisms to a data matrix $\mathbf{A}$, which is a prerequisite

---

[6] The CWM does not provide the formal notions and definitions of section 4.1 on page 24. We introduced our formal description with respect to section 4.3 on page 28, where a formal model for the LOORDSM is introduced. On the one hand, a formalism makes it possible to describe our LOORDSM in a very compact way, on the other hand it inherently includes an interpretation of the CWM.

for all data preparation and data mining activities. The `MiningInputStream` class provides the `getMetaData`-method, which delivers μ_A (represented by the `MiningDataSpecification` class, which is basically a collection of `MiningAttributes`). Furthermore, it provides a cursor, which can be moved by the `next`-method. The `read`-method delivers the vector at the current cursor position. In order to make notation shorter, we refer to a class, which is derived from the `MiningInputStream` class, as *stream*.

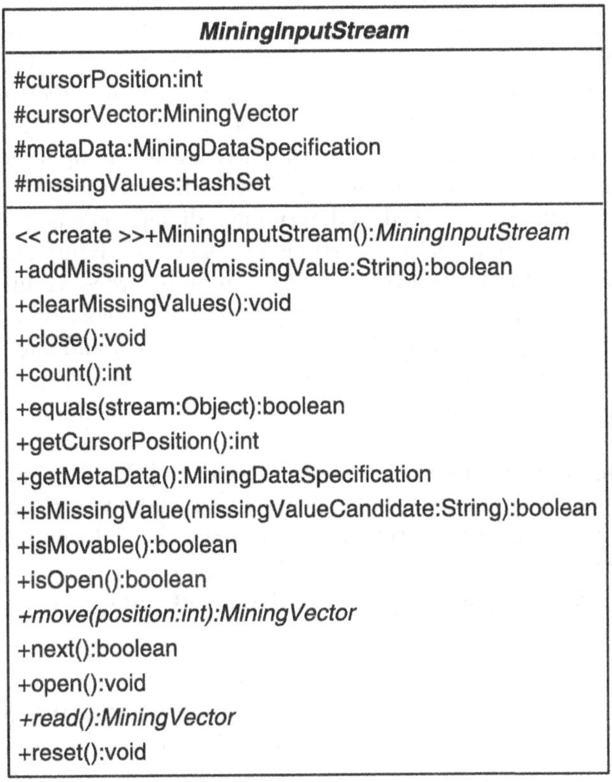

MiningInputStream
#cursorPosition:int
#cursorVector:MiningVector
#metaData:MiningDataSpecification
#missingValues:HashSet
<< create >>+MiningInputStream():*MiningInputStream*
+addMissingValue(missingValue:String):boolean
+clearMissingValues():void
+close():void
+count():int
+equals(stream:Object):boolean
+getCursorPosition():int
+getMetaData():MiningDataSpecification
+isMissingValue(missingValueCandidate:String):boolean
+isMovable():boolean
+isOpen():boolean
+move(position:int):MiningVector
+next():boolean
+open():void
+read():MiningVector
+reset():void

Fig. 4. Modeling data matrices (streams) with WUSAN (UML class diagram)

Fig. 4 depicts a UML class diagram of central stream classes provided by WUSAN. Basic stream functionality is specified by Xelopes' `MiningInputStream` class. The different stream types and their functions are self-explanatory. Xelopes provides several streams, most of which have been re-implemented from scratch in WUSAN to add functionality, for example WUSAN's `UpdatableStream` interface. In our LOORDSM we will use proprietary streams to model the tables to which the ETL process writes transformed data (namely the three SQL streams in fig. 4).

4.3   A Formal Model as Basis for the LOORDSM

Given a coordinate domain $\mathcal{D}(A_1, \ldots, A_m)$ and a semantic basis $\mu_{A_1,\ldots,A_m}$, $m \in \mathbb{N}$ and let

$$p : \mu(A_1, \ldots, A_m) \to \mathcal{P}$$

be a one-to-one and onto mapping. Then the mapping $p \circ \mu_{A_1,\ldots,A_m}$ maps any vector $\mathbf{a} \in \mathcal{D}(A_1, \ldots, A_m)$ to a one-dimensional user-defined domain $\mathcal{P}$. p is called *primary key mapping*, since it assigns a unique primary key to any given vector in $\mathcal{D}(A_1, \ldots, A_m)$. Let $\mathbf{A}$ be a data matrix of dimension $n \times m$ and $\mathbf{p}$ be the corresponding *primary key vector* of size $n \times 1$, i.e. $p_i := p \circ \mu_{A_1,\ldots,A_m}(\mathbf{a}^i)$, $i = 1, \ldots, n$. We construct a new data matrix $(\mathbf{p}|\mathbf{A})$ and define the tuple $D := \big((\mathbf{p}|\mathbf{A}), \mu_{A_1,\ldots,A_m}, p\big)$ as *dimension*. If $m = 1$, D is called *degenerated dimension*.

A dimension is based on a data matrix (for example a database table), the primary keys of which are calculated by the primary key mapping for every vector, which is inserted into the data matrix. As we will see in the next section, the primary key mapping can be used to determine a dimension's behavior in terms of permitting or impeding vector insertions into the underlying data matrix.

A fact table in a star schema (confer [16]) can be regarded as dimension with special features. Compared to a dimension, a fact table's core data matrix contains foreign keys only (except for degenerated dimensions) and may be extended by a set of *calculated attributes*. The value of a calculated attribute depends on the current vector of the core data matrix and at least one additional vector of the core data matrix.

Given an ordered set of *calculated attributes* $\mathcal{C} = \{C_1, \ldots, C_\ell\}$, $\ell \in \mathbb{N}_0$ (i.e. $\mathcal{C}$ may be empty) and an $n \times \ell$ data matrix $\mathbf{C}$ appendant to $\mathcal{C}$. In contrast to $A_1, \ldots, A_m$ the values of the attributes of $\mathcal{C}$ have the following dependencies given a vector $\mathbf{a} \in \mathbf{A}_0 : c_1(\mathbf{a}, \mathbf{A}_0), c_2(\mathbf{a}, c_1, \mathbf{A}_0), \ldots, c_\ell(\mathbf{a}, c_1, \ldots, c_{\ell-1}, \mathbf{A}_0)$, where $c_1, \ldots, c_\ell$ are real functions.[7] Let $C := \big((\mathbf{p}_0|\mathbf{A}_0|\mathbf{C}), \mu_{A_1,\ldots,A_m}, \mu_{C_1,\ldots,C_\ell}, p_0\big)$, where

$$p_0 : \mu(A_1, \ldots, A_m) \to \mathcal{P},$$

be a dimension based on an $n \times (m + \ell)$ data matrix $(\mathbf{A}_0|\mathbf{C})$. It is important to note that p_0 may be a one-to-one and not onto mapping and does not consider the attributes of $\mathcal{C}$, when calculating a primary key. Let $\Delta := \{D_1, \ldots, D_m\}$, $m \in \mathbb{N}$, be an ordered set of dimensions assigned to C. If $a_0^{i,j} = p_j(\mathbf{a}_j^k)$, where $i \in \{1, \ldots, n\}$, $j \in \{1, \ldots, m\}$, and $\mathbf{a}_j^k$ is the k-th row of $\mathbf{A}_j$, i.e. $\mathbf{A}_0$ contains foreign key references to the dimension vectors of Δ, C is denoted as *central table*[8].

---

[7] In OLAP terms, a calculated numeric attribute simply represents a (materialized) measure. The value of a calculated attribute cannot be calculated from the current row alone (if so it should rather be modeled as attribute and the calculation be integrated into ETL transformations). A calculated attribute may use values of other calculated attributes during its calculation. Although c_i, $i = 1, \ldots, \ell$ are real functions, a calculated attribute can be of any attribute type introduced in section 4.1 on page 24.

[8] We rather use the notion of a central table instead of a fact table, since by definition it is possible that C contains no calculated attributes.

The tuple $S = (C, \Delta)$ defines a *star schema*, which is a collection of an ordered set of dimensions Δ and a central table C. The central table contains foreign key references, which reference vectors of the dimensions, and calculated attributes. If a dimension is degenerated, its values can be taken as primary keys and the degenerated dimension may be embedded into the central table.

To finish off with the formal model, we make a note on vector transformations. Since a vector consists of its coordinates and its semantic basis, in general it is necessary to define both, a *coordinate transformation* and a *basis transformation*. In order to map $(\mathbf{a}, \mu_{A_1,\dots,A_m})$, $\mathbf{a} \in \mathcal{D}(A_1, \dots, A_m)$ to $(\mathbf{b}, \mu_{B_1,\dots,B_n})$, $\mathbf{b} \in \mathcal{D}(B_1, \dots, B_n)$ two mappings are required: (i) the coordinate transformation $t : \mathcal{D}(A_1, \dots, A_m) \rightarrow \mathcal{D}(B_1, \dots, B_n)$ (which is a $\mathbb{R}^m \rightarrow \mathbb{R}^n$ mapping), and (ii) the basis transformation T that maps $\mu_{A_1,\dots,A_m}$ to $\mu_{B_1,\dots,B_n}$ (T is actually an operator).

Let $D = \big((\mathbf{p}|\mathbf{A}), \mu_{A_1,\dots,A_m}, p\big)$ be a dimension, which is to be filled during the ETL process. Let $\mu_{\widetilde{A}_1,\dots,\widetilde{A}_\ell}$ be a semantic basis, of which we know that there exists a mapping T such that $T(\mu_{\widetilde{A}_1,\dots,\widetilde{A}_\ell}) = \mu_{A_1,\dots,A_m}$ holds ($\mu_{\widetilde{A}_1,\dots,\widetilde{A}_\ell}$ is referred to as *valid semantic basis* for D). Let $\mu_{\widehat{A}_1,\dots,\widehat{A}_k}$ be another semantic basis that fulfills $\{\widetilde{A}_1, \dots, \widetilde{A}_\ell\} \subseteq \{\widehat{A}_1, \dots, \widehat{A}_k\}$. Then we can define a projection Π such that $\Pi(\mu_{\widehat{A}_1,\dots,\widehat{A}_k}) = \mu_{\widetilde{A}_1,\dots,\widetilde{A}_\ell}$. The mapping $T \circ \Pi$ is denoted as *ETL basis transformation* for dimension D. Analogously, an *ETL coordinate transformation* $t \circ \pi$ can be defined.

4.4 Modeling the LOORDSM in UML

Eventually we introduce the LOORDSM as it has been realized in WUSAN. The different classes have been modeled with respect to the Web usage analysis domain. Fig. 5 on page 32 depicts the LOORDSM as UML class diagram, which has been restricted to crucial classes, methods and variables.

The class `MiningTableSQLStream` extends Xelopes' `MiningInputStream` and models access to a data matrix, whose physical realization is a relational database table. The `createHashKey`-method implements the primary key mapping p, which actually depends on the time, such that for $\mathbf{a} \in \mathbf{A}$ the mapping $p \circ \mu_{A_1,\dots,A_m}(\mathbf{a})$ delivers different unique keys at different times. As a consequence, a `MiningTableSQLStream` may contain duplicate vectors. The `insert`-method receives a vector, calculates and returns its primary key, and inserts the vector into the stream, if no entry with the calculated primary key exists. Due to the mentioned characteristics of p, any vector will be inserted into the stream.

The subclass `MiningExtendedTableSQLStream` implements a one-to-one and onto primary key mapping, which calculates an MD5 digest [26]. Hence, no duplicates are permitted in the stream, and a vector is inserted only, if it does not exist in the stream. The returned key is either the primary key of an existing vector or the key of a vector that has just been inserted into the stream. In our formal model we required p to be bijective for dimensions. Thus, the `MiningExtendedTableSQLStream` class can be taken as basis for dimension classes (unless a dimension is degenerated).

The interface ROLAPObject models a dimension D or a central table C. Its etl-method executes an ETL coordinate transformation and an ETL basis transformation, such that the transformed semantic basis is $\mu_{A_1,...,A_m}$. The getMetaData-method delivers $\mu_{A_1,...,A_m}$. The sub-interface AbstractDimension models dimensions and provides the createTransformation-method, which calculates both, the ETL coordinate and basis transformations. This is done using an ETLToDimensionFactory class. This class contains the hard wired transformation T and calculates the projection Π and the ETL transformation $T \circ \Pi$ dynamically depending on the semantic basis handed over as argument of the createTransformation-method.[9] The classes DegeneratedDimension and Dimension are direct realizations of an AbstractDimension. Degenerated dimensions are not derived from MiningExtendedTableSQLStream, since their data matrix is embedded into the central table. The CentralTable interface models a central table of a star schema and provides the getStarSchema-method, which delivers the schema to which it has been assigned.

Furthermore, fig. 5 on page 32 depicts three specialized subclasses of the Dimension class. A HybridDimension can be used to model normalized dimensions, which consist of a central table and sub-dimensions. It implements the CentralTable interface, since a normalized dimension behaves like a star schema with the subtle distinction that calculated attributes are optional. Due to its hybrid nature, three methods must be overridden: (i) the createHashKey-method must calculate foreign key references to the sub-dimensions beforehand, (ii) the createTransformation-method must calculate not only the central table's transformations, but those of the involved sub-dimensions as well, and (iii) the etl-method must invoke a more complex set of transformations, which executes the dimensions' etl-methods.

The subclass KeyCandidateDimension models dimensions, which inherently contain a primary key. In the Web usage analysis domain the session dimension (session ID as primary key) or the customer dimension (customer ID as primary key) can be frequently found. The createHashKey-method is overridden, since the dimensions' inherent primary key can be used for the primary key mapping p. Finally, the subclass SlowlyChangingDimension models a dimension, whose entries may change over time. Its insert-method is responsible for updating existing entries in the dimension. In the Web usage analysis domain a customer dimension can be modeled as SlowlyChangingDimension.

Fig. 5 on page 32 also depicts the StarSchema class, to which calculated attributes can be assigned optionally. An AbstractDimension can be assigned to several star schemas, whereas a central table can be assigned to only one star schema. In case of a hybrid dimension, the table (viewed as dimension) can still

---

[9] There exist two ways of responding to the problem of data sources, which change over time. If attributes are added to or removed from the data source, such that the chosen valid semantic basis is still contained, it is sufficient to invoke the createTransformation-method for the new semantic basis. If attributes belonging to the chosen valid semantic basis are removed, another valid semantic basis must be chosen to create a new ETLToDimensionFactory for the dimension.

be assigned to other schemas playing the role of a dimension. If a star schema's `etl`-method is invoked for a single vector, it calls the abstract dimensions' `etl`-methods and executes ETL coordinate transformations. If a dimension is hybrid, that is it is the central table of a normalized dimension (confer [16]) or another data mart (involving additional (sub-)dimensions), its `etl`-method automatically invokes the `etl`-method of each additional (sub-)dimension. Note that due to the dependencies of calculated attributes mentioned in the previous section (they do not solely depend on the source stream's current vector), calculated attributes are not part of the core ETL process and must be calculated separately.

5   A Concrete Modeling Example of a Web Warehouse

We suppose that we have transaction log files, which have been recorded for an electronic commerce Web site. The site offers a number of products and services, which are implemented by a Web application server. The log files do not contain a customer's detailed surfing behavior, but records about the transactions users completed during sessions. The log files, which are accessed by the WUSAN system through a `MiningInputStream`, contain the following attributes:

Attribute	Name	Type
A_1	Session ID	categorical
A_2	Customer ID	categorical
A_3	Timestamp	categorical
A_4	Transaction Type	categorical
A_5	Zip-Code	numeric
A_6	City	categorical

Our target is to analyze usage behavior on the level of *transactions*, *sessions*, and *customers*, each of which should be modeled in a separate star schema that can be mapped to multi-dimensional model. Fig. 6 on page 33 depicts the relational snowflake schema, which is modeled using our LOORDSM. The tables *Transaction*, *Session*, and *Customer* all implement the `CentralTable` interface, thus, besides calculated attributes, they may contain foreign key references or degenerated dimensions only. Hence, *Transaction Type*, *Session ID*, and *Customer ID* are modeled as degenerated dimensions. *Duration* is a calculated attribute.

Due to the foreign key dependencies, the order of how we create the classes is crucial. We start with the *Date* and *Location* dimensions, then create the *Customer*, *Session*, and *Transaction* dimensions. Three star schemas can be defined in fig. 6 on page 33:

Star Schema	Central Table	Dimension	Dimension Type
CustomerMart	Customer	Customer ID	degenerated dimension
		Location	normal dimension
		Date	normal dimension
SessionMart	Session	Session ID	degenerated dimension
		Date	normal dimension
		Customer	normalized slowly changing dimension
TransactionMart	Transaction	Transaction Type	degenerated dimension
		Date	normal dimension
		Session	normalized key candidate dimension
		Customer	normalized slowly changing dimension

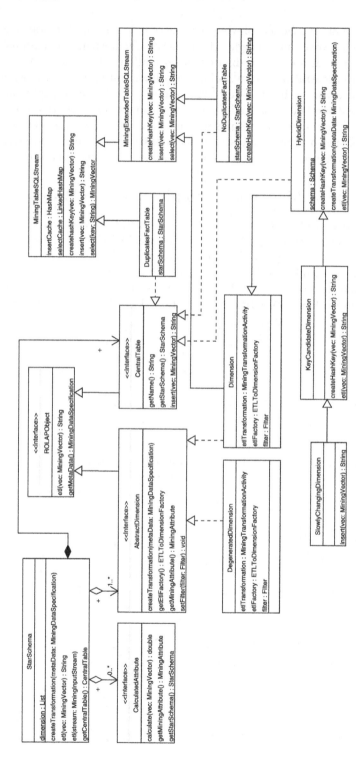

Fig. 5. The core LOORDSM depicted as UML class diagram

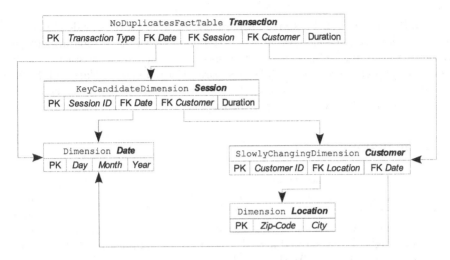

Fig. 6. Modeling a simple Web warehouse using the LOORDSM

It is obvious that our LOORDSM can model all common multi-dimensional relational schema types: star schema, snowflake schema, and 3NF schema [16].

Now comes the crucial part, the modeling of the ETL coordinate and basis transformations. This modeling is done separately for each dimension (including degenerated dimensions). Using dimension `Date` as an example, we must create a transformation T that takes the *Timestamp* attribute A_3 as input and calculates the attributes $B_1 = Day$, $B_2 = Month$, and $B_3 = Year$. Based on T we create an `ETLToDimensionFactory`, whose `etl`-method is invoked for vectors of the semantic basis $\mu_{A_1,\ldots,A_6}$. Internally, Π is created first, which maps $\mu_{A_1,\ldots,A_6}$ to μ_{A_3} and then $T \circ \Pi$, which maps $\mu_{A_1,\ldots,A_6}$ to $\mu_{B_1,\ldots,B_3}$. Analogously, `ETLToDimensionFactorys` must be created for each dimension.

If the *TransactionMart*'s `etl`-method is invoked, the following `etl`-method invocations are triggered (repeated invocations of the same `etl`-method are prevented by a cache):

ETL method of	Type	invoked by	Role
Transaction	central table	TransactionMart	star schema
Transaction Type	degenerated dimension	Transaction	central table
Date	normal dimension	Transaction	central table
Session	key candidate dimension	Transaction	central table
Session ID	degenerated dimension	Session	central table
Date	normal dimension	Session	central table
Customer	slowly changing dimension	Session	central table
Customer ID	degenerated dimension	Customer	central table
Location	normal dimension	Customer	central table
Date	normal dimension	Customer	central table
Customer	slowly changing dimension	Transaction	central table
⋮	⋮	⋮	⋮

An ETL process can be started separately for each mart provided that appropriate data sources are available. For instance, if we have separate stream containing customer data with semantic basis $\mu_{\tilde{A}_1,...,\tilde{A}_\ell}$, we may start an ETL process to populate the *CustomerMart* separately from *SessionMart* and *TransactionMart*. In order to initialize the correct transformations, we must invoke the `createTransformation`-method for $\mu_{\tilde{A}_1,...,\tilde{A}_\ell}$.

6 Conclusions

In this contribution we addressed the issue of modeling and deploying an ETL process in the Web usage analysis domain by introducing a logical object-oriented relational data storage model (LOORDSM). This model has been deployed within our WUSAN system, which has also been briefly summarized. A concrete modeling example showed how the model can be applied in practice. Since our model is founded on CWM's transformation package, all ETL transformations can be conveniently modeled capitalizing on Xelopes' implementation of the CWM transformation package, which provides almost unrestricted power of implementing ETL transformations.

As future work we intend to add the following features: a filtering mechanism, which prevents unwanted data from being written to the warehouse, a process for efficient calculations of calculated attributes, and a library of frequently occurring transformations in order to ease ETL transformation modeling. Furthermore, the caching strategy must be improved to make the ETL process faster. To round off the WUSAN system, additional classes must be implemented to be able to easily access the system's data warehouse for data mining tasks.

References

1. Suhail Ansari, Ron Kohavi, Llew Mason, and Zijian Zheng. Integrating E-Commerce and Data Mining: Architecture and Challenges. In Nick Cercone, Tsau Young Lin, and Xindong Wu, editors, *Proceedings of the 2001 IEEE International Conference on Data Mining, ICDM 2001*, pages 27–34, San José, CA, USA, December 2001. IEEE Computer Society Press.
2. ASCENTIAL. URL http://www.ascential.com. access date: 06/01/2004.
3. Robert Cooley, Bamshad Mobasher, and Jaideep Srivastava. Web Mining: Information and Pattern Discovery on the World Wide Web. In *Proceedings of the 9th International Conference on Tools with Artificial Intelligence, ICTAI 1997*, pages 558–567, Newport Beach, CA, USA, November 1997. IEEE Computer Society Press.
4. Barbara Dinter, Carsten Sapia, Gabriele Höfling, and Markus Blaschka. The OLAP Market: State of the Art and Research Issues. In *Proceedings of the First ACM International Workshop on Data Warehousing and OLAP, DOLAP 1998*, pages 22–27, Washington, DC, USA, November 1998. ACM Press.
5. ETI. URL http://www.eti.com. Access date: 06/01/2004.
6. Narasimhaiah Gorla. Features to Consider in a Data Warehousing System. *Communications of the ACM*, 46(11):111–115, November 2003.

7. Jiawei Han. OLAP Mining: An Integration of OLAP with Data Mining. In Stefano Spaccapietra and Fred J. Maryanski, editors, *Data Mining and Reverse Engineering: Searching for Semantics, Proceedings of the Seventh Conference on Database Semantics, DS-7*, pages 3–20, Leysin, Switzerland, October 1997. Chapman & Hall.

8. Xiaohua Hu and Nick Cercone. A Data Warehouse/Online Analytic Processing Framework for Web Usage Mining and Business Intelligence Reporting. *International Journal of Intelligent Systems*, 19(7):585–606, July 2004.

9. INFORMATICA. URL http://www.informatica.com. Access date: 06/01/2004.

10. Karuna P. Joshi, Anupam Joshi, and Yelena Yesha. On Using a Warehouse to Analyze Web Logs. *Distributed and Parallel Databases*, 13(2):161–180, March 2003.

11. Ralph Kimball and Joe Caserta. *The Data Warehouse ETL Toolkit*. Wiley, Indianapolis, IN, USA, 1 edition, 2004.

12. Ralph Kimball and Richard Merz. *The Data Webhouse Toolkit*. Wiley, Indianapolis, IN, USA, 1 edition, 2000.

13. Ron Kohavi. Mining E-Commerce Data: The Good, the Bad, and the Ugly. In Foster Provost, Ramakrishnan Srikant, Mario Schkolnick, and Doheon Lee, editors, *Proceedings of the Seventh ACM SIGKDD International Conference on Knowledge Discovery and Data Mining, KDD 2001*, pages 8–13, San Francisco, CA, USA, August 2001. ACM Press.

14. Ron Kohavi, Llew Mason, Rajesh Parekh, and Zijian Zheng. Lessons and Challenges from Mining Retail E-Commerce Data. *Machine Learning*, 57(1/2):83–115, October 2004.

15. Thilo Maier and Thomas Reinartz. Evaluation of Web Usage Analysis Tools. *Künstliche Intelligenz*, (1):65–68, January 2004.

16. Tim Martyn. Reconsidering Multi-Dimensional Schemas. *SIGMOD Record*, 33(1): 83–88, March 2004.

17. MICROSOFT-DTS. *Data Transformation Services (DTS)*. Microsoft Corporation. URL http://www.microsoft.com/sql/evaluation/features/datatran.asp. Access date: 06/01/2004.

18. MICROSOFT-MDX. *MDX (Multidimensional Expressions)*. Microsoft Corporation. URL http://msdn.microsoft.com/library/default.asp?url=/library/en-us/olapdmad/agmdxbasics_04qg.asp. access date: 04/19/2004.

19. MONDRIAN-OLAP. URL http://mondrian.sourceforge.net/. Access date: 04/19/2004.

20. OMG. *Common Warehouse Metamodel Specification*. Object Management Group, 2001. URL http://www.omg.org/docs/ad/01-02-01.pdf. Access date: 06/18/2003.

21. Shan L. Pan and Jae-Nam Lee. Using e-CRM for a Unified View of the Customer. *Communications of the ACM*, 46(4):95–99, April 2003.

22. Adrian Payne. The Multi-Channel Integration Process in Customer Relationship Management. White Paper, Cranfield School of Management, Cranfield University, Cranfield, UK, February 2003a. URL http://www.insightexec.com/cgi-bin/library.cgi?action=detail&id=1957. Access date: 03/08/2005.

23. Adrian Payne. A Strategic Framework for Customer Relationship Management. White Paper, Cranfield School of Management, Cranfield University, Cranfield, UK, May 2003b. URL http://www.insightexec.com/cgi-bin/library.cgi?action=detail&id=2254. Access date: 03/05/2005.

24. John Poole, Dan Chang, Douglas Tolbert, and David Mellor. *Common Warehouse Metamodel. Developer's Guide*. Wiley, Indianapolis, IN, USA, 1 edition, 2003.

25. Erhard Rahm and Thomas Stöhr.   Data-Warehouse-Einsatz zur Web-Zugriffsanalyse. In Erhard Rahm and Gottfried Vossen, editors, *Web und Datenbanken. Konzepte, Architekturen, Anwendungen*, pages 335–362. Dpunkt Verlag, Heidelberg, Germany, 1 edition, 2002.

26. Ronald L. Rivest. The MD5 Message-Digest Algorithm, 1992. URL http://theory.lcs.mit.edu/~rivest/Rivest-MD5.txt Access date: 07/09/2004.

27. Jaideep Srivastava, Jau-Hwang Wang, Ee-Peng Lim, and San-Yih Hwang. A Case for Analytical Customer Relationship Management. In Ming-Shan Cheng, Philip S. Yu, and Bing Liu, editors, *Advances in Knowledge Discovery and Data Mining. Proceedings of the 6th Pacific-Asia Conference, PAKDD 2002*, pages 14–27, Taipei, Taiwan, May 2002. Springer.

28. Michael Stonebraker. Too Much Middleware. *SIGMOD Record*, 31(1):97–106, March 2002.

29. Michael Thess. Xeli's Intro. Introduction to Xelopes. White Paper, Prudsys AG, May 2004. URL http://www.xelopes.de. Access date: 07/09/2004.

30. Michael Thess and Michael Bolotnicov. *XELOPES Library Documentation Version 1.2.5*. Prudsys AG, November 2004. URL http://www.xelopes.de. Access date: 07/09/2004.

31. Panos Vassiliadis, Zografoula Vagena, Spiros Skiadopoulos, Nikos Karayannidis, and Timos Sellis. ARKTOS: Towards the Modeling, Design, Control and Execution of ETL Processes. *Information Systems*, 26(8):537–561, December 2001.

32. Panos Vassiliadis, Alkis Simitsis, and Spiros Skiadopoulos. Conceptual Modeling for ETL Processes. In *Proceedings of the 5th ACM International Workshop on Data Warehousing and OLAP*, pages 14–21, McLean, VA, USA, November 2002. ACM Press.

33. Panos Vassiliadis, Alkis Simitsis, Panos Georgantas, and Manolis Terrovitis. A Framework for the Design of ETL Scenarios. In Johann Eder and Michele Missikoff, editors, *Advanced Information Systems Engineering. 15th International Conference, CAiSE 2003*, pages 520–535, Klagenfurt, Austria, June 2003. Springer.

34. Osmar R. Zaïane, Man Xin, and Jiawei Han. Discovering Web Access Patterns and Trends by Applying OLAP and Data Mining Technology on Web Logs. In *Proceedings of the Advances in Digital Libraries Conference, ADL 1998*, pages 19–29, Santa Barbara, CA, USA, April 1998. IEEE Computer Society.

Mission-Based Navigational Behaviour Modeling for Web Recommender Systems[*]

Osmar R. Zaïane[**], Jia Li, and Robert Hayward

University of Alberta, Edmonton AB, Canada
zaiane@cs.ualberta.ca

Abstract. Web recommender systems anticipate the information needs of on-line users and provide them with recommendations to facilitate and personalize their navigation. There are many approaches to building such systems. Among them, using web access logs to generate users' navigational models capable of building a web recommender system is a popular approach, given its non-intrusiveness. However, using only one information channel, namely the web access history, is often insufficient for accurate recommendation prediction. We therefore advocate the use of additional available information channels, such as the content of visited pages and the connectivity between web resources, to better model user navigational behavior. This helps in better modeling users' concurrent information needs. In this chapter, we investigate a novel hybrid web recommender system, which combines access history and the content of visited pages, as well as the connectivity between web resources in a web site, to model users' concurrent information needs and generate navigational patterns. Our experiments show that the combination of the three channels used in our system significantly improves the quality of web site recommendation and, further, that each additional channel used contributes to this improvement. In addition, we discuss cases on how to reach a compromise when not all channels are available.

1 Introduction

A web recommender system is a web-based interactive software agent. It attempts to predict user preferences from user data and/or user access data for the purpose of facilitating users' information needs by providing them with recommendation lists of suggested items. The recommended items could be products, such as books, movies, and music CDs, or on-line resources such as web pages or on-line activities. In general, a web recommender system is composed of two modules: an off-line module and an on-line module. The off-line module pre-processes data to generate user models, while the on-line module uses and updates the models on-the-fly to recognize user goals and predict recommendation lists.

In this chapter, we investigate the design of a hybrid recommender system to recommend on-line resources, with the emphasis of the presence of concurrent

[*] Research funded in part by the Alberta Ingenuity Funds and NSERC Canada.
[**] Corresponding author.

B. Mobasher et al. (Eds.): WebKDD 2004, LNAI 3932, pp. 37–55, 2006.

information needs. Pursuing more than one goal simultaneously (i.e. concurrent information needs) is fairly common for on-line users, but this fact has so far been ignored by web usage-based recommender systems and the research community. We call these simultaneous goals *"missions"* and we use different information channels to identify them, namely the web access usage, the web content, and the web connectivity. Unfortunately, these channels are not all always available and we need to find compromises depending upon the application at hand. Our preliminary goals are to first accurately identify users' multiple information needs, and then assist them to fulfill their needs by predicting their goals and recommend shortcuts to them. Our system has been designed for and tested on both a generic web server log (University of Alberta Department of Computing Science web server log) and an idiosyncratic log created by VIVIDESK$^{(TM)}$, a commercial desktop application that integrates user accesses to multiple on-line applications and resources for health care providers.

One of the earliest and widely used technologies for building recommender systems is *Collaborative Filtering* (CF) [21] [9]. CF-based recommender systems aggregate explicit user ratings or product preferences in order to generate user profiles, which recognize users' interests. A product is recommended to the current user if it is highly rated by other users who have similar interests to the current user. The CF-based techniques suffer from several problems [20]. First of all, they rely heavily on explicit user input (e.g., previous customers' rating/ranking of products), which is either unavailable or considered intrusive. With the sparsity of such user input, the recommendation precision and quality drop significantly. The second challenge is related to the system scalability and efficiency. For a CF-based recommender system, user profile matching has to be performed as an on-line process. For very large datasets, this may lead to unacceptable latency for providing recommendations.

In recent years there has been an increasing interest in applying web usage mining techniques to build web recommender systems [22] [8] [14] [24]. Web usage recommender systems take web server access logs as input, and make use of data mining techniques such as *association rule* and *clustering* to extract implicit, and potentially useful navigational patterns, which are then used to provide recommendations. Web server access logs record user browsing history, which contains plenty of hidden information regarding users and their navigation. They could, therefore, be a good alternative to the explicit user rating or feedback in deriving user models. In web usage recommender systems, navigational patterns are generally derived as an off-line process.

However, a web usage recommender system which focuses solely on access history has its own problems:

- *Incomplete Information* Problem: One restriction with web server logs is that the information in them is very limited. Thus, a number of heuristic assumptions have to be made to identify individual users, visit sessions, and transactions in order to apply any data mining algorithm. One such assumption is that user information needs are fulfilled sequentially while in practice they are often in parallel.

- *Incorrect Information* Problem: When web site visitors are lost, the clicks made by them are recorded in the log, and may mislead future recommendations. This becomes more problematic when a web site is badly designed and more people end up visiting unsolicited pages, making them seem popular.
- *Persistence* Problem: When new pages are added to a web site, because they have not been visited yet, the recommender system may not recommend them, even though they could be relevant. Moreover, the more a page is recommended, the more it may be visited, thus making it look popular and boost its candidacy for future recommendation.

To address these problems, we proposed a hybrid web recommender system [11], which attempts to use three information channels to model user navigational behavior: web access logs, the structure of a visited web site, and the content of visited web pages. In particular, the approach uses the terms within visited web pages to partition visit sessions into overlapping sub-sessions, called *missions*. Our preliminary experiments [11] [12] demonstrate that combining the different information channels has great potential to improve the quality of recommendation. In this chapter, we build upon our previous work to further test and compare the effectiveness of using information from different channels, and from different channels in combination. The experiment is performed on a dataset provided by a generic web site. Our initial approach makes the assumption that all channels are available, which is true only when the recommendation is done on the web server itself, and when web pages are static. In some scenarios, however, the page content is not readily accessible by the recommender agent. When pages are generated dynamically and their content changes, if the content channel needs to be used, the model has to change to attach the content to the use at access time rather than the page itself. In this chapter, we present our initial model and discuss ways to reach a compromise when not all channels – content in particular – are available. We test our approach on a different datasets with different channels available.

A few combined or hybrid web recommender systems have been proposed in the literature [15] [16]. The work in [15] adopts a clustering technique to obtain both site usage and site content profiles in the off-line phase. In the on-line phase, a recommendation set is generated by matching the current active session and all usage profiles. Similarly, another recommendation set is generated by matching the current active session and all content profiles. Finally, a set of pages with the maximum recommendation value across the two recommendation sets is presented as recommendation. This is called a *weighted* hybridization method [3]. In [16], Nakagawa and Mobasher use association rule mining, sequential pattern mining, and contiguous sequential mining to generate three types of navigational patterns in the off-line phase. In the on-line phase, recommendation sets are selected from the different navigational models, based on a localized degree of hyperlink connectivity with respect to a user's current location within the site. This is called a *switching* hybridization method [3]. Whether using the weighted method or the switching method, the combination in these systems happens only in the on-line phase. Our approach, however, combines different information channels in the off-line phase, and therefore, possesses the advantage of high efficiency. There is other work which discusses the combination of different channels, albeit they were not proposed for use with recommender systems. In [6], Chi et al. develop a system that combines multiple data features of each web page to construct user profiles. The user profile in [6] is built mainly upon the content of web pages, represented by keyword vectors; while the web access log is used to provide weights to individual keywords, giving keywords appearing in more frequently visited pages higher weights. Our approach, on the other hand, makes use of content information to identify missions from usage sessions, to better model users' concurrent information needs and navigational patterns. In [17], Nasraoui et al. define a web session similarity that takes web site structure into account, and hence implicitly fuses structure information to the usage clustering process.

Our contributions are as follows: First, we propose a novel web recommender system, which investigates combining and making full use of distinctive information channels available, such as usage data, content data, and structure data, to improve recommendation quality. Second, we propose a novel notion, *mission*, to capture users' concurrent information needs during on-line navigation, and discuss different ways to identify *missions*. Third, a new on-line navigational model – a mission-based model – is proposed and generated, based on the notion of *mission*. The mission-based model has been proved to better capture users' on-line behavior for the purpose of fulfilling information needs.

This chapter is organized as follows: Section 2 presents the off-line module of our system, which pre-processes available usage and web site data to generate users' navigational models, as well as our on-line module, which generates the recommendation list. In particular, in the off-line module, we present the preprocessing step by step and explain our new notion "mission", how missions model concurrent information needs during visits and how missions are detected using the available information channels. Section 3 presents experimental results assessing the performance of our system on two real datasets. Finally, Section 4 concludes.

2   Architecture of a Hybrid Recommender System

As most web usage recommender systems, our system is composed of two modules: an off-line component, which pre-processes data to generate users' navigational models, and an on-line component which is a real-time recommendation engine. Figure 1 depicts the general architecture of our system.

Entries in a web server log are used to identify users and visit sessions, while web pages or resources in the site are clustered based on their content. These clusters of web documents are used to scrutinize the discovered web sessions in order to identify what we call *missions*. A *mission* is a sub-session with a consistent goal. These *missions* are in turn clustered to generate navigational patterns, and augmented with their linked neighbourhood and ranked based on resource connectivity, using the *hub* and *authority* idea [10]. These new clusters

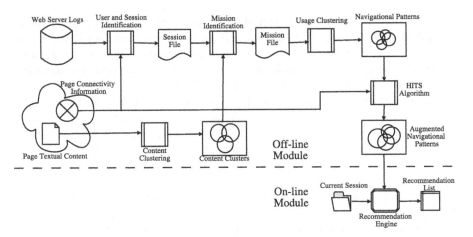

Fig. 1. System Architecture with all three channels available

(i.e., augmented navigational patterns) are provided to the recommendation engine. When a visitor starts a new session, the session is matched with these clusters to generate a recommendation list. The details of the whole process are given below.

2.1   User and Visit Session Identification

A web log is a text file which records information regarding users' requests to a web server. A typical web log entry contains a client address, the requested date address, a time-stamp, and other related information.

For any web access log data, several pre-processing tasks have to be performed before applying data mining techniques for pattern discovery. The pre-processing tasks usually include user identification, visit session identification, and transaction identification. We distinguish two types of web access logs as depicted by our experiments in Section 3: generic web access logs, and session-based access logs. For generic logs, we use similar pre-processing techniques as in [7] to identify individual users and sessions. To sessionize log entries, we chose an idle time of 30 minutes. Session-based access logs, however, have entries identified by users since the users have to log-in, and sessions are already identified since users have also to log-out.

2.2   Visit Mission Identification

The last data pre-processing step proposed in [7] is transaction identification, which divides individual visit sessions into transactions. Two transaction identification approaches are proposed: *Reference Length* approach and *Maximal Forward Reference* approach, both of which have been widely applied in web mining. Rather than dividing sessions into arbitrary transactions, we identify sub-sessions with coherent information needs. We call these sub-sessions *missions*. We assume that a visitor may have different information needs to fulfill during a visit, but we make no assumption on the sequence in which these needs are fulfilled. In the case of transactions in [7], it is assumed that one information need is fulfilled after the other. A *mission* would model a sub-session related to one of these information needs, and would allow overlap between missions, which would represent a concurrent search in the site.

Now how do we identify *missions*? The first approach we proposed to identify *missions* is based on web content [11]. While in the transaction-based model, pages are labeled as *content* pages and *auxiliary* pages, and a transaction is simply a sequence of auxiliary pages that ends with a content page, in the mission-based model we propose, the identified sequence is based on the real content of pages. Indeed, a content page in the transaction-based model is identified simply based on the time spent on that page, or on backtracking in the visitor's navigation. We argue that missions could better model users' navigational behavior than transactions. In our model, users visit a web site with concurrent goals, i.e., different information needs. For example, a user could fulfill two goals in a visit session: a, b, c, d, in which pages a and c contribute to one goal, while pages b and d contribute to the other. Since pages related to a given goal in a visit session are generally supposed to be content coherent, whether they are neighbouring each other or not, we use page content to identify missions within a visit session.

All web site pages are clustered based on their content, and these clusters are used to identify content coherent clicks in a session. Let us give an example to illustrate this point. Suppose the text clustering algorithm groups web pages a, b, c, and e, web pages a, b, c, and f, and web pages a, c and d into three different content clusters (please note that our text clustering algorithm is a soft clustering one, which allows a web page to be clustered into several clusters). Then for a visit session: a, b, c, d, e, f, our system identifies three missions as follows: mission 1: (a, b, c, e); mission 2: (a, b, c, f); and mission 3: (a, c, d). As seen in this example, mission identification in our system is different from transaction identification in that we can group web pages into one mission even if they are not sequential in a visit session. We can see that our mission-based model subsumes the transaction-based model, since missions could become transactions if visitors fulfill their information needs sequentially.

To cluster web pages based on their content, we use a modified version of the DC-tree algorithm [23]. Originally, the DC-tree algorithm was a hard clustering approach, prohibiting overlap of clusters. We modified the algorithm to allow web pages to belong to different clusters. Indeed, some web pages could cover different topics at the same time. In the algorithm, each web page is represented as a keyword vector, and organized in a tree structure called the DC-tree. The algorithm does not require the number of clusters to discover as a constraint, but allows the definition of cluster sizes. This was the appealing property which made us select the algorithm. Indeed, we do not want either too large or too small content cluster sizes. Very large clusters cannot help capture missions from sessions, while very small clusters may break potentially useful relations between pages in sessions.

The mission identification approach above relies on the availability of textual content of web pages, which could not always be satisfied. The purpose of identifying *missions*, however, is to identify users' concurrent information needs in the same visit. With some other specific application access logs, this goal can be achieved by other means. For instance, the URLs recorded in the VIVIDESK$^{(TM)}$ access logs come from different web sites, and a large number of them are dynamically generated. This makes the access to page content for mission identification close to impossible. The alternative, however, is that since VIVIDESK integrates the simultaneous accesses to multiple on-line applications, it records in its logs the application attached to each given access. Therefore, we use the application identifier as an indicator of a mission. Our experiments (see Section 3) show that this is a good approach to identify missions for VIVIDESK$^{(TM)}$ data. Moreover, this generalizes our notion of *mission*. In addition, this highlights the importance to have application related logs rather than just relying on information poor web server logs.

VIVIDESK$^{(TM)}$ (www.vividesk.com) is a commercial system developed by the Centre of Health Evidence at the University of Alberta as a gate to a multitude of applications and on-line resources, and is used by hospital personnel and other health practitioners. It has its specific session-based activity log which records details about user accesses to on-line pages via different applications. The log entries encompass more specific details than typical web server logs and pertain to different web sites rather than just one. Moreover, since users need to authenticate and then safely quit the application, users and exact sessions are automatically identified.

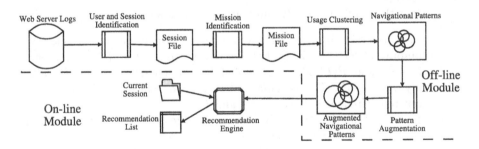

Fig. 2. System Architecture when web content is not available

Figure 2 shows the general architecture of our system when web page content is not available and clustering of web pages based on content coherence for mission identification is not possible. This is the case for the VIVIDESK$^{(TM)}$ data.

2.3   Navigational Pattern Discovery

According to how missions are identified, we propose two ways to discover navigational patterns from discovered missions. If missions are identified based on content coherence, we could therefore discover content coherent navigational patterns which are sets of web pages that are frequently visited together and that have related content. These patterns are used by the recommender system to recommend web pages, if they were not already visited. To discover these navigational patterns, we simply group the missions we uncovered from the web server logs into clusters of sub-sessions having commonly visited pages. Each of the resulting clusters could be viewed as a user's navigation pattern. In this scenario, the patterns discovered from missions possess two characteristics: usage cohesive and content coherent. Usage cohesiveness means the pages in a cluster tend to be visited together, while content coherence means pages in a cluster tend to be related to a topic or concept. This is because missions are grouped according to content information. Since each cluster is related to a topic, and each page has been represented in a keyword vector, we are able to easily compute the topic vector of each cluster, in which the value of a keyword is the average of the corresponding values of all pages in the cluster. The cluster topic is widely used in our system, in both the off-line and on-line phases (see below for details). In the case where we discover missions in the absence of textual content, the navigational patterns discovered hold only usage cohesion characteristic and do not guarantee content coherence. Thus, no cluster topic vector is computed.

The clustering algorithm we adopt for grouping missions is *PageGather* [19]. This algorithm is a soft clustering approach allowing overlap of clusters. Instead of trying to partition the entire space of items, it attempts to identify a small number of high quality clusters based on the *clique* clustering technique [19].

The algorithm could be briefly summarized as follows:

- For each pair of web pages *P1* and *P2* in the visit missions (collectively), we compute $P(P1|P2)$, the probability of a visitor visiting *P1* after already visiting *P2* and $P(P2|P1)$, the probability of a visitor visiting *P2* after already visiting *P1*. The minimum of these two values is recorded as the co-occurrence frequency between *P1* and *P2*.
- We create a similarity matrix between web pages where the distance (similarity) between pages is either zero if the two pages are directly linked in the web site structure (i.e. there is a hyperlink from one to the other) or set to the co-occurrence frequency between the two pages otherwise.
- We create a graph *G* in which each page is a node and each nonzero cell in the matrix is an arc.
- In order to reduce noise, we apply a threshold to remove edges corresponding to low co-occurrence frequency.
- In this graph *G*, a cluster corresponds to a set of nodes whose numbers are directly connected with arcs. A clique – a subgraph in which every pair of nodes has an edge between them – is a cluster in which every pair of pages co-occurs often.

2.4 Navigational Pattern Improved with Connectivity

The missions we extracted and clustered to generate navigational patterns are primarily based on the sessions from the web server logs. These sessions exclusively represent web pages or resources that were visited. It is conceivable that there are other resources not yet visited, even though they are relevant and could be interesting to have in the recommendation list. Such resources could be, for instance, newly added web pages or pages that have links to them not evidently presented due to bad design. Thus, these pages or resources are never presented in the missions previously discovered. Since the navigational patterns, represented by the clusters of pages in the missions, are used by the recommendation engine, we need to provide an opportunity for these rarely visited or newly added pages to be included in the clusters. Otherwise, they would never be recommended. To alleviate this problem, our general system model expands the clusters to include the connected neighbourhood of every page in a mission cluster. The local neighborhood of a page, obtained by tracing a small number of links from the originating page, is a good approximation to the "semantic neighborhood" of the page [13]. In our case, the connected neighbourhood of a page p is the set of all the pages directly linked from p and having similar content of p, and all the pages that directly link to p also with similar content. Figure 3(A) illustrates the concept of neighbourhood expansion, and Figure 3 (B) shows the process of the augmentation. The cluster expansion is only possible when content and structure channels are available. In detail, this approach of expanding the

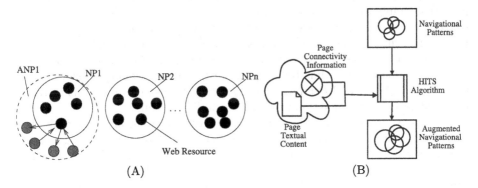

Fig. 3. (A) Navigational Patterns(NPs) and Augmented Navigational Patterns(ANPs) (B) The Augmentation Process

neighbourhood is performed as follows: we consider each previously discovered navigational pattern (i.e., a cluster of content coherent and visitation cohesive missions) as a set of seeds. Each seed is supplemented with pages it links to and pages that link to it as well as having similar content. The result is what is called a connectivity graph which now represents our augmented navigational pattern. This process of obtaining the connectivity graph is similar to the process used by the HITS algorithm [10] to find the *authority* and *hub* pages for a given topic. The difference is that we do not consider a given topic, but start from a mission cluster as our set of seeds. Moreover, it was shown in [1] that HITS, using pure connectivity analysis, introduces a problem known as "topic drift". We eliminate this problem in our case by computing relevance weights of all supplemented pages. The relevance weight of a page equals the similarity of the page content to the corresponding mission cluster, which is represented by the cosine normalization of web pages and mission clusters keyword vectors. We then prune nodes whose relevance weights are below a threshold from the connectivity graph. For simplicity, we use *Median Weight* (i.e. the median of all relevance weights) as the pruning threshold [1]. The pruning process avoids augmenting the navigational patterns with pages that focus on other topics and guarantees that the augmented patterns are still coherent and focused. After expanding and pruning the clusters representing the navigational patterns, we also augment the keyword vectors that label the clusters. The new keyword vectors that represent the augmented navigational patterns have also the terms extracted from the content of the augmented pages.

We take advantage of the built connectivity graph by cluster to apply the HITS algorithm in order to identify the *authority* and *hub* pages within a given cluster. These measures of *authority* and *hub* allow us to rank the pages within the cluster. This is important because at real time during the recommendation, it is crucial to rank recommendations, especially if they are numerous. Long recommendation lists are not advisable.

Authority and *hub* are mutually reinforcing [10] concepts. Indeed, a good *authority* is a page pointed to by many good *hub* pages, and a good *hub* is a page that points to many good *authority* pages. Since we would like to be able to recommend pages newly added to the site, in our framework, we consider only the *hub* measure. This is because a newly added page would be unlikely to be a good authoritative page, since not many pages are linked to it. However, a good new page would probably link to many *authority* pages; it would, therefore, have the chance to be a good *hub* page. Consequently, we use the *hub* value to rank the candidate recommendation pages in the on-line module.

Some may argue to use the content similarity (if applicable) to rank the candidate recommendations. However, the success of Google (www.google.com) encourages us to embed web structure analysis into this task. In Google, *PageRank* [2] – a pure web linkage analysis algorithm – is combined with the textual content information of web pages to provide search results. In general, when a user submits a query, Google searches all pages containing the keyword(s) in the query. The resulting pages are ranked according to their *PageRank* scores, which have been pre-computed. The higher its *PageRank* value, the earlier a page is presented to the user. Traditionally, a search engine can be viewed as an application of information retrieval with the focus on "matching": a search engine is supposed to return all those pages that match users' query, ranked by degree of match. On the other hand, the semantics of a recommender system is "interesting and useful" [3]. However, Google blurs this distinction by incorporating *PageRank* into its ranking, which uses web structure information to measure the authoritativeness or importance of web pages. From this point, Google can be viewed as a form of hybrid recommender system combining content and structure analysis with a one-input interface (By contrast, regular recommender systems have a zero-input interface). Indeed, this linkage analysis could compensate the possible limitation of our content coherent mission identification to web pages that are related by the virtue of their functionality rather than content. Ranking recommendation candidates based on this connectivity analysis could also allow rarely visited or newly added pages to be include in recommendations. This is important because rarely visited pages and newly added pages do not have corresponding entries in the web server access log and are typically excluded from any potential recommendation. Our approach gives them the chance to be picked up as recommended pages.

2.5 The Recommendation Engine

The previously described process consists of pre-processing done exclusively off-line. When a visitor starts a new session in the web site, we identify the navigation pattern after a few clicks and try to match on-the-fly with already captured navigational patterns. If they were matched, we recommend the most relevant pages in the matched cluster. When page content is not obtainable, the available clusters are based solely on access history, and we identify navigational patterns by finding the clusters that contain the last page referenced in the current user's mission. However, in the presence of content, identifying the navigational pattern of the current visitor consists of recognizing the current focused topic of interest to the user. A study in [4] shows that looking on either side of an anchor (i.e., text encapsulated in a *href* tag) for a window of 50 bytes would capture the topic of the linked pages. Based on this study, we consider the anchor clicked by the current user and its neighbourhood on either side as the contextual topic of interest. The captured topics are also represented by a keyword vector which is matched with the keyword vectors of the clusters representing the augmented navigational patterns. From the best match, we get the pages with the best *hub* value and provide them in a recommendation list, ranked by the *hub* values. The *hub* value is chosen for ranking instead of the *authority* value because the *authority* value does not favor newly added pages and disadvantages them. Indeed, newly added pages are not linked from other pages since they were unknown and thus would never have a high value of *authority*. However, newly added pages could certainly link to good authorities.

To avoid supplying a very large list of recommendations, the number of recommendations is adjusted according to the number of links in the current page: we simply make this number proportional to the number of links in the current page. Our goal is to have a different recommendation strategy for different pages based on how many links the page already contains. Our general strategy is to give $\sqrt{n}$ best recommendations (n is the number of links), with a maximum of 10. The limit of 10 is to prevent adding noise and providing too many options. The relevance and importance of recommendations is measured with the *hub* value already computed off-line.

3   Experimental Evaluation

We evaluate our recommendation framework on both a generic web site dataset with all three information channels available (the University of Alberta Department of Computing Science web server, abbreviated as the UofA CS web server) and an application-specific enriched log with only the usage channel available (VIVIDESK$^{(TM)}$ session-based logs). For the UofA CS web server access logs, data were collected for 8 months (Sept. 2002 – Apr. 2003), and partitioned into months. On average, each monthly partition contains more than 40,000 pages, resulting in on average 150,000 links between them. The log of each month averaged more than 200,000 visit sessions, which generated an average of 800,000 missions per month. The modified DC-tree content clustering algorithm generated about 1500 content clusters, which we used to identify the missions per month. For VIVIDESK$^{(TM)}$ logs, data were collected for one and a half years (May 2001 – Sept. 2002), totaling 16024 login sessions. Data are also partitioned into months.

3.1   Methodology

Given the data partitioned per month as described above, we adopt the following empirical evaluation: one or more months data is used for building our models (i.e., training the recommender system), and the following month or months for evaluation. The reason why we divide the data based on a time frame (months) rather than use standard cross-validation on the data set is that we want to measure the prediction ability of our system for the future rather than merely the past. Moreover, the web site evolves over time. More specifically, the idea is that given a session s from a month m, if the recommender system, based on data from month $m - 1$ and some prefix of the session s, can recommend pages p_i that contain some of the pages in the suffix of s, then the recommendation is considered accurate. Moreover, the distance in the number of clicks between the suffix of s and the recommended page p_i is considered a gain (i.e., a shortcut). More precisely, we measure the *Recommendation Accuracy* and the *Shortcut Gain* as described below.

   Recommendation Accuracy is the ratio of correct recommendations among all recommendations, and the correct recommendation is the one that appears in the suffix of a session from which the prefix triggers the recommendation. As an example, consider that we have S visit sessions in the test log. For each visit session s, we take each page p and generate a recommendation list $R(p)$. $R(p)$ is then compared with the remaining portion of s (i.e., the suffix of s). We denote this portion $T(p)$ (T stands for Tail). The recommendation accuracy for a given session would be how often $T(p)$ and $R(p)$ intersect. The general formula for *recommendation accuracy* is defined as:

$$Recommendation\ Accuracy = \frac{\sum_s \frac{|\bigcup_p (T(p) \cap R(p))|}{|\bigcup_p R(p)|}}{S}$$

The *Shortcut Gain* measures how many clicks the recommendation allows users to save if the recommendation is followed. Suppose we have a session a, b, c, d, e, and at page b, the system recommends page e; then if we follow this advice, we would save two hops (i.e., pages c and d). There is an issue in measuring this shortcut gain when the recommendation list contains more than one page in the suffix of the session. Should we consider the shortest gain or the longest gain? To solve this problem, we opted to distinguish between *key* pages and *auxiliary* pages. A *key* page is a page that may contain relevant information and in which a user may spend some time. An *auxiliary* page is an intermediary page used for linkage and in which a user would spend a relatively short time. In our experiment, we use a threshold of 30 seconds as this distinction. Given these two types of pages, a shortcut gain is measured as being the smallest jump gain towards a *key* page that has been recommended. If no *key* page is recommended, then it is the longest jump towards an *auxiliary* page. The set of pages in the session we go through with the assistance of the recommender system is called the improved session s'. For the total S visit sessions in the test log, *Shortcut Gain* can be computed as:

$$Shortcut\ Gain = \frac{\sum_s \frac{|s| - |s'|}{|s|}}{S}$$

In addition, we compute the *Coverage* of a recommender system, which measures the ability of a system to produce all pages that are likely to be visited by users. The concept is similar to what is called *Recall* in information retrieval. *Coverage* is defined as:

$$Recommendation\ Coverage = \frac{\sum_s \frac{|\bigcup_p (T(p) \cap R(p))|}{|\bigcup_p T(p)|}}{S}$$

3.2 Experimental Results

Experiments on the UofA CS Web Server Dataset

We first evaluated the performance of our system on the UofA CS web server dataset. Our first experiment varies the *Coverage* to see the tendency of the *Recommendation Accuracy*, as depicted in Figure 4(A). For the purpose of comparison, we also implement an Association Rule Recommender System, the most commonly used approach for web mining based recommender systems, and record its performance in the same figure. As expected, the accuracy decreases when the we increase coverage. However, our system was consistently superior to the *Association Rule* system by at least 30%.

We next varied the *coverage* to test the *Shortcut Gain*, both with our system and with the *Association Rule* System, as illustrated in Figure 4(B).

From Figure 4(B), we can see that in the low boundary where the *Coverage* is lower than 8%, the *Shortcut Gain* of our system is close to that of the *AR* system. With the increase of the *Coverage*, however, our system can achieve an

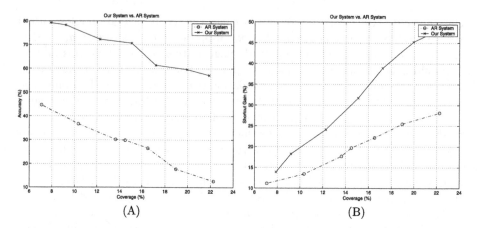

Fig. 4. Performance Comparison: our system vs. *Association Rule* Recommender System. (A): *Recommendation Accuracy* (B): *Shortcut Gain.*

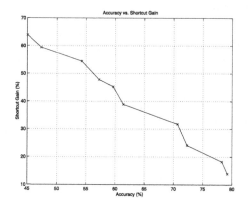

Fig. 5. *Accuracy* vs. *Shortcut Gain*

increasingly superior *Shortcut Gain* than the latter, although the performance of both systems continues to improve.

Figure 5 depicts the relationship of *Recommendation Accuracy* and *Shortcut Gain* in our system. It shows that *Recommendation Accuracy* is inversely proportional to the *Shortcut Gain*. Our study draws the same conclusion from the *Association Rule* recommender system. We argue this is an important property of a usage-based web recommender system, and therefore, how to adjust and balance between the *Accuracy* and *Shortcut Gain* for a web recommender system to achieve the maximum benefit is a question that should be investigated. Some web sites, e.g., those with high link density, may favour a recommender system with high *Accuracy*, while some others may favor a system with high *Shortcut Gain.*

In the above tests, the three distinctive information channels – usage, content, and structure – are provided to, and used in our system. In a second battery of tests we measured the effect of the individual information channels. We first compared three recommender systems, one using all channels, one using only usage and one using only content. We refer to our recommender using the three channels as *Hybrid123*. For this comparison, we implemented an association rule-based usage recommender system as in the previous tests (referred to as *Usage*), as well as a web recommender system based purely on content similarity (referred to as *Content*). The *Usage* system works as follows: an efficient association rule algorithm [5] is applied to the access logs to generate a set of rules. Whenever the pages in the antecedent of an rule have appeared in the user's current session, those pages in its consequence are recommended. For the *Content* system, all pages in the web site are extracted and grouped into clusters solely based on their textual content similarity, using a high-quality content clustering algorithm [18]. If one or more pages in a cluster have been visited, the pages in the same clusters are selected to be recommended. The *Recommendation Accuracy* and *Shortcut Gain* of the three systems are depicted in Figure 6. In the experiment, we varied the *Coverage* to test the trend and consistency of the system quality.

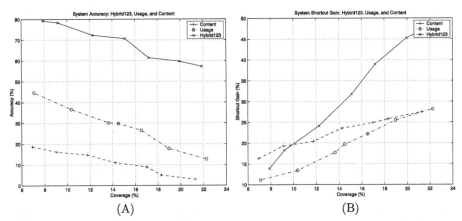

Fig. 6. *Hybrid123, Usage,* and *Content.* (A): *Recommendation Accuracy* (B): *Shortcut Gain.*

Figure 6 (A) shows the *Recommendation Accuracy* of the three contenders. As expected, the accuracy decreases when we increase *Coverage*. However, *Hybrid123* is consistently the best among the three systems, superior to *Usage* by at least 30% – while *Usage* always ranks second.

From Figure 6 (B), we can see that in the low boundary, the *Shortcut Gain* of *Content* is the best of the three systems, and the other two are close. With the increase of *Coverage*, the *Shortcut Gain* of all three systems continues to improve, but in different degrees. *Hybrid123* can achieve an increasingly superior *Shortcut Gain* to that of *Usage*, and exceeds *Content* after *Coverage* is larger than about 10%. The major reason that the *Shortcut Gain* improvement of *Content* is lowest is that with the increase of *Coverage*, more and more pages containing only the same terms, but without any logical relationship are selected to be recommended.

In our next experiment, we illustrate the advantage of incorporating web content and web structure information in our system. To do so, we implemented additional two recommender prototypes. The first is similar to *Hybrid123* but is stripped from its connectivity information channel. That is, we do not make use of linkage information to augment and improve the navigational patterns built on usage and content information. We name this hybrid system *Hybrid-3*. The second is also a similar system to *Hybrid123* but does not make use of content information to identify a mission. Rather, the navigational patterns in the system is built upon traditional transactions identified according to the approach in [7]. Then, the patterns are improved with structure information, as with *Hybrid123*. This hybrid system is called *Hybrid-2*. The *Recommendation Accuracy* and *Shortcut Gain* of the three systems are depicted in Figure 7.

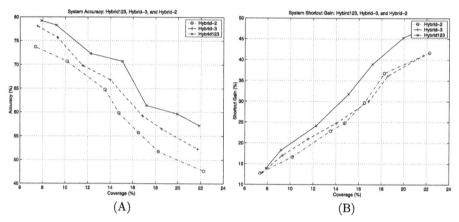

Fig. 7. *Hybrid123, Hybrid-3,* and *Hybrid-2.* (A): *Recommendation Accuracy* (B): *Shortcut Gain.*

Figure 7 (A) shows the *Recommendation Accuracy* of the three systems. The consistent best performance of *Hybrid123* illustrates the validity of content and connectivity information to improve recommendations in our hybrid system, and also indicates that content is more useful for recommendation accuracy improvement. The *Shortcut Gains* of the three systems are depicted in Figure 7 (B). We notice that with the increase of *Coverage, Hybrid123* can achieve an increasingly superior *Shortcut Gain* compared to both *Hybrid-3* and *Hybrid-2*, while the two systems keep similar performance in terms of *Shortcut Gain*. This figure verifies our justification for using distinctive information channels in building a hybrid recommender system, and shows that content and structure information make a similar contribution to the improvement in *Shortcut Gain* in our system.

In summary, this experiment shows that our system can significantly improve the quality of web site recommendation by combining the three information channels, while each channel included contributes to this improvement.

Experiments on the VIVIDESK Log

We then tested our system on VIVIDESK$^{(TM)}$ log data. As explained before, the visited page content information is not available and we used a more general definition of *mission*, namely the applications used during a VIVIDESK$^{(TM)}$ session. However, VIVIDESK$^{(TM)}$ also records in its logs keystrokes made by users. These text data, while not the real content of pages, can be associated with the visited resources and used to separate sessions into missions. Thus, we implemented two recommender systems: one using the simple definition of mission by means of the applications (*App-Mission*), and one using the extra text data to generate missions (*Text-Mission*). In addition, we implemented the same system but using transactions as defined in [7] (*Tran*) to verify the advantage of missions over transactions. In our reported experiment, we also varied the *Coverage* to see the tendency of the *Recommendation Accuracy* and *Shortcut Gain*.

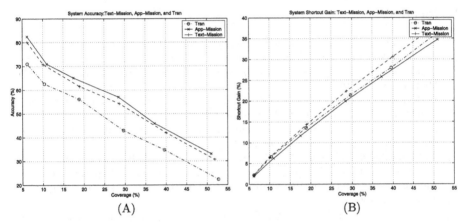

Fig. 8. *Text-Mission, App-Mission,* and *Tran.* (A): *Recommendation Accuracy* (B): *Shortcut Gain.*

As depicted in Figure 8, we notice that *App-Mission* could achieve a higher *Recommendation Accuracy* than simple transaction identification, but lead to a lower *Shortcut Gain*. However, because we can get a much higher *Recommendation Accuracy* with a slight loss of *Shortcut Gain*, we can be confident that mission identification is a better model for user navigational behaviour. The reason why *App-Mission* lead to a lower *Shortcut Gain* is that we identify missions solely based on invoked applications with the absence of content. However, users may need more than one application to fulfill one information need. Thus, identifying missions based on applications may break some interrelationship between web resources across applications. However, bigger jumps are achieved when we used the text entered by the users as means to identify missions. This text is the text entered for instance in HTML form input fields. The *Shortcut Gain* achieved by *Text-Mission* is even higher than the transaction-based approach. This justifies our advocacy of using additional information channels for recommendation improvement.

4 Conclusion

In this paper, we present a framework for a combined web recommender system, in which users' navigational patterns are automatically learned from web usage data and content data. These navigational patterns are then used to generate recommendations based on a user's current status. The items in a recommendation list are ranked according to their importance, which is in turn computed based on web structure information. Our preliminary experiments show that the combination of usage, content, and structure of data in a web recommender system has the potential to improve the quality of the system, as well as to keep the recommendation up-to-date. However, there are various ways to combine these different channels. Our future work in this area will include investigating different methods of combination.

References

1. K. Bharat and M. R. Henzinger. Improved algorithms for topic distillation in a hyperlinked environment. In *Proceedings of SIGIR-98, 21st ACM International Conference on Research and Development in Information Retrieval*, pages 104–111, Melbourne, AU, 1998.
2. S. Brin and L. Page. The anatomy of a large-scale hypertextual web search engine. In *The 7th World-Wide Web Conference*, 1998.
3. R. Burke. Hybrid recommender systems: Survey and experiments. In *User Modeling and User-Adapted Interaction*, 2002.
4. S. Chakrabarti, B. Dom, D. Gibson, J. Kleinberg, P. Raghavan, and S. Rajagopalan. Automatic resource list compilation by analyzing hyperlink structure and associated text. In *Proceedings of the 7th International World Wide Web Conference*, 1998.
5. M.-S. Chen, J.-S. Park, and P. Yu. Efficient data mining for path traversal patterns. *IEEE Transactions on Knowledge and Data Engineering*, 10(2):209–221, 1998.
6. E. H. Chi, A. rosien, and J. Heer. Lumberjack: Intelligent discovery and analysis of web user traffic composition. In *The Fourth International WEBKDD Workshop: Web Mining for Usage Patterns and User Profiles*, pages 1–15, 2002.
7. R. Cooley, B. Mobasher, and J. Srivastava. Data preparation for mining world wide web browsing patterns. *Knowledge and Information Systems*, 1(1):5–32, 1999.
8. X. Fu, J. Budzik, and K. J. Hammond. Mining navigation history for recommendation. In *Intelligent User Interfaces*, pages 106–112, 2000.
9. J. L. Herlocker, J. A. Konstan, A. Borchers, and J. Riedl. An algorithmic framework for performing collaborative filtering. In *Proceedings of the 22nd annual international ACM SIGIR conference on Research and development in information retrieval*, pages 230 – 237, 1999.
10. J. M. Kleinberg. Authoritative sources in a hyperlinked environment. *Journal of the ACM*, 46(5):604–632, 1999.
11. J. Li and O. R. Zaïane. Combining usage, content, and structure data to improve web site recommendation. In *5th International Conference on Electronic Commerce and Web Technologies (EC-Web 2004)*, 2004.
12. J. Li and O. R. Zaïane. Using distinct information channels for mission-based web recommender system. In *Sixth ACM SIGKDD Workshop on Webmining and Web Analysis (WebKDD 2004)*, pages 35–46, Seattle, WA, USA, August 2004.

13. H. Lieberman. Autonomous interface agents. In *Proceedings of the ACM Conference on Computers and Human Interface, CHI-97*, Atlanta, Georgia, 1997.
14. C. Lin, S. Alvarez, and C. Ruiz. Collaborative recommendation via adaptive association rule mining, 2000.
15. B. Mobasher, H. Dai, T. Luo, Y. Sun, and J. Zhu. Integrating web usage and content mining for more effective personalization. In *EC-Web*, pages 165–176, 2000.
16. M. Nakagawa and B. Mobasher. A hybrid web personalization model based on site connectivity. In *Fifth WebKDD Workshop*, pages 59–70, 2003.
17. O. Nasraoui, H. Frigui, R. Krishnapuram, and A. Joshi. Extracting web user profiles using relational competitive fuzzy clustering. *International Joint Artificial Intelligence Tools*, 9(4), 2000.
18. P. Pantel and D. Lin. Document clustering with committees. In *The 25th Annual International ACM SIGIR Conference on Research and Development in Information Retrieval*, 2002.
19. M. Perkowitz and O. Etzioni. Adaptive web sites: Automatically synthesizing web pages. In *AAAI/IAAI*, pages 727–732, 1998.
20. B. M. Sarwar, G. Karypis, J. A. Konstan, and J. Riedl. Analysis of recommendation algorithms for e-commerce. In *ACM Conference on Electronic Commerce*, pages 158–167, 2000.
21. U. Shardanand and P. Maes. Social information filtering: Algorithms for automating "word of mouth". In *Proceedings of ACM CHI'95 Conference on Human Factors in Computing Systems*, volume 1, pages 210–217, 1995.
22. J. Srivastava, R. Cooley, M. Deshpande, and P.-N. Tan. Web usage mining: Discovery and applications of usage patterns from web data. *SIGKDD Explorations*, 1(2):12–23, 2000.
23. W. Wong and A. Fu. Incremental document clustering for web page classification, 2000.
24. A. L. C. Yi-Hung Wu, Yong-Chuan Chen. Enabling personalized recommendation on the web based on user interests and behaviors. In *11th International Workshop on research Issues in Data Engineering*, 2001.

Complete This Puzzle: A Connectionist Approach to Accurate Web Recommendations Based on a Committee of Predictors

Olfa Nasraoui[1] and Mrudula Pavuluri[2]

[1] Dept. of Computer Science and Engineering
Speed Scientific School, University of Louisville
Louisville, KY 40292
olfa.nasraoui@louisville.edu
[2] Dept. of Electrical and Computer Engineering
The University of Memphis
Memphis, TN 38152-3180
mpavulur@memphis.edu

Abstract. We present a *Context Ultra-Sensitive Approach based on two-step Recommender systems (CUSA-2-step-Rec)*. Our approach relies on a committee of profile-specific neural networks. This approach provides recommendations that are accurate and fast to train because only the URLs relevant to a specific profile are used to define the architecture of each network. Similar to the task of completing the missing pieces of a puzzle, each neural network is trained to predict the missing URLs of several complete ground-truth sessions from a given profile, given as input several incomplete subsessions. We compare the proposed approach with collaborative filtering showing that our approach achieves higher coverage and precision while being faster, and requiring lower main memory at recommendation time. While most recommenders are inherently context sensitive, our approach is context *ultra*-sensitive because a *different* recommendation model is designed for *each profile* separately.

1 Introduction

The Web information age has brought a dramatic increase in the sheer amount of information (content), the accessibility to this information (usage), as well as the intricate complexities governing the relationships within this information (structure). Hence, not surprisingly, information overload has turned into a common nuisance when searching and browsing the WWW. One of the most promising and potent remedies against information overload comes in the form of *personalization*. Personalization aims to customize a website's interactions with a user depending on the user's explicit and/or implicit interests. The move from *traditional* physical stores of products or information (such as grocery stores or libraries) to virtual stores of products or information (such as *e-commerce sites* and *digital libraries*) has practically eliminated physical constraints traditionally limiting the number and variety of products in a typical inventory. Unfortunately, the move from the physical to the virtual space has drastically limited the traditional three dimensional layout of

B. Mobasher et al. (Eds.): WebKDD 2004, LNAI 3932, pp. 56–72, 2006.
© Springer-Verlag Berlin Heidelberg 2006

products for which access is further facilitated thanks to the sales representative or librarian who *know* their *products and* their *customers*, to a dismal *planar* interface *without* the sales representative or librarian. As a result, the customers are drowned by the huge number of options, most of which they may never even get to know. Hence, in both the e-commerce sector and digital libraries, Web personalization has become more of a necessity than an option. One of the most successful examples of personalization comes in the form of *recommender systems*. Several approaches to automatically generate Web recommendations based on user's Web navigation patterns or ratings exist. Some involve learning a usage model from Web access data or from user ratings. For example, lazy modeling is used in collaborative filtering which simply stores all users' information and then relies on *K-Nearest-Neighbors* (*KNN*) to provide recommendations from the previous history of similar users. *Frequent itemsets*, session *clusters*, or user *profiles* can also form a user model obtained using data mining. Pazzani and Billsus [3] presented a collaborative filtering approach based on users' ratings of web pages, and Naives Bayes as the prediction tool. Mobasher et al. [1] use pre-discovered association rules and an efficient data structure to provide recommendations based on web navigation patterns. Among the most popular methods, the ones based on collaborative filtering and the ones based on fixed support association rule discovery may be the most difficult and expensive to use. This is because, for the case of high-dimensional and extremely sparse Web data, it is difficult to set suitable support and confidence thresholds to yield reliable and complete web usage patterns. Similarly, collaborative models may struggle with sparse data, and do not scale well to the number of users.

In this paper, we investigate several single-step and two-step recommender systems. The *Context Sensitive Approaches based on single-step Recommender systems (CSA-1-step-Rec)* simply predict the URLs that are part of the nearest estimated profile as recommendations. The nearest profile prediction model simply bases its recommendations on the closest profile. The *Context Ultra-Sensitive Approaches based on two-step Recommender systems (CUSA-2-step-Rec)* first maps a user session to one of the pre-discovered profiles, and then uses one of several profile-specific URL-predictor neural networks (such as Multilayer Perceptron or Hopfield Autoassociative memory networks) in the second step to provide the final recommendations. Based on this classification, a different recommendation model is designed for each profile separately. Each neural network is trained to complete the missing URLs of several complete ground-truth sessions from a given profile, given as input several incomplete subsessions. This learning is analogous to completing some missing parts of a puzzle. The two-step recommendation method not only handles *overlap* in user interests, but also can mend the effects of some types of misclassifications in the first nearest profile assignment step, and even mend the effect of a coarse profile dichotomy due to the profile discovery stage.

The rest of the paper is organized as follows. In Section 2, we present an overview of profile discovery using Web usage mining. In Section 3, we present the single-step profile prediction based recommendation process, and the two-step recommender system based on a committee of profile-specific URL-predictor neural networks. In Section 4, we present an empirical evaluation of the recommendation strategies on real web usage data, and finally, in Section 5, we present our conclusions.

2 Profile Discovery Based on Web Usage Mining

Our approach is based on first extracting user *profiles* or *ratings* using a method, such as Web usage mining. In this case, the profile discovery can be executed *offline* by mining user access log files using the following steps:

(1) Preprocess log file to extract user *sessions*,
(2) *Categorize* sessions by *clustering*,
(3) Summarize the session categories in terms of *user profiles*,

After automatically grouping sessions into different clusters, we summarize the session categories in terms of *user profile vectors*, p_i: The kth component/weight of this vector (p_{ik}) captures the *relevance* of URL_k in the ith profile, as estimated by the conditional probability that URL_k is accessed in a session belonging to the ith cluster.

3 Description of the Single-Step and Two-Step Recommendation Strategy Options

Let $U = \{url_1, url_2, ..., url_{N_U}\}$ be a set of N_U urls on a given web site visited in web user sessions $s_j, j = 1, ..., N_s$, as defined in (1). Let $P = \{p_1, p_2, ..., p_{N_P}\}$ be the set of N_P Web user profiles computed by the profile discovery engine. Each profile consists of a set of URLs associated with their relevance weights in that profile. The problem of recommendation can be stated as follows. Given a current Web user session vector, $s_j = [s_{j1}, s_{j2}, ..., s_{jN_U}]$, predict the set of URLs that are most relevant according to the user's interest, and recommend them to the user, usually as a set of Hypertext *links* dynamically appended to the contents of the Web document returned in response to the most recent Web query. It may be useful to associate the kth recommended URL with a corresponding URL relevance *score*, r_{jk}. Hence it is practical to denote the recommendations for current Web user session, s_j, by a vector $r_j = [r_{j1}, r_{j2}, ..., r_{jN_U}]$. In this study, we limit the scores to be binary.

3.1 Context Sensitive Approach Based on Single-Step Profile Prediction Recommender System (*CSA-1-step-Rec*)

3.1.1 Single-Step Nearest-Profile Prediction Based Recommender System

The simplest and most rudimentary approach to profile based Web recommendation is to simply determine the most similar profile to the current session, and to recommend the URLs in this profile, together with their URL relevance weights as URL recommendation scores.

Figure 1 shows the structure of such a recommendation system, where the profile prediction model simply consists of a nearest-profile estimator based on computing a session to profile similarity, and selecting the profile with highest similarity as the predicted profile.

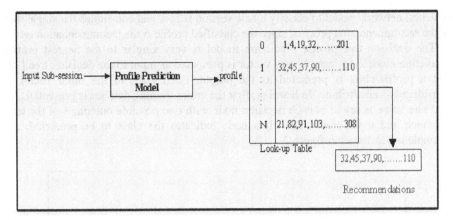

Fig. 1. Context-Sensitive Approach based on single-step profile prediction based Recommender System *(CSA-1-step-Rec)*. The Profile Prediction Model can be a Nearest-Profile classifier or any of the models shown in Figs 2 or 3.

The similarity score between an input session, s, and the ith profile, p_i, can be computed using the cosine similarity as follows,

$$S_{si}^{\cos ine} = \frac{\sum_{k=1}^{N_U} p_{ik}s_k}{\sqrt{\sum_{k=1}^{N_U} p_{ik} \sum_{k=1}^{N_U} s_k}} \qquad (1)$$

If a hierarchical Web site structure should be taken into account, then a modification of the cosine similarity, introduced in [3,4], that can take into account the Website structure can be used to yield the following input membership,

$$S_{si}^{web} = \max \left\{ \frac{\sum_{l=1}^{N_U} \sum_{k=1}^{N_U} p_{il}S_u(l,k)s_k}{\sum_{k=1}^{N_U} p_{ik} \sum_{k=1}^{N_U} s_k}, S_{si}^{\cos ine} \right\} \qquad (2)$$

where S_u is a URL to URL similarity matrix that is computed based on the amount of overlap between the paths leading from the root of the website (main page) to any two URLs, and is given by

$$S_u(i,j) = \min \left(1, \frac{|p_i \cap p_j|}{\max(1, \max(|p_i|, |p_j|) - 1)} \right) \qquad (3)$$

We refer to the special similarity in (2) as the *Web Session Similarity*.

3.1.2 Single-Step Decision-Tree Based Profile Prediction Recommender System

The nearest profile prediction model makes the critical assumption that sessions in different profiles are linearly separated. While this may be applicable for certain web mining methods, it may not be true for others. In order to be able to reliably map new unseen sessions to a set of mined profiles, without such assumptions about the profiles or how they separate the sessions, we can resort to classification methods that are not based on distance or similarity computations. In this paper, we explore both decision trees and neural networks for this task. Once trained, using the decision tree or neural network model to classify a new session is fast, and constitutes the single step of the recommendation process, since the classified profile *is* the recommendation set.

The decision tree profile prediction model is very similar to the nearest profile prediction model. An input binary vector is presented as input to the decision tree [22] and a profile/class is predicted as the output. Each URL in the input vector is considered as an attribute. In learning, first the entire training data set is presented. An attribute value is tested at each decision node with two possible outcomes of the test, a branch and a sub-tree. The class node indicates the class to be predicted. An example is illustrated in figure 2.

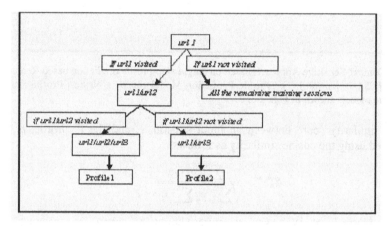

Fig. 2. Example of a Profile Prediction Model based on a decision tree that can be used within *CSA-1-step-Rec*

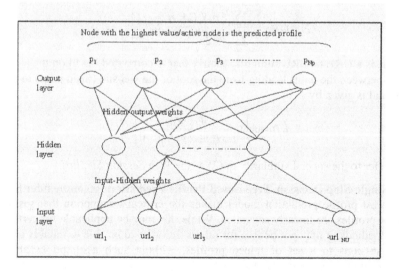

Fig. 3. Architecture of a Profile Prediction Model based on a Multi-Layer Perceptron that can be used within *CSA-1-step-Rec*

3.1.3 Single-Step Neural Network Based Profile Prediction Recommender System

In the neural network [21] based approach of profile prediction, a feed-forward multilayer perceptron is used and is trained with Back-Propagation. The inputs (session URLs) and output (class or profile) to the prediction model remain the same as the ones described above. The neural network replaces the classification model block in Figure 1. Hence the input layer of the network consists of as many input nodes as the number of valid URLs (i.e. N_U nodes), an output layer having one output node for each profile (i.e. N_p nodes), and a hidden layer with $(N_U + N_p)/2$ nodes. Figure 3 shows the architecture of the neural network used to predict the most relevant profile. The index of the output node with highest activation indicates the final class/profile.

3.2 Context Ultra-Sensitive Approach Based on Two-Step Recommender System with a Committee of Profile-Specific URL-Predictor Neural Networks (*CUSA-2-step-Rec*)

The single-step Profile prediction recommendation procedure is intuitively appealing and simple. In particular, its implementation and deployment in a live setting is very efficient. Essentially, it amounts to a look-up table. However, it has several flaws: (*i*) the degree of similarity between the current session and the nearest profile that is identified may not be taken into account, (*ii*) the above procedure does not take into account sessions that are similar to more than a single profile, (*iii*) it cannot handle sessions which are different from all known profiles, and (*iv*) the set of recommendations derive directly from the contents of a single (assigned) profile for all sessions assigned to this profile, without any further distinction between the specific access patterns. For this reason, we propose a two-step approach that in addition to exploiting the profile information, is able to recommend more highly personalized recommendations that depend not only on the assigned profile (*people-to-people* collaboration filtering), but also explicitly, on the input session itself (*item-to-item* collaboration filtering),.

3.2.1 Description of the Multi-layer Perceptron URL-Predictor Neural Network

A Multilayer Perceptron neural network [21] can be used to predict the recommendation *URLs*. The architecture of this network, shown in Figure 4, is different from the network used in the *profile* prediction scenario of Figure 3. This is because the number of output nodes is now equal to the number of input nodes. The neural network is trained to complete the missing URLs of several complete ground-truth sessions, given as input several incomplete subsessions. This learning is analogous to completing some missing parts of a puzzle, as illustrated in Figure 12. Each training input consists of a user sub-session (*ss*) derived from a ground-truth complete session *S*, while training by example teaches the network output nodes to conform to the remainder of this session (*S-ss*). This means that there is one output node per URL. Hence, the architecture of the network can become extremely complex, as there would be N_U input and N_U output nodes. Training such a network may prove to be unrealistic on large websites that may consist of thousands of URLs. To overcome this problem, a separate network is learned for each profile *independently*, with an architecture of its own. The number of input and output nodes depends only on the number of significant URLs in that profile, and possibly those related to its URLs by URL-level or conceptual/semantic similarity. The number of hidden nodes is set to the average of number of input and output nodes. Figure 4 shows the architecture of each URL-predictor neural network. There will be a committee of N_p specialized networks of similar kind used in developing this URL recommendation prediction model, as illustrated in Figure 5. Each of these networks is completely specialized to forming the recommendations for a single profile, hence offering a local, more refined model, that enjoys the advantages of better accuracy, simplicity (fewer nodes and connections), and ease of training (as a result of simplicity).

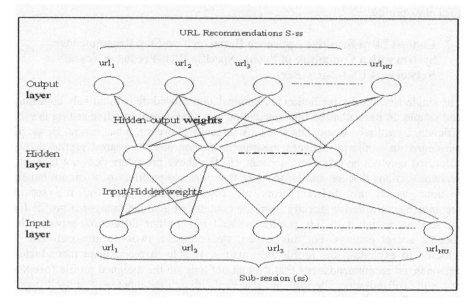

Fig. 4. Architecture of a Profile-Specific URL-Predictor Neural Network used in *CUSA-2-step-Rec*

3.2.2 Learning the Profile-Specific URL-Predictor Neural Network Models

The URL-Predictor network for each profile is learnt independently with a separate set of training data. Learning each network involves presenting a *sub-session* consisting of some of the URLs visited by the user belonging to that profile as input and adjusting the network weights by *back propagation* to recommend URLs that are not part of the sub-session given as input, but which are a part of the ground truth complete session, as output of the network. For each ground truth complete session, we find all the sub-sessions for window sizes 1-9, and use them to generate independent training and testing sets. Cosine similarity is used to map each sub-session to the closest profile, and the URL-Predictor network specialized for that profile is invoked to obtain the recommendations. A URL is considered to be recommended if its activation value exceeds a *'0.5'* at the corresponding output node of the invoked network.

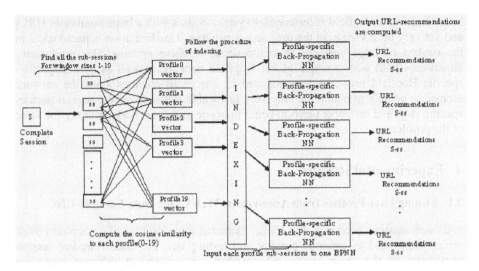

Fig. 5. Context Ultra-Sensitive Approach based on Two-Step Recommendation Process *(CUSA-2-step-Rec)* using a Committee of Profile-Specific URL-Predictor Neural Networks (Any URL-Predictor model can be substituted for the Multi-Layer Perceptron, e.g. a Hopfield network)

3.3   Recommendations Based on Autoassociative Memory Hopfield Networks

Hopfield networks are a special kind of recurrent neural networks that can be used as associative memory [21]. A Hopfield network can retrieve a complete pattern stored through the training process from an imperfect or noisy version of it. In some sense, a recommender system performs a similar operation, when it recommends certain URLs from an incomplete session. Given N_{url} fully connected (via symmetric weights w_{ij} between each two units i and j) neurons, each serving simultaneously as input and as output, and assuming that the activation values, x_i, are bipolar (+1/-1), the optimal weights to memorize N_p patterns, can be determined by *Hebbian* learning as follows

$$w_{ij} = \sum_{p=1}^{N_p} x_i^p x_j^p \qquad \text{for all } i \neq j \text{ (0, otherwise)} \tag{4}$$

During testing/recall, when a new noisy pattern x_{new} is presented as input, we set the activation at node i at iteration 0 to be $x_i^0 = x_{new\text{-}i}$, then the units are adjusted by iteratively computing, at each iteration t

$$x_i^{t+1} = \sum_{j=1}^{N_{url}} w_{ij} x_j^t \tag{5}$$

until the network converges to a stable state. However, the desired behavior of recall in a Hopfield network is expected to hold only if all the possible complete session prototypes can be stored in the Hopfield network's connection weights, and if these complete sessions do not interact (or *cross-talk*) excessively. Severe deterioration starts occurring when the number of patterns exceeds a certain fraction of the number of nodes:

$$N_p > 0.138 N_{url}, \tag{6}$$

hence limiting a Hopfield recommender system to sites with a large number of URLs and yet very little variety in the user access patterns. This limitation is paradoxical in the context of large websites or transactional database systems. Our preliminary simulations with both a single global Hopfield network as well as several profile-specific Hopfield networks have resulted in low recall qualities since the network seemed to be able to memorize only very few stable states. However several profile-specific Hopfield networks perform better than one global network, but only for some of the profiles.

4 Experimental Results

4.1 Mining User Profiles from Anonymous Web Usage Data Using H-UNC

1703 web sessions accessing 343 URLs, extracted from log files of a university Web server, were used to generate training and testing sets. For each *complete* session considered as the *ground-truth*, all possible *sub-sessions* of different sizes are generated. The test dataset forms an independent 20% of the sub-sessions. Hierarchical Unsupervised Niche Clustering (H-UNC) [2] partitioned the web sessions into 20 clusters, each characterized by one of 20 profile vectors that were thoroughly checked and validated for consistency.

4.1.1 Justifications for Using H-UNC to Mine User Profiles

H-UNC [2] was used because it is the only algorithm previously used successfully for web usage mining, while satisfying all of the following stringent requirements to ensure the completeness and quality of the discovered user profiles: (i) ability to discover an unknown and unspecified number of clusters/profiles, (ii) ability to resist unknown amounts of noise in the data, (iii) ability to handle specialized and non-differentiable similarity measures (in this case the Web session similarity takes into account domain knowledge in the form of the structure of the website, hence knowledge about the website structure is directly infused into the profile discovery phase via the similarity measure), (iv) ability to discover the clusters/profiles in sparse session data sets based on a soft and error-tolerant density criterion that can discover dense URL-itemsets (and hence profiles) even in small regions (subspaces) of the high-dimensional space. H-UNC is also fully integrated within a comprehensive web usage mining package, coded in Java, that also includes extensive pre-processing and post-processing tools. One of the other main advantages of using H-UNC's post-processing capabilities, is that we could verify and validate each discovered profiles. Until it is made available to download from a public URL, it can be obtained by e-mailing the first author.

4.2 Comparative Simulation Results for *CUSA-2-step-Rec*, *CSA-1-step-Rec*, and *K-NN* Collaborative Filtering

We used the following parameters in training the multilayer perceptron URL-Predictor neural networks: Maximum number of epochs = 2000, Learning Rate = 0.7 (for Input to Hidden layer) and 0.07 (for Hidden to Output layer), and a Momentum factor of 0.5. The Collaborative filtering approach is based on using K Nearest

Neighbors (K-NN) followed by top-N recommendations for different values of K and N. First the closest K complete sessions from the entire history of accesses are found. Then the URLs present in these top K sessions are sorted in decreasing order of their frequency, and the top N URLs are treated as the recommendation set. We show only the best results obtained for K-NN at K=50 neighbors and N=10 URLs.

Figures 6 and 7, depicting the 20-profile averaged precision and coverage measures, show that the two-step profile-specific URL-predictor multilayer perceptron neural network recommender system *(CUSA-2-step-Rec)* wins in terms of *both* precision and coverage, particularly *above input sub-session size 2*. Figure 9 depicts the average *F1* measure, which is an equal aggregation of precision and coverage, for each input sub-session size. It may at first appear unusual that a recommendation strategy scores highly on both precision and coverage, and that an increase in precision did not seem to compromise coverage in any way. However, by looking at the details of the design of the profile-specific URL-predictor neural network, we explain this relentless increase in precision by the fact that the neural network output is trained to predict only the URLs that the user has *not* seen before, i.e. '*S-ss*', where *S* is the *complete* session, and *ss* is the sub-session (URLs *visited* by the user). Clearly, as the sub-session size increases, more URLs are presented to the output of the neural network, making the prediction task easier, since fewer URLs need to be predicted compared to smaller input sub-sessions. Similarly, coverage increases, since with more input URLs, the neural network is able to predict more of the missing URLs to complete the puzzle. However, this does not happen at the expense of precision. On the contrary, giving more hints about the user in the form of more of the visited URLs makes the prediction task easier, and hence, will only result in more accurate predictions.

We notice that the single-step recommender systems *(CSA-1-step-Rec)* do not have this nice feature, i.e., precision and coverage will generally have opposing trends. The performance of k-NN fares competitively with all the single-step recommender strategies, but only for longer session sizes. This is not surprising, considering that k-NN can yield very accurate predictions, because it too is based on local context-sensitive models. However, k-NN is notorious for its *excessive computational and memory costs, at recommendation time*, in contrast to all the other investigated techniques. While lazy in the learning phase, involving nothing more than storing the previously seen cases, k-NN takes its toll during the recommendation phase, when it needs to compare a new session with all past cases to produce recommendations.

Figures 10 and 11 depict the *F1* measures for each profile separately obtained with *CUSA-2-step-Rec* with specialized multilayer perceptron neural networks and k-NN, respectively. These figures show that the prediction quality may vary widely between different profiles, since the sessions in some profiles are noisier, and hence are more difficult to predict. We also note that some profiles do not generate any testing sessions beyond a certain size because of their particular session length distribution. Table 1 summarizes the characteristics of the session lengths for each profile. The median length for most profiles is larger than 5 and for six of the profiles (0, 3, 4, 5, 11, and 15), it is greater than 9. For these profiles, half of the sessions have length greater than or equal to 9. Moreover, because we generate a large number of subsession combinations from each session for testing, we end up with a reasonably large number of test sessions (in the hundreds), especially between session size 2 and 8. We notice from Fig. 10 and 11, that at longer session lengths (above 5), the F1 measure with *CUSA-2-step-Rec* -NN far exceeds that of k-NN. This can be explained by the fact that while the performance of k-NN eventually saturates and even starts decreasing beyond a certain session length, that of the *CUSA-2-step-Rec* –NN approach can only improve, since each specialized network is essentially trained to complete the missing pieces (URLs) of a complete session, when given as input only some of the pieces. This is illustrated in Figure 12. Hence, it is only natural in this context that when more pieces are shown, a specialized neural network is better able to predict the missing pieces. The degradation of precision that results from higher coverage in k-NN approaches is avoided because the neural networks in *CUSA-2-step-Rec* are *trained* to be *precise*, while *excessive* coverage is controlled thanks to the *specialization* of each NN to only one of the profiles. Finally, we note that, if *all* input sub-session lengths are taken into account, then it is clear that a combination of *several different* recommender strategies, each applied only within its *optimal* range of sub-session length, will outperform each one of the recommender strategies acting on its own. In fact, in this case, even the very simple *CSA-1-step-Rec* strategy based on *nearest profile identification* outperforms all other strategies for very short input sessions (< 2 URLs). This is crucial to the retention and guidance of users who may be in their very initial browsing stages.

Finally, in Table 2, we show the performance (averaged over all session lengths) of the *CUSA-2-step-Rec* approach when specialized *Hopfield* networks are used for each profile instead of the *multilayer perceptron* neural networks. It is important to note that, while *testing* both types of neural networks was performed in a similar fashion, *training* them was a different matter. The Hopfield networks in our context are analogous to auto-associative memory banks. Hence, they were trained to

Table 1. Number of URLs, sessions, minimum, maximum and median session lengths of each profile

profile	Number of Nodes (URLs)	Number of Sessions	Minimum Length	Maximum Length	Median Length
0	189	106	1	40	10
1	194	104	1	40	6
2	171	177	1	132	7
3	101	61	1	40	10
4	134	58	1	40	9
5	153	50	1	132	10
6	104	116	1	24	5
7	64	51	1	23	7
8	139	134	1	36	4
9	73	41	1	25	3
10	134	95	1	19	4
11	98	185	1	36	9
12	170	74	1	132	5
13	136	38	1	132	5
14	163	33	1	31	6
15	86	51	1	37	9
16	105	77	1	132	2
17	23	68	1	6	1
18	5	65	1	3	1
19	24	120	1	10	2

memorize each complete session, and not to complete missing parts of a complete sessions from a large number of incomplete subsessions as in the multilayer perceptron neural networks.

We notice that while some profiles can be handled using the Hopfield networks, the performance for many profiles is poor, even sinking to complete failure for profiles 10, 17, 18, and 19. We attribute this failure to the excessive amount of cross-talk between the patterns to be memorized by the Hopfield networks for these profiles compared to the low number of nodes/URLs, especially in light of the constraint in (6). For example, as shown in Table 1, the Hopfield network for profile 18 had to memorize a large number of patterns: $N_p = 65$ training sessions in contrast with only $N_{url} = 5$ nodes. We have also trained a *single global* Hopfield network for all profiles to predict the URLs of incomplete sessions. Note that in this case, the constraint in (6) is severely violated with $N_p = 1703$ training patterns and $N_{url} = 343$ nodes. *Not surprisingly*, the average similarity between the memorized and retrieved sessions, obtained in this case, was *nil*.

Table 2. Average cosine similarity between complete session and session retrieved from an incomplete input using several specialized Hopfield networks (one per profile). The similarity obtained when a *single global* Hopfield network is used for all profiles was *nil*.

Profile	0	1	2	3	4	5	6	7	8	9	10	11	12	13	14	15	16	17	18	19
Similarity	.57	.4	.6	.18	.47	.13	.43	.62	.29	.31	0	.68	.26	.27	.28	.54	.30	0	0	0

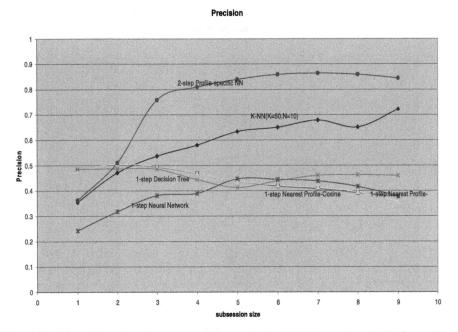

Fig. 6. Precision Values for all recommendation strategies (*CSA-1-step-Rec, CUSA-2-step-Rec,* and *K-NN*)

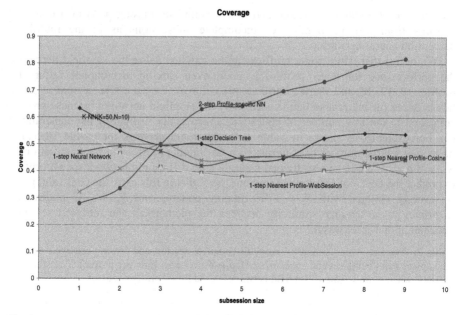

Fig. 7. Coverage Values for all recommendation strategies (*CSA-1-step-Rec, CUSA-2-step-Rec,* and *K-NN*)

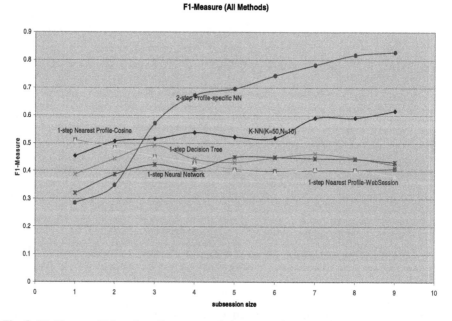

Fig. 8. F1-Measure Values for all recommendation strategies (*CSA-1-step-Rec, CUSA-2-step-Rec,* and *K-NN*)

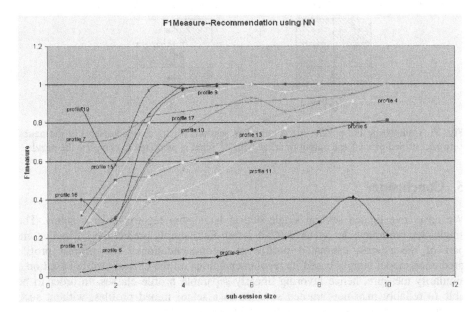

Fig. 9. Individual averaged F1-Measure Values for each profile with the *CUSA-2-step-Rec* strategy

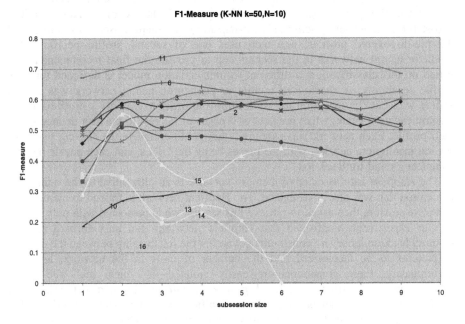

Fig. 10. Individual averaged F1-Measure Values for each profile with the *K-NN* (K = 50, N = 10) strategy

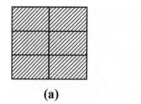 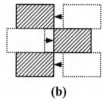

（a）   （b）

Fig. 11. Completing the puzzle: (a) A complete session, (b) Input (incomplete) to the neural network (striped pieces) and output (marked with "?") that is predicted to complete the puzzle

5   Conclusions

We have investigated several single-step and two-step recommender systems. The single-step recommender systems *(CSA-1-step-Rec)* simply predict the URLs that are part of the nearest estimated profile as recommendations. The nearest profile prediction model simply based its recommendations on the closest profile based on a similarity measure, hence favoring linearly separable profile classes. In order to be able to reliably map new unseen sessions to a set of mined profiles, without such assumptions about the profiles or how they separate the sessions, we can resort to more powerful classification methods. In this paper, we explored both decision trees and neural networks for this task. Once trained, using the decision tree or neural network model to classify a new session constitutes the single step of the recommendation process, since the classified profile *is* the recommendation set. The two-step recommender system *(CUSA-2-step-Rec)* first maps a user session to one of the pre-discovered profiles, and then uses one of several profile-specific URL-predictor neural networks in the second step to provide the final recommendations. Based on this classification, a different recommendation model is designed for each profile separately. A *specialized* multilayer perceptron neural network was trained offline with back-propagation *for each profile* in order to provide a profile-specific recommendation strategy that predicts web pages of interest to the user depending on their profile. Each network was essentially trained to complete the *missing* pieces of several incomplete puzzles, with the pieces being the URLs, and each puzzle being a complete ground-truth session.

The *Hopfield* auto-associative memory network is an alternative to the multilayer perceptron that was also investigated. The Hopfield network is trained to memorize a complete session, then asked to retrieve this session when presented with only part of it. Our experiments confirmed that Hopfield networks can only form a reliable memory bank under severe constraints governing the relationship between the number of patterns to be memorized and the number of units in the network, and that unfortunately, these constraints are easily violated in typical real web usage environments. Nevertheless, *several profile-specialized* Hopfield networks in a *CUSA-2-step-Rec* framework performed significantly better than a *single* global network. The latter failed to form a reliable memory of the web usage patterns.

Unlike most previous work, the proposed two-step profile-specific URL-predictor neural network recommender system allows a more refined context sensitive recommendation process. The idea of using a separate network specialized to each profile seems to be novel, since it provides an even higher level of context-awareness in personalization than the level already offered through collaborative filtering based personalization. It is reasonable to expect that this modular design could be extended by replacing the URL-Predictor neural network modules by different learning paradigms that are faster to train, while not compromising the accuracy of predictions. The proposed model could also be made even faster to train and more accurate by encouraging the discovery of even more high-resolution profiles.

We finally classify our recommendation approaches with respect to the two-dimensional taxonomy presented in [16]. First, because the user is *anonymous* at all times, our approaches are all *ephemeral* with respect to the *persistence dimension*. Second, with respect to the *automation dimension*, our approaches are *fully automatic*. Furthermore, with regard to the four different families of recommendation techniques identified in [16] (*non-personalized, attribute based, item-to-item correlation, and people-to-people correlation*), the 1-step recommenders (*CSA-1-step-Rec*) can be considered as people-to people collaborative filtering. However, they use a cluster/profile summarization model, hence providing better scalability. On the other hand, the *CUSA-2-step-Rec* model uses people-to people collaborative filtering that is summarized through a cluster model, in the first stage to map a new user to a profile. Then it uses a specialized item-to-item recommendation model to produce the final recommendations. Therefore, the *CUSA-2-step-Rec* approach can be considered as a *hybrid* between *people-to-people* and *item-to-item* recommendations, and this fact, in addition to the quality of the preliminary Web usage mining results, may account for its good performance.

Acknowledgements

This work is supported by a National Science Foundation CAREER Award IIS-0133948 to Olfa Nasraoui.

References

1. M. Perkowitz and O. Etzioni. Adaptive web sites: Automatically learning for user access pattern. Proc. 6th int. WWW conference, 1997.
2. R. Cooley, B. Mobasher, and J. Srivastava, Web Mining: Information and Pattern discovery on the World Wide Web, Proc. IEEE Intl. Conf. Tools with AI, Newport Beach, CA, pp. 558-567, 1997.
3. Nasraoui, R. Krishnapuram, and A. Joshi. Mining Web Access Logs Using a Relational Clustering Algorithm Based on a Robust Estimator, 8th International World Wide Web Conference, Toronto, pp. 40-41, 1999.
4. Nasraoui, R. Krishnapuram, H. Frigui, and A. Joshi. Extracting Web User Profiles Using Relational Competitive Fuzzy Clustering, International Journal on Artificial Intelligence Tools, Vol. 9, No. 4, pp. 509-526, 2000.
5. Nasraoui, and R. Krishnapuram, A Novel Approach to Unsupervised Robust Clustering using Genetic Niching, Proc. of the 9th IEEE International Conf. on Fuzzy Systems, San Antonio, TX, May 2000, pp. 170-175.

6. Nasraoui and R. Krishnapuram. A New Evolutionary Approach to Web Usage and Context Sensitive Associations Mining, International Journal on Computational Intelligence and Applications - Special Issue on Internet Intelligent Systems, Vol. 2, No. 3, pp. 339-348, Sep. 2002.

7. M. Pazzani and D. Billsus, Learning and revising User Profiles: The identification of Interesting Web Sites, Machine Learning, Arlington, 27, pp. 313-331, 1997.

8. D.H. Kraft, J. Chen., M.J. Martin-Bautista, and M.A. Vila, Textual Information Retrieval with User Profiles Using Fuzzy Clustering and Inferencing, in *"Intelligent Exploration of the Web"*, Szczepaniak, P.S., Segovia, J., Kacprzyk, J., and Zadeh, L.A. (eds.), Physica-Verlag, Heidelberg, Germany, 2002.

9. B. Mobasher, H. Dai, T. Luo, and M. Nakagawa, Effective personalizaton based on association rule discovery from Web usage data, ACM Workshop on Web information and data management, Atlanta, GA, Nov. 2001.

10. J. H. Holland. *Adaptation in natural and artificial systems*. MIT Press, 1975.

11. L. Zadeh (1965). Fuzzy sets. Inf. Control 8, 338-353.

12. G. J. Klir and B. Yuan, *Fuzzy Sets and Fuzzy Logic*, Prentice Hall, 1995, ISBN 0-13-101171-5.R. Agrawal and R. Srikant (1994), Fast algorithms for mining association rules, Proceedings of the 20th VLDB Conference, Santiago, Chile, pp. 487-499.

14. G. Linden, B. Smith, and J. York, *Amazon.com* Recommendations Item-to-item collaborative filtering, IEEE Internet Computing, Vo. 7, No. 1, pp. 76-80, Jan. 2003

15. J. Breese, H. Heckerman, and C. Kadie, Empirical Analysis of Predictive Algorithms for Collaborative Filtering, Proc. 14th Conf. Uncertainty in Artificial Intelligence, pp. 43-52, 1998.

16. J.B. Schafer, J. Konstan, and J. Reidel, Recommender Systems in E-Commerce, Proc. ACM Conf. E-commerce, pp. 158-166, 1999.

17. J. Srivastava, R. Cooley, M. Deshpande, and P-N Tan, Web usage mining: Discovery and applications of usage patterns from web data, SIGKDD Explorations, Vol. 1, No. 2, Jan 2000, pp. 1-12.

18. Zaiane, M. Xin, and J. Han, Discovering web access patterns and trends by applying OLAP and data mining technology on web logs, in "Advances in Digital Libraries", 1998, Santa Barbara, CA, pp. 19-29.

19. M. Spiliopoulou and L. C. Faulstich, WUM: A Web utilization Miner, in Proceedings of EDBT workshop WebDB98, Valencia, Spain, 1999.

20. J. Borges and M. Levene, Data Mining of User Navigation Patterns, in *"Web Usage Analysis and User Profiling"*, Lecture Notes in Computer Science", H. A. Abbass, R. A. Sarker, and C.S. Newton Eds., Springer-Verlag , pp. 92-111,1999.

21. S. Haykin, *Neural Networks: A Comprehensive Foundation*, Macmillan, New York, 1994.

22. J. R. Quinlan. Induction of Decision Trees. Machine Learning, Vol. 1, pp. 81--106, 1986.

Collaborative Quality Filtering: Establishing Consensus or Recovering Ground Truth? *

Jonathan Traupman and Robert Wilensky

Computer Science Division
University of California, Berkeley
387 Soda Hall
Berkeley, CA 94720-1776
jont@cs.berkeley.edu, wilensky@cs.berkeley.edu

Abstract. We present a algorithm based on factor analysis for performing collaborative quality filtering (CQF). Unlike previous approaches to CQF, which estimate the consensus opinion of a group of reviewers, our algorithm uses a generative model of the review process to estimate the latent intrinsic quality of the items under reviews. We run several tests that demonstrate that consensus and intrinsic quality are, in fact different and unrelated aspects of quality. These results suggest that asymptotic consensus, which purports to model peer review, is, in fact, not recovering the ground truth quality of reviewed items.

1 Introduction

Despite the vast number of reviews of products, stores, media, and articles on the Internet, little has been done to separate worthwhile expertise from biased or uninformed opinions. When assigning a total score to an item, nearly all review sites simply average the scores given by each reviewer. A few, such as the Internet Movie Database [1], use a Bayesian mean, which takes into account both the number of reviews written as well as the scores given to a particular film. None of these systems make any attempt to determine the ability of the reviewers to estimate the quality of items they review. Such a method would be necessary to emulate peer review, which weights the opinions of experts most heavily.

Collaborative Quality Filtering (CQF) [2,3] attempts to improve these estimates for item quality by giving more accurate reviewers more weight than less accurate ones. Unlike standard collaborative filtering, CQF systems do not create personal recommendations for users. Instead, they use individual reviews to estimate the underlying quality of the item being reviewed. Clearly, collaborative quality filtering is less useful for items where people's tastes tend to differ, such as movies, books, and music. However, for items where there is agreement about what constitutes quality, it can be a more accurate method of estimating quality than the simple or Bayesian means in common use today. Indeed, one goal of CQF research is to rationalize subjective processes, such as reviewing academic papers or ranking journals and institutions.

---

* This research was supported by the Digital Libraries Initiative under grant NSF CA98-17353.

B. Mobasher et al. (Eds.): WebKDD 2004, LNAI 3932, pp. 73–86, 2006.

In [2] and [3], a CQF algorithm is described that works by what we will call "asymptotic consensus": an iterative method that gives greater weights to reviewers who give scores closer to the weighted mean for each item.

Here, we present a new algorithm for CQF based on factor analysis. In comparing these two algorithms, we have discovered what we believe to be a fundamental division in approaches to CQF. While both approaches use a set of reviews to compute estimates of item quality, they differ in what they consider to be a "high quality" item.

The first approach, exemplified by the asymptotic consensus algorithm, takes the view that quality is not an a priori property of an item. Instead, the quality estimates assigned by these algorithms attempt to reflect the consensus opinion of the reviewers. Algorithms in this family try to maximize the agreement among reviewers about the quality of an item by giving greater weight to reviewers whose opinions best reflect the consensus.

The second approach assumes that quality is an intrinsic property of an item that can be judged by reviewers but is not defined by them. Algorithms such as factor analysis estimate this intrinsic quality by assuming a generative model of reviews and then estimating the intrinsic qualities that best explain the observed data. The notion that quality is an intrinsic property of an item raises interesting philosophical issues, which we cannot do justice to here. However, we note that this view posits that quality is not a completely arbitrary social construction (even if the ideals with respect to which quality is judged are socially construed). That is, reviewers are making a determination about properties of an artifact, but their collective consensus doesn't establish the underlying reality. We view it as a positive if the reviewing process is in fact uncovering some underlying truth, rather than fabricating an arbitrary social agreement. Ideally, the social process and the uncovering of intrinsic properties would converge.

We believe that both of these approaches will find uses in different applications, but the vastly different results we have seen suggest that users of CQF systems need to consider carefully just what type of "quality" they hope to measure. For example, while the asymptotic consensus algorithm purports to model academic review, these results suggest it is measuring consensus rather than recovering an objective notion of quality. For a system intended to retrieve the highest quality articles, a CQF algorithm that accurately estimates intrinsic quality may in fact be more useful.

2   Related Work

Riggs and Wilensky [2,3] coined the term *Collaborative Quality Filtering* to refer to the process of estimating the quality of an item using reviewer preference data, in contrast to standard collaborative filtering, which suggests items users may like based on their preferences. They presented a CQF system that works by asymptotic consensus, which we compare to our method.

Most existing systems for ranking item quality use either the mean of the reviews for an item or a Bayesian mean [1] of reviews as a proxy for quality. In the world of publishing, citation analysis [4,5] has been used to measure the influence and thus the quality of articles and journals. However, citations are, at best, an indirect measure of quality and provide little information for more recently published works.

Collaborative Filtering makes recommendations instead of estimating item quality, but uses techniques that can be applied to CQF. Early, "memory-based," systems work by finding users with similar tastes and then making recommendations based on these preferences. These systems filter items as diverse as email [6], NetNews [7], movies [8] and music [9]. Herlocker [10] compares the performance of a number of these techniques.

More recently, model-based approaches, including latent semantic analysis [11] and factor analysis [12], have been applied to collaborative quality filtering with good results. The March 1997 issue of CACM [13] presents good summaries of early work on collaborative filtering and the recent special issue of ACM Transactions on Information Systems [14] highlights some contemporary results in this field.

While not a CQF system, [15] applies a hybrid approach, combining both collaborative and content-based filtering, to academic publications. However, like most collaborative filtering systems, it provides recommendations based on similar taste rather than on estimates of intrinsic quality. In a similar vein to CQF is online reputation management systems such as [16]. Like CQF, these systems estimate a single intrinsic characteristic — in this case, trustworthiness. However, reputation is computed based on users' opinions of each other rather than on reviews of items.

3   Factor Analysis

Our CQF system is based on the widely used factor analysis (FA) method, a dimensional reduction technique that takes a high dimensional data vector as input and returns a vector of factors of typically much lower dimension. These factors form a basis for a subspace that captures as much of the variance in the original data space as possible. Our implementation uses an iterative EM algorithm, an approach widely discussed in available literature [17,18], so we skip its derivation and simply present a summary of our implementation.

3.1   Factor Analysis of Dense Datasets

The data sets used in collaborative quality filtering are typically very sparse, since most reviewers will only rate a small fraction of the available items. However, it is helpful to understand factor analysis on dense datasets before examining the modifications necessary to make it work with sparse data.

The factor analysis model consists of a set of M independent, identically distributed data points, one for each item being reviewed. Each data point is associated with two random variables: R, a length N vector of observed reviews, and Q, the latent intrinsic quality that the FA algorithm estimates from the reviews. In the general case, Q may be a vector of length P, with $P < N$, but in our application, we choose to have $P = 1$, representing the single factor of "intrinsic quality."

The entire dataset consists of the $M \times N$ matrix $\mathbf{R}$. Each row, R_m, is a vector of N reviews for item m. Each element, $R_{m,n}$, is the review given to item m by reviewer n. The output of our algorithm is a $M \times 1$ matrix, Q, where each scalar row, Q_m, is the estimated quality of item m.

We assume that each Q_m is independent and distributed normally with a mean of zero and unit variance. The distribution of R_m conditioned on Q_m is also normal with mean $\mu + \Lambda Q_m$ and diagonal covariance matrix Ψ. Λ and μ are N element vectors and Ψ is a $N \times N$ diagonal matrix. We use a maximum likelihood approach to estimate the values of these three parameters.

The μ parameter can be estimated simply as the sample mean:

$$\mu = \frac{1}{M} \sum_{m=1}^{M} R_m \tag{1}$$

The other parameters, Λ, and Ψ, are estimated using the EM algorithm.

For the E-step, we calculate the conditional expectations, $\mathrm{E}(Q_m|R_m)$, and the estimated variances, $\mathrm{Var}(Q_m|R_m)$. [18] shows that:

$$\mathrm{E}(Q_m|R_m) = (I + \Lambda^T \Psi^{-1} \Lambda)^{-1} \Lambda^T \Psi^{-1}(R_m - \mu) \tag{2}$$
$$\mathrm{Var}(Q_m|R_m) = (I + \Lambda^T \Psi^{-1} \Lambda)^{-1} \tag{3}$$

We can then use these two expected values to obtain the necessary estimates of the sufficient statistics used in the M-step:

$$\langle Q_m \rangle = \mathrm{E}(Q_m|R_m) \tag{4}$$
$$\langle Q_m^2 \rangle = \mathrm{Var}(Q_m|R_m) + \mathrm{E}(Q_m|R_m)^2 \tag{5}$$

Note that some of these equations are slightly different than classical derivations of factor analysis because our Q_m are scalars, not vectors.

The M-step uses these estimates to update the parameter estimates:

$$\Lambda^{(t+1)} = \left(\sum_{m=1}^{M} R_m \langle Q_m \rangle \right) \left(\sum_{m=1}^{M} \langle Q_m^2 \rangle \right)^{-1} \tag{6}$$

$$\Psi^{(t+1)} = \frac{1}{M} \, \mathrm{diag}\left(\sum_{m=1}^{M} R_m R_m^T - \Lambda^{(t+1)} \sum_{m=1}^{M} \langle Q_m \rangle R_m^T \right) \tag{7}$$

These new estimates are then used by the next iteration's E-step. EM is proven to converge to a local maximum and in practice converges fairly rapidly.

Once the EM algorithm converges, the estimate of $E(Q_m|R_m)$ is our estimate of the quality of the item m. The first term in the equation for $E(Q_m|R_m)$:

$$(I + \Lambda^T \Psi^{-1} \Lambda)^{-1} \Lambda^T \Psi^{-1} \tag{8}$$

can be interpreted as a length N vector of weights, each of which represent the amount of confidence we have in a reviewer.

3.2 Factor Analysis of Sparse Datasets

Because the data sets we will be using for CQF are typically very sparse, we need to make a few modifications to the standard FA algorithm. These modifications are derived from the sparse FA algorithm described by [12], which in turn is based on [19]. The main difference between our derivation and [12] is our use of a diagonal covariance matrix Ψ, which allows individual variance values for each reviewer, instead of a single scalar variance that applies to all reviewers.

While our approach is very similar algorithmically to [12], it is important to note that we are applying it to a different problem. The collaborative filtering system in [12] finds factors across users to make personalized recommendations. We use factor analysis to find factors across items for estimating item quality.

We introduce a set of $N \times N$ diagonal *trimming matrices*, T_m, one for each item m in the dataset. Each diagonal element, $T_{m,n}$, is one if and only if there is as a review of item m by reviewer n in the dataset and zero otherwise. All non-diagonal elements of T_m are zero.

The sparse estimate for μ now becomes:

$$\mu = \left(\sum_{m=1}^{M} T_m \right)^{-1} \left(\sum_{m=1}^{M} R_m \right) \tag{9}$$

Similarly, we have updated equations for the E-step:

$$\bar{\Lambda}_m = T_m \Lambda \tag{10}$$
$$E(Q_m|R_m) = (I + \bar{\Lambda}_m^T \Psi^{-1} \bar{\Lambda}_m)^{-1} \bar{\Lambda}_n^T \Psi^{-1}(R_m - \mu) \tag{11}$$
$$\text{Var}(Q_m|R_m) = (I + \bar{\Lambda}_m^T \Psi^{-1} \bar{\Lambda}_m)^{-1} \tag{12}$$

Note that because the rows of the trimming matrix are unique, the terms used to calculate $\text{Var}(Q_m|R_m)$ and $E(Q_m|R_m)$ are different for each row of the data matrix. The unfortunate result is that the E-step becomes much more computational expensive.

These estimated can then be used to compute the sufficient statistics $\langle Q_m \rangle$ and $\langle Q_m^2 \rangle$ used in the M-step in the same fashion as the dense case.

The update equations for the M-step are also similar to their dense counterparts:

$$\Lambda^{(t+1)} = \left(\sum_{m=1}^{M} T_m \langle Q_m^2 \rangle \right)^{-1} \left(\sum_{m=1}^{M} R_m \langle Q_m \rangle \right) \tag{13}$$

$$\Psi^{(t+1)} = \left(\sum_{m=1}^{M} T_m \right)^{-1} \text{diag} \left(\sum_{m=1}^{M} R_m R_m^T - T_m \Lambda^{(t+1)} \langle Q_m \rangle R_m^T \right) \tag{14}$$

Canny [12] presents a more complicated form of 13 that can handle the general case of a vector Q_m. He also includes normalization terms necessary for his collaborative filtering application, which significantly degrades the performance of our application.

The estimated quality of the items being reviewed is, as in the dense case, simply the expected values $E(Q_m|R_m)$. Calculating the reviewer weight vector requires a little more effort than the dense case:

$$\left(\sum_{m=1}^{M} T_m \right)^{-1} \left(\sum_{m=1}^{M} (I + \bar{\Lambda}_m^T \Psi^{-1} \bar{\Lambda}_m)^{-1} \bar{\Lambda}_m^T \Psi^{-1} \right) \tag{15}$$

where $\bar{\Lambda}_m$ is defined as in equation 11. Without this summation and normalization, reviewers with few reviews receive unrealistically high weights.

3.3 Smoothing

To further improve performance with sparse data, we implemented a simple smoothing method loosely based on the technique of deleted interpolation [20], commonly used to smooth Hidden Markov Models.

We smooth Λ and Ψ using a linear combination of the estimates produced by the EM algorithm and prior estimates of these parameters:

$$\Lambda_n = (1 - w_n)\Lambda_{\text{EM},n} + w_n\Lambda_{\text{prior},n} \tag{16}$$

The equation for Ψ is identical. Each weight, w_n, is the reciprocal of the number of reviews written by reviewer n, which gives more weight to the EM estimates for reviewers with many reviews and more weight to the prior for reviewers with few reviews.

We determine the prior estimates of Λ and Ψ by running the EM factor analysis algorithm on a subset of the dataset restricted to reviewers with 100 or more reviews, then take the mean of the resulting Λ and Ψ vectors.

3.4 Implementation and Performance

We implement factor analysis in C++ as a Matlab plug-in. An 867MHz Pentium III with 512MB of RAM requires approximately 111 minutes to process the full dataset. Smoothing reduces the number of iterations needed for convergence and thus decreases the time by about two thirds. For extremely large datasets, factor analysis can easily be parallelized.

For processing large datasets that change and grow over time, a previous run's Λ and Ψ values can be used to bootstrap subsequent runs, drastically reducing the number of EM iterations required. A large review website, for example, would only need to run the full EM algorithm once. As new items, reviewers, and reviews are added to the site, the existing parameter values can be used to bootstrap EM on the new dataset. As long as new information is only a small fraction of the total data set, only one or two iterations should be necessary to re-estimate the parameter values.

4 Methodology

Testing CQF algorithms present several challenges in addition to the implementation problems related to dataset size and sparseness. Existing datasets, such as the data from epinions.com that we used, do not come with ground truth, making it impossible to measure how well an algorithm recovers intrinsic quality. Likewise, it is easy to create synthetically generated datasets with known ground truth, but not obvious how to model agreement among reviewers and thus consensus.

4.1 Testing Consensus

To test an algorithm's ability to measure consensus, we use a dataset gathered by crawling the epinions.com site in 2001. Since the factor analysis algorithm will fail with a singular Ψ matrix if there are any reviewers with fewer than two reviews, we trim out reviewers with only one review, leaving us with 104,889 items and 53,796 reviewers.

In addition to the individual reviews of items, the epinions.com dataset also includes readers' evaluations of the reviewers, which we use as a measure of consensus. Users of the site are allowed to indicate reviewers that they trust. The number of users that trust a reviewer thus becomes a metric for the community's opinion of a reviewer's reviews. Since the reviews of a prolific reviewer who has rated many items are more likely to be seen and therefore trusted, we divide the raw number of users trusting each reviewer by the number of reviews the reviewer has written to determine an average trust score.

It must be noted that average trust is not necessarily a good indicator of a reviewer's ability to accurately judge the quality of an item. A reader's decision to trust a reviewer is also influenced by subjective factors, such as the length, thoroughness, and quality of the written reviews. However, we believe one important influence on trust scores is how closely a reviewer's opinions match those of the site's readers. Reviewers who consistently write reviews that agree with the consensus opinion will likely be trusted by large numbers of readers.

4.2 Testing Intrinsic Quality

The epinions.com dataset does not contain any information about the ground truth intrinsic quality of the items it contains, nor do any sets of user reviews that we know of. Therefore, we use synthetically generated datasets to test each algorithm's ability to recover the ground truth quality.

One of the biggest risks when using synthetic datasets is that the choice of models for generating the data may bias the set to favor one algorithm over another. For example, if we created a synthetic dataset with a zero mean, unit variance Gaussian distributed ground truth and reviews generated by a simple linear transformation of this ground truth, we would imagine that factor analysis would perform superbly, since that is exactly the model that factor analysis assumes.

To more completely and fairly evaluate these algorithms, we create two synthetic datasets, both considerably different than the simplistic approach described above. These two datasets use different distributions of ground truth quality, which allows us to measure how well our algorithm performs when presented with data whose distribution differs from what its model assumes.

When creating the synthetic datasets, we were primarily concerned with making it as similar as possible to the real epinions.com dataset. The sparseness of reviews in the real and synthetic datasets are identical: an item, m, has a review by reviewer n in the synthetic datasets if and only if n reviewed m in the real dataset.

The distribution of reviews in the epinions.com set is skewed (the average review is 1 on a scale of -2 to 2), so we added similar skew to our synthetic sets. However, the way we accounted for this skew is different in our two synthetic datasets. For the first set, we assumed that the observed skew is a result of the review process and not indicative of the intrinsic quality. In this set, the ground truth is normally distributed with a mean of zero and variance of one, and thus has no skew. Because the asymptotic consensus algorithm and the mean both assume a bounded quality scale, we truncate the ground truth values to lie between -2 and 2.[1]

An alternative explanation for the observed skew in the epinions.com data is that it is a reflection of skew in the intrinsic quality of the items being reviewed. Our second synthetic dataset explores this possibility. The ground truth of this dataset is generated so that the frequency of each score is the same as the frequency of that score in the observed data.

We created the reviews by adding randomly generated noise term to the ground truth of the item being reviewed. This noise was distributed normally from mean and variance parameters associated with each reviewer. For the first dataset, the mean parameters are normally distributed with mean and variance one, which gives us the overall bias toward higher valued reviews observed in the epinions.com data. In the second dataset this bias is already present in the ground truth, so the distribution of the mean parameter has mean zero and variance one. For both datasets, the noise variance parameters were generated from the square of a zero mean, unit variance normal distribution.

5   Results

We performed two sets of tests on several variants of both the factor analysis and asymptotic consensus CQF algorithms. The first set of experiments tests the abilities of the algorithms to recover the ground truth intrinsic quality of the items reviewed. For this test, we use our two synthetically generated datasets, which include ground truth information. The second experiment measures the algorithms' ability to estimate the consensus opinion of the reviewers. This test uses the epinions.com review data and uses the average trust statistic as a measure of how closely a reviewer's opinions are aligned with that of the consensus.

5.1   Recovering Ground Truth

To test a CQF algorithm's ability to recover ground truth intrinsic quality, we compared its estimates of item quality to the known ground truth using our two synthetically generated datasets. Dataset 1 has no bias in its ground truth, while the ground truth for dataset 2 has a bias equal to the bias we observed in the epinions.com data. We compared our factor analysis CQF algorithm, the asymptotic consensus algorithm, and also simple mean of an item's reviews, which serves as a baseline.

---

[1] The question of whether to model intrinsic quality by a bounded or an unbounded distribution is another philosophical difference between our factor analysis approach and earlier CQF systems. We believe that allowing both intrinsic quality and reviewer scores to be unbounded more closely matches our intuitive understanding of quality. After all, at any time it is possible to encounter an item of higher quality than any previous seen item, though the probability of such an encounter becomes smaller as more items are seen. However, we chose to bound both the ground truth intrinsic quality and the reviewer scores for this experiment, in order to level the field for all three methods and more closely model the epinions.com data. Experiments we conducted using unbounded intrinsic quality but bounded reviews showed no significant differences from results we present here.

We compare the algorithms' quality estimates to the ground truth by measuring their correlation. The use of correlation, as opposed to a simpler metric like mean absolute error, allows us to ignore differences in scale and normalization among the systems tested.

We tested factor analysis both with and without the smoothing technique described in Sect. 3.3. We found that the α parameter, a smoothing technique for asymptotic consensus that gives greater weight to reviewers with more reviews, had no effect on performance in this test, so these results are omitted for clarity. We did not test the β and γ factors because they had little effect according to [2].

We discovered that both the mean and the asymptotic consensus algorithm delivered better results when we adjusted for reviewer bias by normalizing each reviewer's average score to zero, so we also tested versions of these algorithms with the observed data adjusted for bias. We did not adjust for the bias with factor analysis because this calculation is already part of the factor analysis algorithm.

To show how sparseness affected these algorithms, we varied the minimum number of reviews necessary for a reviewer to be considered by the algorithms. The most sparse run used all reviewers with at least two reviews, while other runs only used reviewers with a minimum of 3, 5, 7, 10, 15, 20, 35, 50, 75, and 100 reviews.

The results of our tests can be seen in Fig. 1, which shows that factor analysis is significantly better than both the mean and the asymptotic consensus algorithm at recovering ground truth quality. Smoothing improves performance with sparse data, but slightly degrades performance with denser datasets. The asymptotic consensus algorithm provides little gain versus the mean on this test, but adjusting for reviewer bias provides a significant improvement to both the mean and asymptotic consensus algorithms.

The results are roughly the same on both of our datasets. The mean and the asymptotic consensus algorithm showed better performance on the second dataset, where the skew in the observed data is due to similar skew in the ground truth. This result is not surprising, since the distribution of observed data and ground truth data are much more similar in this dataset than in the first one.

However, factor analysis also shows a slight increase in overall performance compared to the first dataset. We believe that this result demonstrates that factor analysis is a robust technique that excels at recovering intrinsic quality even when the distribution of that ground truth data is quite different than what the factor analysis model assumes.

As one might expect, all of the algorithms predict the quality of items with many reviews far more accurately than items with only a few reviews. However, because approximately 90% of items in these datasets have 10 or fewer reviews, an algorithm's ability to accurately estimate the quality of items with very few reviews has significant impact on its total performance.

Fig. 2 shows a more detailed view of the algorithms performance for a specific degree of sparseness — a minimum of 10 reviews per reviewer — and plot the correlation between the actual ground truth and the quality estimates for items with different numbers of reviews ranging from 1 to 50. These results show that factor analysis provides the greatest advantage for the common case of items with few reviews. This distribution of reviews per item also partly explains why asymptotic consensus is barely better than the mean in Fig. 1. While asymptotic consensus consistently outperforms the mean by a small amount for items with several reviews, its estimates are, by definition, identical

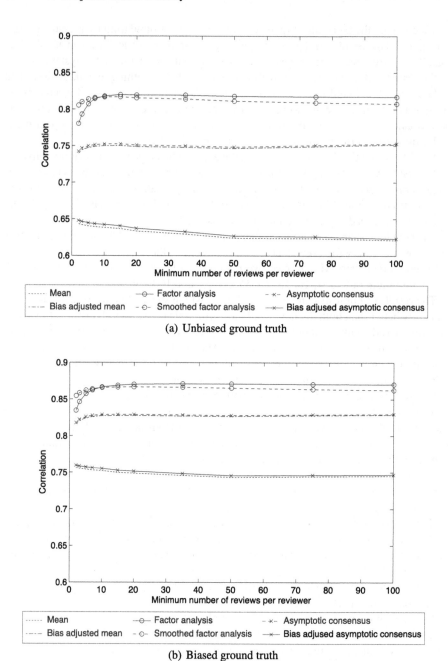

(a) Unbiased ground truth

(b) Biased ground truth

Fig. 1. Comparison of CQF algorithms on a dataset with (a) unbiased ground truth and (b) biased ground truth

to the means for items with only a single review. Because more than half of the items have a single review, its overall performance is only slightly better than the mean.

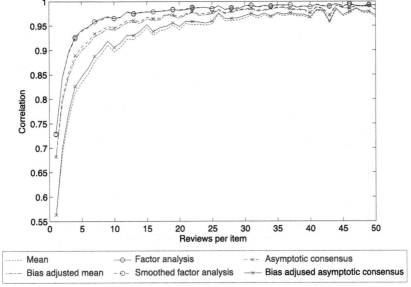

(a) Unbiased ground truth

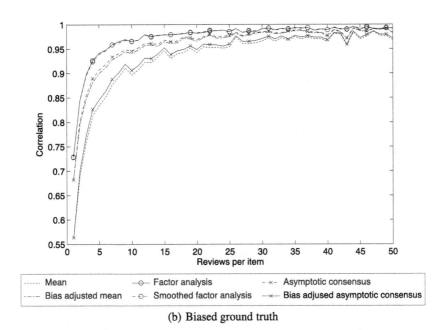

(b) Biased ground truth

Fig. 2. Detailed comparison of mean, asymptotic consensus, and factor analysis algorithms on dataset with (a) unbiased ground truth and (b) biased ground truth. Minimum of 10 reviews per reviewer.

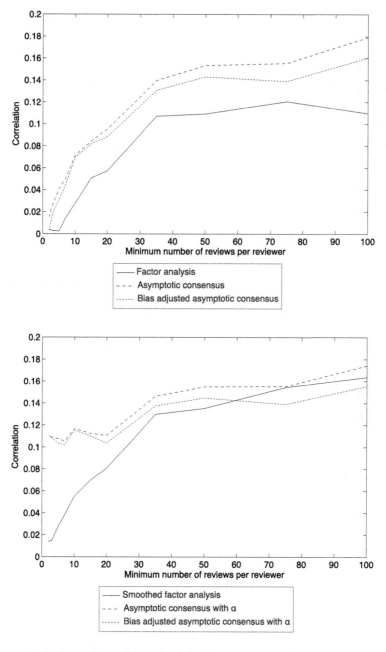

Fig. 3. Comparison of algorithms' abilities to estimate reviewer consensus

5.2 Estimating Consensus

To measure a CQF system's ability to estimate the consensus of a group of reviewers, we measured the correlation between the reviewer weights returned by an algorithm and the average trust score assigned to the reviewer in the epinions.com dataset.

For this test, we compared factor analysis, both with and without smoothing, to several variants of the asymptotic consensus algorithm. For asymptotic consensus, we used both the raw reviewer data and the data where we adjusted each reviewer's bias to zero. We also compared using asymptotic consensus's α parameter to not using it. Because the mean does not calculate weights for individual reviewers, we omitted it from this experiment. The results of comparing these six algorithm variants is shown in Fig. 3.

None of the algorithms did particularly well on this test, with a maximum correlation of about 0.18. We believe this has as much to do with average trust being a rather poor indicator of consensus as it does with any weakness in the particular algorithms.

As expected, asymptotic consensus is clearly best at estimating reviewer consensus. Using the α parameter—a smoothing parameter that discounts reviewers with few reviews—provides a significant boost with highly sparse datasets. Smoothing also provides a noticeable benefit for factor analysis, though even the smoothed version lags behind asymptotic consensus.

Interestingly, asymptotic consensus performs slightly worse on this test when we center the reviewer data to zero out any reviewer bias. While unbiased reviews allow better predictions of intrinsic quality, they actually hurt the algorithm's ability to predict consensus. Upon reflection, this isn't surprising: if the consensus opinion is also biased, we should expect the best prediction will be made from biased data.

In general, techniques that were most successful at estimating intrinsic quality—namely factor analysis and using unbiased data—had a detrimental impact when estimating consensus. Others which had no effect on estimating quality, like the α parameter, had large effects on this test. We feel the simplest explanation for this behavior is that intrinsic quality and consensus are actually very different concepts of quality.

6 Conclusion

Our experiments suggest that while both asymptotic consensus and factor analysis are purported to be filtering on quality, they are in fact computing quite different things. The asymptotic consensus algorithm converges to an estimate of the consensus of a group of reviewers, while factor analysis tries to recover objective quality. While the lack of objective ground truth for either intrinsic quality or consensus makes evaluation difficult, the preponderance of evidence suggests that these two aspects of quality are actually distinct.

Neither approach is necessarily "correct"; each may be suitable for different types of applications. However, as the stated goal of asymptotic consensus is to serve as a model of scholarly review, one might hope that reviewer consensus and intrinsic quality would converge. Unfortunately, our results suggest that they are likely to be different. Should these results withstand further scrutiny, in particular, a test against real peer review data, they would raise interesting questions about what such processes are in fact measuring.

We believe that for such applications, factor analysis, or another approach that recovers intrinsic quality, may be the better technique.

References

1. Internet Movie Database: (Top 250 films) http://www.imdb.com/top_250_films.
2. Riggs, T.: Collaborative quality filtering in open review systems. Master's thesis, University of California, Berkeley, Computer Science Division (2001)
3. Wilensky, R., Riggs, T.: An algorithm for automatically rating reviewers. In: Proc. of the First Joint Conf. on Digital Libraries, Roanoke, Virginia (2001)
4. Katerattanakui, P., et al.: Objective quality ranking of computing journals. Communications of the ACM **46** (2003) 111–114
5. Brown, L., Gardner, J.: Using citation analysis to assess the impact of journals and articles on contemporary accounting research. Journal of Accounting Research **23** (1995) 84–109
6. Goldberg, D., et al.: Using collaborative filtering to weave and information tapestry. Communications of the ACM **35** (1992) 61–70
7. Resnick, P., et al.: GroupLens: An Open Architecture for Collaborative Filtering of Netnews. In: Proc. of ACM 1994 Conf. on Computer Supported Cooperative Work, Chapel Hill, North Carolina, ACM (1994) 175–186
8. Hill, W., et al.: Recommending and evaluating choices in a virtual community of use. In: Proc. of the SIGCHI Conf. on Humand Factors in Computing Systems. (1995) 194–201
9. Shardanand, U., Maes, P.: Social information filtering: Algorithms for automating "word of mouth". In: Proc. of ACM CHI'95 Conf. on Human Factors in Computing Systems. Volume 1. (1995) 210–217
10. Herlocker, J.L., et al.: An algorithmic framework for performing collaborative filtering. In: SIGIR '99: Proc. of the 22nd Annual International ACM SIGIR Conf. on Research and Development in Information Retrieval, August 15-19, 1999, Berkeley, CA, USA, ACM (1999) 230–237
11. Hofmann, T.: Latent semantic models for collaborative filtering. ACM Transactions on Information Systems **22** (2004) 89–115
12. Canny, J.: Collaborative filtering with privacy via factor analysis. In: Proc. of the 25th Annual International ACM SIGIR Conf. on Research and Development in Information Retrieval. (2002) 238–245
13. Resnick, P., Varian, H.R.: Recommender systems. Communications of the ACM (1997)
14. Konstan, J.A.: Introduction to recommender systems: Algorithms and evaluation. ACM Transactions on Information Systems **22** (2004) 1–4
15. Middleton, S.E., et al.: Ontological user profiling in recommender systems. ACM Transactions on Information Systems **22** (2004) 54–88
16. Zacharia, G., et al.: Collaborative reputation mechanisms in electronic marketplaces. In: HICSS. (1999)
17. Rubin, D.B., Thayer, D.T.: EM algorithms for ML factor analysis. Psychometrika **47** (1982) 69–76
18. Jordan, M.I.: An introduction to probabilistic graphic models. (Unpublished textbook manuscript)
19. Ghahramani, Z., Jordan, M.I.: Learning from incomplete data. Technical Report AIM-1509, Massachusettes Institute of Technology, Artificial Intelligence Laboratory (1994)
20. Jelinek, F., Mercer, R.L.: Interpolated estimation of markov source parameters from sparse data. In Gelsema, E.S., Kanal, L.N., eds.: Pattern Recognition in Practice. North-Holland Publishing Company (1980) 381–397

Spying Out Accurate User Preferences for Search Engine Adaptation

Lin Deng, Wilfred Ng, Xiaoyong Chai, and Dik-Lun Lee

Department of Computer Science
Hong Kong University of Science and Technology
{ldeng, wilfred, carnamel, dlee}@cs.ust.hk

Abstract. Most existing search engines employ static ranking algorithms that do not adapt to the specific needs of users. Recently, some researchers have studied the use of clickthrough data to adapt a search engine's ranking function. Clickthrough data indicate for each query the results that are clicked by users. As a kind of implicit relevance feedback information, clickthrough data can easily be collected by a search engine. However, clickthrough data is sparse and incomplete, thus, it is a challenge to discover accurate user preferences from it. In this paper, we propose a novel algorithm called "Spy Naïve Bayes" (SpyNB) to identify user preferences generated from clickthrough data. First, we treat the result items clicked by the users as *sure positive* examples and those not clicked by the users as unlabelled data. Then, we plant the sure positive examples (the spies) into the unlabelled set of result items and apply a naïve Bayes classification to generate the *reliable negative* examples. These positive and negative examples allow us to discover more accurate user's preferences. Finally, we employ the SpyNB algorithm with a ranking SVM optimizer to build an adaptive metasearch engine. Our experimental results show that, compared with the original ranking, SpyNB can significantly improve the average ranks of users' click by 20%.

1 Introduction

The information on the Web is huge and growing rapidly. An effective search engine is an important means for users to find the desired information from billions of Web pages. Besides standalone search engines, metasearch engines are also very useful because they allow users to access multiple search engines simultaneously with a uniform interface.

Adapting a search engine to cater for specific users and queries is an important research problem and has many applications. In general, there are two aspects of search engine adaptation that need to be addressed. The first aspect is *query specific* adaptation; that is, how to return the best results for a query from the underlying search engines that have different coverage and focuses. The second aspect is *user specific* adaptation that aims to meet the diversified preferences of different users in the search results. A well-adapted metasearch engine should be able to optimize its ranking function for different query categories and different

B. Mobasher et al. (Eds.): WebKDD 2004, LNAI 3932, pp. 87–103, 2006.

user communities. The challenging task is how to adapt the ranking function of a metasearch engine to cater for different users' preferences.

Some previous studies employed users' explicit relevance feedback to adapt the search engine's ranking function [1,2]. However, users are usually unwilling to give explicit feedback because of the manual efforts involved, making the feedback data too few to be representative. To overcome this problem, researchers have recently studied the use of clickthrough data, which is a kind of implicit relevance feedback data, to optimize the ranking functions [3,4,5] in an automatic manner.

Formally, clickthrough data are represented as a triplet (q, r, c), where q is the input query, r is the ranked result links $(l_1, \ldots, l_n)$, and c is the set of links that a user has clicked on. Figure 1 illustrates an example from clickthrough data of the query "apple" and three links l_1, l_7 and l_{10} are in bold, indicating that they have been clicked by the user. The main advantage of using clickthrough data is that it does not require extra effort from the user, and thus can be obtained at a very low cost. However, clickthrough data are ambiguous when used as a sign of user preferences. As a consequence, it is more difficult to interpret clickthrough data and discover user preferences than explicit relevance feedback data.

In essence of search engine adaptation using clickthrough data, there are two steps. The first step is to identify user preferences (i.e., the user prefers one result over another). The second step is to optimize the ranking function based on the preferences obtained in the first step. There exists an effective algorithm called ranking SVM [4] for the second step, but little research has been done for the first step. In this paper, we focus on the accurate elicitation of user preferences from clickthrough data. In particular, we propose a novel learning technique called *Spy Naïve Bayes* (SpyNB), which analyzes the titles, abstracts and URLs of the returned links to identify any actual irrelevant links. We show that SpyNB is an effective way to discover accurate user preferences from clickthrough data by incorporating SpyNB (for the first step) with a ranking SVM (for the second step) to construct an adaptive metasearch engine ranker. Notice that SpyNB can be used to adapt the ranking function of a standalone search engine. However, metasearch is chosen in this paper, since it does not only serve as an important search tool but allows us to focus on the adaptive ranking of the results without considering crawling and indexing, which are not the goal of our paper. In addition, metasearch allows us to choose underlying search engines with different strengths, coverages and focuses, thus giving us a new dimension to observe the effectiveness of SpyNB.

Finally, we develop a metasearch engine prototype that comprises MSNSearch, WiseNut and Overture for conducting experimental performance evaluations. The empirical results show that SpyNB algorithm can accurately elicit user preferences from clickthrough data and thus improve the ranking quality of a metasearch engine. Importantly, the ranking quality produced with SpyNB is shown to be significantly better than that of Joachims algorithm and the original rankings from the underlying search engines.

Links	The list of search results with titles, abstracts and URLs of webpages
l₁ (clicked)	**Apple** **Opportunities at Apple. Visit other Apple sites ...** *http://www.apple.com/*
l₂	Apple - QuickTime - Download Visit the Apple Store online or at retail locations ... *http://www.apple.com/quicktime/download/*
l₃	Apple - Fruit Apples have a rounded shape with a depression at the top ... *http://www.hort.purdue.edu/ext/senior/fruits/apple1.htm*
l₄	www.apple-history.com A brief history of the company that changed the computing world ... *http://www.apple-history.com/*
l₅	MacCentral: Apple Macintosh News Steve Jobs unveils Apple mini stores. ... *http://www.macworld.com/news/*
l₆	Adams County Nursery, apple trees One of the most widely planted apple cultivars worldwide. *http://www.acnursery.com/apples.htm*
l₇ (clicked)	**Apple .Mac Welcome** **... member specials throughout the year. See ...** *http://www.mac.com/*
l₈	AppleInsider ... Apple seeds Mac OS X Server 10.3.6 build 7R20. *http://www.appleinsider.com/*
l₉	ROSE APPLE Fruit Facts The rose apple is too large to make a suitable container plant. ... *http://www.crfg.org/pubs/ff/roseapple.html*
l₁₀ (clicked)	**Apple - Support** **Support for most Apple products provided by Apple Computer** *http://www.info.apple.com/*

Fig. 1. A clickthrough for the query "apple". Links in bold are clicked by the user.

The rest of this paper is organized as follows. In Section 2, we briefly review the related works. In Section 3, we present our SpyNB algorithm to identify user preferences from clickthrough data. In Section 4, we revisit the idea of a ranking SVM. In Section 5, the experimental results related to the effectiveness of our SpyNB algorithm are reported. Section 6 concludes the paper.

2   Related Work

Related work on search engine adaptation using clickthrough data falls into two subareas. The first one is the analysis of clickthrough data to identify user's preferences. The second one is the study of the optimization of a search engines' ranking function using the identified preferences. For ranking function optimization, ranking SVM[4] is an effective algorithm, which can learn an optimized ranking function using user preferences as input. Recently, an RSCF algorithm [5] has been proposed to extend ranking SVM to a co-training framework in order to tackle the lack of clickthrough data for training.

For clickthrough data analysis, a simple algorithm was proposed by Joachims [4], which elicits preference pairs from clickthrough data. We call this method "*Joachims algorithm*" throughout this paper. Joachims algorithm assumed that the user scans the ranked results strictly from top to bottom. Therefore, if a user skips link l_i and clicks on link l_j which ranks lower than link l_i ($i < j$), Joachims algorithm assumed that the user must have observed link l_i and decided not to click on it. Then preference pairs are elicited as $l_j <_{r'} l_i$, where $<_{r'}$ represents the target ranking of search results.

For example, in the clickthrough of the "apple" query shown in Figure 1, the user does not click on l_2, l_3, l_4, l_5, and l_6, but clicks on l_7. Therefore according to Joachims algorithm, l_7 is more relevant to the user than the other five links. In other words, l_7 should rank ahead of those five links in the target ranking. Similarly, l_{10} should rank ahead of l_2, l_3, l_4, l_5, l_6, l_8, and l_9 in the target ranking. All preferences obtained using Joachims algorithm are shown in Figure 2.

Preference pairs arising from l_1	Preference pairs arising from l_7	Preference pairs arising from l_{10}
Empty Set	$l_7 <_{r'} l_2$	$l_{10} <_{r'} l_2$
	$l_7 <_{r'} l_3$	$l_{10} <_{r'} l_3$
	$l_7 <_{r'} l_4$	$l_{10} <_{r'} l_4$
	$l_7 <_{r'} l_5$	$l_{10} <_{r'} l_5$
	$l_7 <_{r'} l_6$	$l_{10} <_{r'} l_6$
		$l_{10} <_{r'} l_8$
		$l_{10} <_{r'} l_9$

Fig. 2. Preferences derived from the clickthrough of Figure 1 using Joachims algorithm

3   Learning Preferences from Clickthrough Data

We first discuss some inadequacies of Joachims algorithm. We then introduce a new interpretation of clickthrough data, and based on that the SpyNB algorithm for learning preferences from clickthrough data.

3.1   Inadequacy of Joachims Algorithm

As depicted in Section 2, Joachims algorithm is simple and efficient. However, we argue that the assumption made by Joachims algorithm of how users scan search results is too strong in reality, since users' behaviors are diverse. Therefore, there could be a problem in that Joachims algorithm assumes that the user scans search results *strictly* from top to bottom, as in reality a user may leap over several results. In short, the up-to-down scanning may not in reality be *strict*.

Moreover, we notice that Joachims algorithm is unfair to the high-ranking links, which means that the high-ranking links (e.g. l_1, l_2) are more likely to be "penalized" than the low-ranking links (e.g. l_9, l_{10}). Consider the preference example shown in Figure 2. Link l_1 and l_{10} are both clicked links; however l_1 appears on the left hand side of preference pairs (meaning it should be ranked high in target ranking) much *less* than l_{10}. (l_1, 0 times; l_{10}, 7 times.) On the other hand, link l_2 and l_9 are both unclicked links; however, l_2 appears on the right hand side of preference pairs (means it should be ranked low in target ranking) *more* than l_9. (l_2, twice; l_9, 1 times.) Therefore, the high-ranking links (e.g. l_1, l_2) are more likely to be ranked low after learning. We note the phenomenon where Joachims algorithm is apt to penalize the high-ranking links.

3.2   New Clickthrough Interpretation

In order to address the above problems, we propose to interpret the clickthrough data in a new manner. We note that the user typically clicks on the links whose titles, abstracts or URLs are interesting to them. Therefore, we assume the clicked links are liked by the user. Moreover, users in general are unlikely to click all the links that match his interests. For example, after a user has obtained the desired information, he stops scanning the results. Thus, we further assume that the unclicked links contain both the links that the user likes and dislikes. Finally, we assume that the disliked links are the links that are most different in content to the clicked links.

Based on the new interpretation, we label the clicked links as *positive* and the unclicked links as *unlabeled* samples. Then the problem of discovering user's preferences becomes how to identify the reliable *negative* samples from the unlabeled set, where *negative* indicates that the link does not match user's interests. After the reliable negatives are identified, the user preference can be reflected in the way that the user prefers all links in the positive set to those in the negative set. Let P denote the positive set, U denote the unlabeled set and RN denote the reliable negative set, where $RN \subset U$. The pairwise preferences can be represented as:

$$l_i <_{r'} l_j, \quad \forall \ l_i \in P, \ l_j \in RN \tag{1}$$

Equation (1) indicates that all links in the positive set should rank ahead of those from the negative set in the target ranking.

3.3   Spy Naïve Bayes

The problem now can be formulated as how to identify the reliable negative examples from an unlabeled set using only positive and unlabeled data. Recently, *partially supervised classification* [6,7,8,9] provides a novel paradigm for constructing classifiers using positive examples and a large set of unlabeled examples. Finding reliable negative examples can be solved by partially supervised classification techniques, such as Spy technique [8], 1-DNF [9], and the Rocchio method [6]. In particular, we incorporate the spy technique with naïve Bayes to design a *Spy Naïve Bayes* (SpyNB) algorithm for identifying the reliable negative examples. We choose the spy technique, because it has been shown to be effective for common text classification [8]. However, clickthrough data have some unique characteristics compared to common texts. For instance, the titles and abstracts are both very short texts, and the size of positive set (the number of clicked links) is also very small. Consequently, the identified RN is not reliable if only a small portion of positive examples are used as spies. Thus we further employ a voting procedure to strengthen SpyNB. In this section, we elaborate on the SpyNB algorithm in detail.

We first illustrate how the Naïve Bayes [10] (NB for short) is adapted in click-through analysis as follows. Let "+" and "−" denote the positive and negative classes, respectively. Let $L = \{l_1, l_2, \cdots, l_N\}$ denote a set of N links (documents) in the search results. Each link l_i can be described as a word vector, $W = (w_1, w_2, \cdots, w_M)$, in the *vector space model* [11], where we count the occurrences of w_i appearing in the titles, abstracts and URLs. Then, a NB classifier is built by estimating the prior probabilities ($Pr(+)$ and $Pr(-)$), and likelihood ($Pr(w_j|+)$ and $Pr(w_j|-)$), as shown in Algorithm 1.

Algorithm 1 Naïve Bayes Algorithm

Input:
  $L = \{l_1, l_2, \ldots, l_N\}$ /* a set of links */
Output:
  Prior probabilities: $Pr(+)$ and $Pr(-)$;
  Likelihoods: $Pr(w_j|+)$ and $Pr(w_j|-)$ $\forall j \in \{1, \ldots, M\}$
Procedure:
  1: $Pr(+) = \frac{\sum_{i=1}^{N} \delta(+|l_i)}{N}$;
  2: $Pr(-) = \frac{\sum_{i=1}^{N} \delta(-|l_i)}{N}$;
  3: **for** each attribute $w_j \in W$ **do**
  4:   $Pr(w_j|+) = \frac{\lambda + \sum_{i=1}^{N} Num(w_j, l_i)\delta(+|l_i)}{\lambda M + \sum_{j=1}^{M}\sum_{i=1}^{N} Num(w_j, l_i)\delta(+|l_i)}$;
  5:   $Pr(w_j|-) = \frac{\lambda + \sum_{i=1}^{N} Num(w_j, l_i)\delta(-|l_i)}{\lambda M + \sum_{j=1}^{M}\sum_{i=1}^{N} Num(w_j, l_i)\delta(-|l_i)}$;
  6: **end for**

In Algorithm 1, $\delta(+|l_i)$ indicates the class label of link l_i. Its value is 1 if l_i is positive; and 0 otherwise. $Num(w_j, l_i)$ is a function counting the number of keywords w_j appearing in link l_i. λ is the smoothing factor, where $\lambda = 1$ is known as Laplacian smoothing [12], which we use in our experiments.

When testing, NB classifies a link l by calculating the posterior probability using Bayes rule:

$$Pr(+|l) = \frac{Pr(l|+)Pr(+)}{Pr(l)}$$

where $Pr(l|+) = \prod_{j=1}^{|w_l|} Pr(w_{l_j}|+)$ is the product of the likelihoods of the keywords in link l. Then, link l is predicted to belong to class "+", if $P(+|l)$ is larger than $P(-|l)$; and "−" otherwise.

When the training data contain only positive and unlabeled examples, spy technique is used to learn an NB classifier [8]. The idea behind spy technique is shown in Figure 3. First, a set of positive examples S are selected from P and put in U, to act as "spies". Then, the unlabeled examples in U together with S are regarded as negative to train a NB classifier using Algorithm 1. The obtained classifier is then used to assign probabilities $Pr(+|l)$ to each example in $U \cup S$. After that, a threshold T_s is decided on by the probabilities assigned to S. An unlabeled example in U is selected as a reliable negative example if its probability is less than T_s, and thus RN is obtained. The examples in S act as "spies", since they are regarded as positive examples and are put into U pretending to be negative examples. During classification, the unknown positive examples in U are assumed to have comparative probabilities with the spies. Therefore, the reliable negative examples RN can be identified.

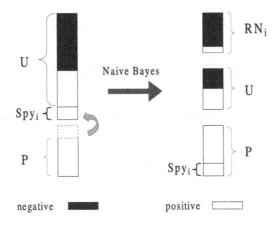

Fig. 3. Spy technique of SpyNB

Due to the unique characteristics of clickthrough data, we further employ a voting procedure (Figure 4) to make Spy Naïve Bayes more robust. The idea of voting procedure is as follows. The algorithm runs an n-time iteration, where $n = |P|$ is the number of positive examples. In each iteration, a positive example p_i in P is selected to act as a spy. It is then put into U to train an NB classifier NB_i. The probability $Pr(+|p_i)$ assigned to the spy p_i can be used as a threshold T_s to select a candidate for a reliable negative example set (RN_i). That is, any unlabeled example u_j with a smaller probability of being a positive example than the spy $(Pr(+|u_j) < T_s)$ is selected into RN_i. Consequently, n candidate reliable negative sets: $RN_1, RN_2, \cdots, RN_n$ are identified. Then, a voting procedure is taken to combine all RN_i into the final RN. An unlabeled example is included in the final RN, if and only if, it appears in at least a certain portion (T_v) of RN_i. The advantage of adopting the voting procedure in SpyNB is that the procedure makes full use of all positive examples in P. Also, the procedure makes decisions on RN by taking opinions from all possible spies and thus minimizes the influence of a random selection of spies.

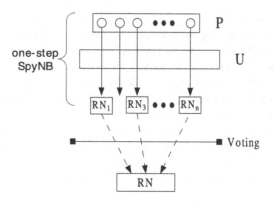

Fig. 4. Voting procedure of SpyNB

Algorithm 2 Spy Naïve Bayes (SpyNB) Algorithm

Input:
  P – a set of positive examples; U – a set of unlabeled examples; T_v – a voting threshold; T_s – a spy threshold
Output:
  RN – the set of reliable negative examples
Procedure:
  1: $RN_1 = RN_2 = \cdots = RN_{|P|} = \{\}$ and $RN = \{\}$;
  2: **for** each example $p_i \in P$ **do**
  3:   $P_s = P - \{p_i\}$;
  4:   $U_s = U \cup \{p_i\}$;
  5:   Assign each example in P_s the class label 1;
  6:   Assign each example in U_s the class label -1;
  7:   Build a NB classifier on P_s and U_s;
  8:   Classify each example in U_s using the NB classifier;
  9:   Spy threshold $T_s = Pr(+|p_i)$;
 10:   **for** each $u_j \in U$ **do**
 11:     **if** $Pr(+|u_j) < T_s$ **then**
 12:       $RN_i = RN_i \cup \{u_j\}$;
 13:     **end if**
 14:   **end for**
 15: **end for**
 16: **for** each $u_j \in U$ **do**
 17:   $Votes$ = the number of RN_i such that $u_j \in RN_i$
 18:   **if** $Votes > T_v \times |P|$ **then**
 19:     $RN = RN \cup \{u_j\}$;
 20:   **end if**
 21: **end for**

The SpyNB algorithm is given in Algorithm 2. Steps 2 to 15 use the Spy technique to generate n candidates of reliable negative example sets RN_i. Steps 16 to 21 combine all RN_i into the final RN using the voting procedure.

To analysis the time complexity of SpyNB algorithm, let $|P|$ denote the number of clicked links (positive examples), $|U|$ denote the number of unclicked links (unlabeled examples) and N denote the number of all links. Training naïve Bayes (Algorithm 1) requires only one time scan of all links, thus the time complexity of training is $O(N)$. The predication of naïve Bayes costs $O(|U|)$ time, where $|U| < N$. Thus the steps 2 to 15 of SpyNB algorithm cost $O(|P| \times (N + |U|)) = O(|P| \times N)$ time. With similar analysis, the time complexity of steps 16 to 21 of SpyNB algorithm is $O(|P| \times |U|)$, which is smaller than $O(|P| \times N)$.

Thus overall, the time complexity of the SpyNB algorithm is $O(|P| \times N)$. We know that the time complexity of Joachims algorithm is $O(N)$. It seems that SpyNB algorithm is not as efficient as Joachims algorithm. However, we note that in most realistic cases, $|P|$ (the number of links clicked by the user) is usually very small, and actually can be considered as having a constant bound. For example, the empirical clickthrough data reported in [5] has merely an average of 2.94 clicks per query. Therefore, without losing the generality, we can assume no user clicks more than 10 (or any large enough integer) links for a query. Then, $|P| < 10$ and the time complexity of SpyNB algorithm becomes $O(10 \times N) = O(N)$.

In short, although the SpyNB algorithm is more sophisticated than Joachims algorithm, due to the characteristics of clickthrough data, the *practical* complexity of SpyNB is still at the same level as Joachims algorithm, according to the previous analysis.

4   Optimizing Ranking Functions

After preferences are identified by SpyNB, we employ a ranking SVM [4] to optimize the ranking function using the identified preferences. We now briefly revisit the basic idea of ranking SVM as follows.

For a training data set, $T = \{(q_1, r_1'), (q_2, r_2'), \ldots, (q_n, r_n')\}$, where q_i in T is a query and r_i' is the corresponding target ranking, ranking SVM aims at finding a linear ranking function $f(q, d)$, which holds as many preferences in T as possible. $f(q, d)$ is defined as the inner product of a *weight vector* $\vec{w}$ and a *feature vector* of query-document mapping $\phi(q, d)$. $\phi(q, d)$ describes how well a document d of a link in the ranking matches a query q (will be detailed in Section 5.2). $\vec{w}$ gives a weighting of each feature.

Given a weight vector, $\vec{w}$, retrieved links can be ranked by sorting the values: $f(q, d) = \vec{w} \cdot \phi(q, d)$. Then, the problem of finding a ranking function, f, becomes finding a weight vector, $\vec{w}$, that makes the maximum number of the following inequalities hold:

$$\text{For all} \quad (d_i, d_j) \in r_k' \ , \ (1 \le k \le n)$$
$$\vec{w} \cdot \phi(q_k, d_i) > \vec{w} \cdot \phi(q_k, d_j) \tag{2}$$

where $(d_i, d_j) \in r'_k$ is a document pair corresponding to the preference pair $(l_i <_{r'_k} l_j)$ of q_k, which means d_i should rank higher than d_j in the target ranking of r'_k. Figure 5 illustrates the effect of different weight vectors on ranking three documents, d_1, d_2 and d_3, while the target ranking is $d_1 <_{r*} d_2 <_{r*} d_3$. As we can see, $\vec{w_1}$ is better than $\vec{w_2}$: the documents are correctly ranked as (d_1, d_2, d_3) by $\vec{w_1}$, but are ranked as (d_2, d_1, d_3) by $\vec{w_2}$ in which $d_1 < d_2$ does not hold.

However, solving $\vec{w}$ with the constraints in Equation (2) is *NP-hard* [13]. An approximate solution can be obtained by introducing non-negative *slack variables*, ξ_{ijk}, to the inequalities to tolerate some ranking errors. The inequalities are rewritten as:

$$\text{For all} \quad (d_i, d_j) \in r'_k \ , \quad (1 \le k \le n)$$
$$\vec{w} \cdot \phi(q_k, d_i) > \vec{w} \cdot \phi(q_k, d_j) + 1 - \xi_{ijk}, \quad \xi_{ijk} \ge 0 \qquad (3)$$

and ranking SVM is then formulated as a constrained optimization problem, which is stated as minimizing the target function:

$$V(\vec{w}, \xi) = \frac{1}{2}\vec{w} \cdot \vec{w} + C\sum \xi_{ijk}, \qquad (4)$$

subject to the constraints given in Equation (3).

The idea of solving the above optimization problem is: let δ be the distance between the two closest projected documents along a weight vector. In Figure 5, δ_1 and δ_2 are the distances between the two closest projections along $\vec{w_1}$ and $\vec{w_2}$, respectively. If there are several weight vectors that are able to make all the rankings hold subject to the condition in Equation (3), the one that maximizes the margin δ is preferred. This is because the larger value of δ, the more definite the ranking, and hence the better the quality of the weight vector $\vec{w}$. The summation term, $\sum \xi_{ijk}$, of slack variables in target function (4) is the sum of the errors in ranking pairs. Therefore, minimizing this term can be viewed as minimizing the total training errors made. Finally, parameter C is introduced to allow a trade-off between the margin size δ and the total training errors.

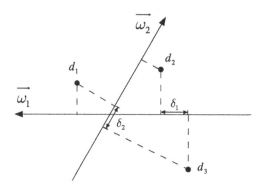

Fig. 5. Ranking the documents d_1, d_2, and d_3 with the weight vectors $\vec{w_1}$ and $\vec{w_2}$

As output, ranking SVM gives a weight vector $\vec{w}$, which can be used to rank future retrieved results by sorting the value: $f(q, d) = \vec{w} \cdot \phi(q, d)$. The ranking SVM algorithm is implemented in a SVM-Light software, which can be downloaded from [14].

5   Experimental Evaluations

We conduct extensive experiments to evaluate our method. Section 5.1 describes how we set up the experiment. Section 5.2 explains the specification of the implemented ranking function. Section 5.3 introduces a baseline method mJoachims algorithm and Section 5.4 reports the experimental results.

5.1   Experiment Setup

In order to evaluate the effectiveness of our method, we develop a metasearch engine that comprises three search engines: MSNSearch[1], WiseNut[2] and Overture[3]. At the time of this writing, MSNSearch is regarded as one of the best major search engines in the world; WiseNut is a new and growing search engine; and Overture is an advertising search engine which ranks results based on the prices paid by the sponsors. We choose the three search engines that have different strengths in terms of retrieval quality and focus, as we can test our methods in a *query-specific* adaptation context.

Our metasearch engine works as follows. When a query is submitted to the system, top 100 links from each search engine are retrieved. Then the combined list presented to the user is produced in a round-robin manner [15] to ensure that there is no bias towards any source. If a result is returned by more than one search engine, we only present it once. The titles, abstracts and URLs of the retrieved results are displayed in a uniform style. Therefore, the users do not know which search engine a particular link is from.

To collect clickthrough data, we asked five graduate students in our department to test the system. The users are considered to share the same interests as they come from the same community. We gave the users three categories of queries for searching: Computer Science (CS), news and shopping, and each category contains 30 queries. This setting aims to test the methods in a *query-specific* context. However, in essential, the result can also apply to *user-specific* context. Figure 6 shows some statistics of the clickthrough we collected.

5.2   Linear Ranking Function

Our metasearch engine adopts a linear ranking function to rank search results. Suppose q is a submitted query, and d is a document (link) retrieved from underlying search engines. The links are ranked according to the value

---

[1] http://search.msn.com

[2] http://www.wisenut.com

[3] http://www.overture.com

Query category	Computer Science	News	Shopping
Number of queries	30	30	30
Number of clicks	123	87	130
Average clicks per query	4.1	2.9	4.3
Average rank clicked on	5.87	5.6	5.59

Fig. 6. Statistics of experiment data

$f(q, d) = \vec{w} \cdot \phi(q, d)$, where $\phi(q, d)$ is a feature vector representing the match between query q and document d, and $\vec{w}$ is a weigh vector that can be learned by our personalization approach. We then define the feature vector $\phi(q, d)$ as three kinds of features, namely, *Rank Features*, *Common Features* and *Similarity Features*:

1. **Rank Features** (3 numerical and 12 binary features).
   Let search engine $E \in \{M, W, O\}$ (M stands for MSNsearch, W for WiseNut, and O for Overture) and $T \in \{1, 3, 5, 10\}$. We define numerical features $Rank\_E$ and binary features Top_E_T of document d as follows:

$$Rank\_E = \begin{cases} \frac{11-X}{10} & \text{if } d \text{ ranks } X \text{ in } E,\ X <= 10 \\ 0 & \text{otherwise.} \end{cases}$$

$$Top\_E\_T = \begin{cases} 1 & \text{if } d \text{ ranks top } T \text{ in } E; \\ 0 & \text{otherwise.} \end{cases}$$

2. **Common Features** (2 binary features).

$$Com\_2 = \begin{cases} 1 & \text{if } d \text{ ranks top 10 in two search engines;} \\ 0 & \text{otherwise.} \end{cases}$$

$$Com\_3 = \begin{cases} 1 & \text{if } d \text{ ranks top 10 in three search engines;} \\ 0 & \text{otherwise.} \end{cases}$$

3. **Similarity Features** (1 binary and 2 numerical features).

$$Sim\_U = \begin{cases} 1 & \text{if any word in query appears in URL;} \\ 0 & \text{otherwise.} \end{cases}$$

$Sim_T = $ Cosine similarity between query and title.

$Sim_A = $ Cosine similarity between query and abstract.

Overall, $\phi(q, l)$ contains 20 features as shown below:

$$(Rank\_M, Top\_M\_1, \ldots, Top\_M\_10, Rank\_W, \ldots,$$
$$Rank\_O, \ldots, Com\_2, Com\_3, Sim\_U, \ldots, Sim\_A) \tag{5}$$

The corresponding weight vector $\vec{w}$ contains 20 weight values, each of which reflects the importance of a feature in Equation (5). There are other ways to define $\phi(q, d)$ and $\vec{w}$. Our definition only reflects the intuition about what we think are important for a metasearch engine to rank search results and still easy for implementation.

5.3 mJoachims Algorithm

As pointed out in Section 3.1, Joachims algorithm unfairly penalizes the high-ranking links, which in practice may lead to problems. To verify this point, we modify a bit the way of Joachims algorithm generating preference pairs, and call it "mJoachims algorithm". The mJoachims algorithm adds some preferences to standard Joachims algorithm with the high-ranking links appearing in the left hand side, for alleviating the penalty. In particular, suppose l_i is a clicked link, l_j is the next clicked link right after l_i (that is, none of clicked links exists between l_i and l_j), and l_k is any skipped link ranks between l_i and l_j, then the preferences derived with mJoachims algorithm are those derived with standard Joachims algorithm added with the pairs of $l_i <_{r'} l_k$ ($i < k < j$). Figure 7 shows the preference pairs derived using mJoachims algorithm from the clickthrough of Figure 1. The difference between Joachims and mJaochims algorithm can be seen by comparing Figure 2 and Figure 7.

Preference pairs arising from l_1	Preference pairs arising from l_7	Preference pairs arising from l_{10}
$l_1 <_{r'} l_2$	$l_7 <_{r'} l_2$	$l_{10} <_{r'} l_2$
$l_1 <_{r'} l_3$	$l_7 <_{r'} l_3$	$l_{10} <_{r'} l_3$
$l_1 <_{r'} l_4$	$l_7 <_{r'} l_4$	$l_{10} <_{r'} l_4$
$l_1 <_{r'} l_5$	$l_7 <_{r'} l_5$	$l_{10} <_{r'} l_5$
$l_1 <_{r'} l_6$	$l_7 <_{r'} l_6$	$l_{10} <_{r'} l_6$
	$l_7 <_{r'} l_8$	$l_{10} <_{r'} l_8$
	$l_7 <_{r'} l_9$	$l_{10} <_{r'} l_9$

Fig. 7. Preferences derived using mJoachims algorithm

5.4 Experimental Results

The experiment consists of three parts. We first compare the effectiveness of SpyNB with Joachims and mJoachims algorithm on ranking quality. Secondly, we analyze the effect of training data size on the performance of algorithms. Finally, we make some interesting observation on the learned ranking functions.

Evaluation on Ranking Quality. In order to evaluate SpyNB algorithm on ranking quality, we incorporate SpyNB, Joachims and mJoachims algorithms with ranking SVM, and obtain 3 learned ranking functions. Particularly, we set the voting threshold of SpyNB (T_v in Algorithm 2) as 50% just by random. Then we evaluate the ranking functions by using them to *rerank* the original clickthrough, and see if the ranking quality can be improved.

   We measure ranking quality in terms of *the average rank of users' clicks*, denoted as Ψ. Intuitively, a good ranking function should rank the user desired links high. Thus, the smaller the value of Ψ, the better the ranking quality. To show the actual improvement, we define a metric *relative average rank of users' clicks*, denoted as Ψ^r, as the Ψ derived from a personalized ranking function divided by the Ψ of the original search result. $\Psi^r < 1$ indicates that an actual improvement is achieved.

The results are shown in Figure 8. First, the values of Ψ^r of SpyNB are all about $0.8 < 1$, which means the ranking function derived with SpyNB can improve the ranking quality by about 20% for all 3 categories. This result indicates that SpyNB algorithm can effectively discover user's preferences from clickthrough data.

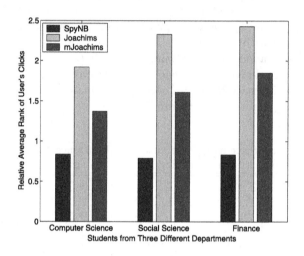

Fig. 8. Comparison on Relative Average Rank of Users' Clicks of three methods

Moreover, we find that Joachims algorithm and mJoachims algorithm fail to achieve actual improvement after reranking the original search results, since their Ψ^r values are greater than 1. We explain this finding as because their strong assumptions do not hold on our empirical clickthrough data. Thus the preferences identified by the existing algorithms are incorrect. Particularly, mJoachims algorithm is relatively better than Joachims algorithm, which can be interpreted that Joachims algorithm is apt to penalize high-ranking links, while mJoachims algorithm alleviates this penalty. Finally, we can conclude that the preferences discovered by SpyNB algorithm are much more accurate than those by Joachims and mJoachims algorithms.

Effect of Varying Data Size. In order to study the impact of data set size on the ranking function optimizer, we randomly select n queries to evaluate our SpyNB algorithm and the Joachims algorithm, where n is set to 6, 12, 18, 24 and 30. The experimental settings are the same as those described in Section 5.4. We also compute the Ψ^r parameter and present the results in Figure 9.

From Figure 9, we can see that when the data size is small, the performance of SpyNB is not satisfactory (i.e. $\Psi^r > 1$). The reason is that when the data size is too small, the training data is not representative enough for learning an effective ranking function. When the data size is growing, the performance of

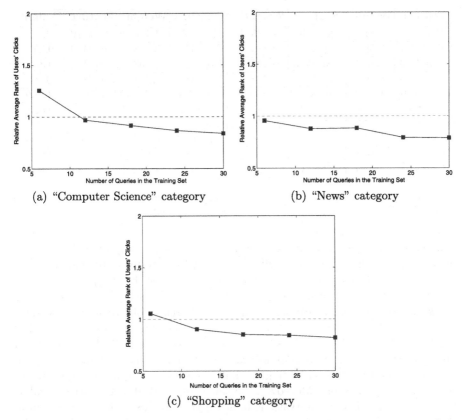

(a) "Computer Science" category   (b) "News" category

(c) "Shopping" category

Fig. 9. Relative Average Rank Ψ^r of SpyNB and Joachims algorithm on varying data size

SpyNB is gradually improved, and when the training data szie increase to 30, the Ψ^r value decreases to around 0.8, which means that SpyNB can achieve about 20% improvement compared with the original ranking. Moreover, we note that the performance curves at point of 30 become quite flat, so we suppose the best performance of SpyNB will converge at some level a bit samller than 0.8. On the other hand, this result also indicates that the least number of clickthrough data for training SpyNB is quite small: just 30 training clickthrough can train an effective SpyNB ranking function optimizer.

Learned Weights of Ranking Functions. As detailed in Section 5.2, the learned ranking function in our experiment is a weight vector comprising 20 components. We list the weight vectors learned on the query categories of "Computer Science", and "Shopping" in Figure 10 and Figure 11 respectively.

Intuitively, the features with high absolute weights have a large impact on the resulted ranking. In particular, a higher positive (negative) weight indicates that the links with this feature would be ranked higher (lower) in the combined list. As we can see, the weight vector of the "Computer Science" category and the

Feature	Weight	Feature	Weight
Rank_M	1.811	Rank_W	1.275
Top_M_1	0.566	Top_W_1	0.480
Top_M_3	-0.003	Top_W_3	0.229
Top_M_5	0.063	Top_W_5	-0.138
Top_M_10	-0.021	Top_W_10	-0.458
Rank_O	0.415	Sim_A	0.357
Top_O_1	-0.677	Sim_T	0.785
Top_O_3	0.447	Sim_U	0.288
Top_O_5	-0.087	Com2	0.186
Top_O_10	-0.440	Com3	-0.226

Feature	Weight	Feature	Weight
Rank_M	1.154	Rank_W	-0.217
Top_M_1	0.108	Top_W_1	0.355
Top_M_3	0.563	Top_W_3	0.362
Top_M_5	-0.045	Top_W_5	-0.364
Top_M_10	-0.757	Top_W_10	-1.429
Rank_O	1.019	Sim_A	0.025
Top_O_1	0.718	Sim_T	0.520
Top_O_3	0.586	Sim_U	-0.106
Top_O_5	0.528	Com2	0.240
Top_O_10	-0.864	Com3	0

Fig. 10. Learned weight vector of the "Computer Science" category

Fig. 11. Learned weight vector of the "Shopping" category

"Shopping" category are quite distinguishable, which clearly indicates that the underlying search engines have different strengths in terms of topical specialty.

We can also draw some user preference information of the group of users in our experiment from the learned weight vector. Generally speaking, the numerical *Rank Features Rank_M*, *Rank_O* and *Rank_W* reflect the relative importance of MSNSearch, Overture and WiseNut respectively. As we can see from Figure 10 and Figure 11, the values of *Rank_M* are the largest for both the "Computer Science" and the "Shopping" categories. The value of *Rank_O* is small for the "Computer Science" category, but large (almost equal to *Rank_M*) for the "Shopping" category. Moreover, the values of *Rank_W* are relative small for both categories. These observations indicate that MSNSearch are strong in all the queries in both categories, Overture is particularly good at shopping queries, and WiseNut does not perform outstandingly in any query category. These conclusions are consistent with the common knowledge that MSNSearch is one of the best general search engines in the world, Overture is an advertising search engine, and WiseNut is a growing search engine which still needs to perfect itself.

As another interesting observation, we can see that the similarity between query and title seems to be more important than the similarity between query and abstract, for the reason that the values of *Sim_T* are larger than those of *Sim_A* in Figure 10 and Figure 11. This observation can be explained as follows: the abstracts sometimes are not very informative and the titles usually have larger influences on users' relevance judgement than the abstracts. In short, analysis of the learned weight vector can be useful to understand the users' preferences and behaviors.

6   Conclusions

In this paper, we first identify some problems of an existing algorithm for discovering user's preferences from clickthrough data. We then introduce a new clickthrough interpretation and propose a novel SpyNB algorithm for discovering preferences based on analyzing the texts (titles, abstracts) of clickthrough data. Furthermore, we present an approach to adapting a search engine's ranking function using SpyNB algorithm plus a ranking SVM optimizer.

To evaluate our methods, we conducted controlled experiments, particularly in a query-specific adaptation context. The experimental results demonstrated that our method significantly improved the ranking quality in terms of the average rank of users' clicks by 20% compared with the original ranking and even more when compared with existing Joachims algorithm.

There are several directions we are going to study in the future. First, we would like to test a more sophisticated Spy Naïve Bayes technique by extending current black-and-white (0 or 1) voting procedure to incorporate continuous probability into vote values. Moreover, we plan to conduct online interactive experiments to further evaluate our method and also evaluate our method in a user-specific adaptation context.

References

1. Bartell, B., G.Cottrell, Belew, R.: Automatic combination of multiple ranked retrieval systemss. In: Proc. of the 17th ACM SIGIR Conference. (1994) 173–181
2. Cohen, W., Shapire, R., Singer, Y.: Learning to order things. Journal of Artifical Intelligence Research **10** (1999) 243–270
3. Boyan, J., Freitag, D., Joachims, T.: A machine learning architecture for optimizing web search engines. In: Proc. of AAAI workshop on Internet-Based Information System. (1996)
4. Joachims, T.: Optimizing search engines using clickthrough data. In: Proc. of the 8th ACM SIGKDD Conference. (2002) 133–142
5. Tan, Q., Chai, X., Ng, W., Lee, D.: Applying co-training to clickthrough data for search engine adaptation. In: Proc. of the 9th DASFAA conference. (2004) 519–532
6. Li, X., Liu, B.: Learning to classify text using positive and unlabeled data. In: Proc. of 8th International Joint Conference on Artificial Intelligence. (2003)
7. Liu, B., Dai, Y., Li, X., Lee, W.S.: Building text classifiers using positive and unlabeled examples. In: Proc. of the 3rd International Conference on Data Mining. (2003)
8. Liu, B., Lee, W.S., Yu, P., Li, X.: Partially supervised classification of text documents. In: Proc. of the 19th International Conference on Machine Learning. (2002)
9. Yu, H., Han, J., Chang, K.: PEBL: Positive example based learning for web page classification using svm. In: Proc. of the 8th ACM SIGKDD Conference. (2002)
10. Mitchell, T.: Machine Learning. McGraw Hill, Inc. (1997)
11. Baeza-Yates, R., Ribeiro-Neto, B.: Modern Information Retrieval. Addison-wesley-Longman, Harlow, UK (1999)
12. McCallum, A., Nigam, K.: A comparison of event models for naive bayes text classification. In: Proc. of AAAI/ICML-98 Workshop on Learning for Text Categorization. (1998) 41–48
13. Hoffgen, K., Simon, H., Horn, K.V.: Robust trainability of single neurons. Journal of Computer and System Sciences **50** (1995) 114–125
14. Joachims, T.: Making large-scale SVM learning practical. In: *B. Scholkoph et al., editor,* Advances in Kernel Methods – Support Vector Learning, MIT Press (1999) http://svmlight.joachims.org/.
15. Joachims, T.: Evaluating retrieval performance using clickthrough data. In: Proc. of the SIGIR Workshop on Mathematical/Formal Methods in Information Retrieval. (2002)

Using Hyperlink Features to Personalize Web Search

Mehmet S. Aktas[1], Mehmet A. Nacar[1], and Filippo Menczer[1,2]

[1] Computer Science Department
[2] School of Informatics
Indiana University
Bloomington, IN 47405 USA
{maktas, mnacar, fil}@indiana.edu

Abstract. Personalized search has gained great popularity to improve search effectiveness in recent years. The objective of personalized search is to provide users with information tailored to their individual contexts. We propose to personalize Web search based on features extracted from hyperlinks, such as anchor terms or URL tokens. Our methodology personalizes PageRank vectors by weighting links based on the match between hyperlinks and user profiles. In particular, here we describe a profile representation using Internet domain features extracted from URLs. Users specify interest profiles as binary vectors where each feature corresponds to a set of one or more DNS tree nodes. Given a profile vector, a weighted PageRank is computed assigning a weight to each URL based on the match between the URL and the profile. We present promising results from an experiment in which users were allowed to select among nine URL features combining the top two levels of the DNS tree, leading to 2^9 pre-computed PageRank vectors from a Yahoo crawl. Personalized PageRank performed favorably compared to pure similarity based ranking and traditional PageRank.

1 Introduction

The explosive growth of documents in the Web makes it difficult to determine which are the most relevant documents for a particular user, given a general query. Recent search engines rank pages by combining traditional information retrieval techniques based on page content, such as the word vector space [1,2], with link analysis techniques based on the hypertext structure of the Web [3,4].

Personalized search has gained great popularity to improve search effectiveness in recent years [10,12,29]. The objective of personalized search is to provide users with information tailored to their individual contexts. We propose to personalize Web search based on features extracted from hyperlinks, such as anchor terms or URL tokens. Our methodology personalizes PageRank vectors by weighting links based on the match between hyperlinks and user profiles. In particular, here we describe a profile representation using Internet domain features extracted from URLs.

B. Mobasher et al. (Eds.): WebKDD 2004, LNAI 3932, pp. 104–115, 2006.

We identify two aspects of link analysis. One is the global importance of pages as estimated from analyzing the Web link graph structure. There is a major body of research exploring retrieval techniques based on link popularity such as PageRank [3] and HITS [4]. Another aspect of link analysis is the structure of the hyperlinks themselves. For example, anchor text has been shown to be a very good predictor of content of the linked page [27,28]. One can expect that keywords in the anchor text of a link might be highly related with the content of that page. The accuracy and quality of a page can also be estimated by looking at its URL. Web pages published under an educational institution Web site might be deemed to have higher prestige compared to those published under free Web hosting sites. In this research, we combine these two aspects of link analysis: PageRank and hyperlink structure to improve search effectiveness through personalized search.

The PageRank algorithm provides a global ranking of Web pages based on their importance estimated from hyperlinks [5,3,6]. For instance, a link from page "A" to page "B" is considered as if page "A" is voting for the importance of page "B". So, as the number of links to page "B" increases, its importance increases as well. In PageRank, not only the number of inlinks but their sources decide the importance of a page. In this scenario, the global ranking of pages is based on the Web graph structure. Search engines such as Google[1] utilize the link structure of the Web to calculate the PageRank values of the pages. These values are then used to rank search results to improve precision. Comprehensive reviews of the issues related to PageRank can be found in [7,8,9].

The PageRank algorithm [5,3] attempts to provide an objective global estimate of Web page importance. However, the importance of Web pages is subjective for different users and thus can be better determined if the PageRank algorithm takes into consideration user preferences. The importance of a page depends of the different interests and knowledge of different people; a global ranking of a Web page might not necessarily capture the importance of that page for a given individual user. Here we explore how to personalize PageRank based on features readily available from page URLs. For instance a user might favor pages from a specific geographic region, as may be revealed by Internet (DNS) domains. Likewise, topical features of Internet domains might also reflect user preferences. A user might prefer pages that are more likely to be monitored by experts for accuracy and quality, such as pages published by academic institutions. Current search engines cannot rank pages based on individual user needs and preferences.[2]

In order to address the above limitations of global PageRank, we introduce a methodology to personalize PageRank scores based on hyperlink features such as Internet domains. In this scenario, users specify interest profiles as binary feature vectors where a feature corresponds to a DNS tree node or node set. We pre-compute PageRank scores for each profile vector by assigning a weight to each URL based on the match between the hyperlink and the profile features. A

---

[1] http://www.google.com

[2] See Section 2 for an exception to this, currently under beta-testing by Google.

weighted PageRank vector is then computed based on URL weights, and used at query time to rank results. We present promising results from an experiment in which users were allowed to select among nine hyperlink features combining the top two levels of the DNS tree, leading to 2^9 pre-computed PageRank vectors.

In the next section we discuss work relevant to PageRank computation and personalizing PageRank. Section 3 presents our method of computation for personalized PageRank vectors and outlines how user profiles are created based on Internet domains. Section 4 details the design and architecture of our implementation as well as a user study conducted to evaluate our methodology. Experimental results are presented in Section 5.

2 Background

The idea of a personalized PageRank was first introduced in [5] and has been studied by various researchers [10,11,12] as a query-dependent ranking mechanism. If personal preferences are based on n binary features, there are 2^n different personalized PageRank vectors for all possible user preferences. This requires an enormous amount of computation and storage facilities. In an attempt to solve this problem, a method was introduced that computes only a limited amount of PageRank vectors offline [12]. This method provides for a methodology where personalized PageRank vectors can be computed at query time for all other possible user preferences. The main concern of the work presented here is to introduce a methodology for personalizing PageRank vectors based on hyperlink features. To this end, we limit the choices of user preferences to topical and geographic features of Internet domains.

Techniques for efficient and scalable calculation of PageRank scores are an area of very active research [13,14,15,16]. While this is important and relevant to the issue of personalized PageRank discussed here, it is outside the scope of the present paper. For the experiments presented here we use a collection from a relatively small crawl ($\sim 10^5$ pages, cf. Section 4), and it is not necessary to recompute PageRank frequently. Therefore scalability is not discussed further.

Web personalization and customization are related, but distinct concepts. The objective of personalization is to provide users with information tailored to their individual contexts. Mostafa [21] defines customization systems as involving more functionalities than personalization. This includes factors such as location and time to identify the structure and presentation of information. Methodologies for the system to learn about the user's informational context can be defined as information request, use and demand patterns. Our system requires that the user provides personal information by creating an individual profile based on domain profiles. Therefore we view our approach as an example of personalization and not customization.

Personalization can be achieved in various ways. Erinaki and Vazirgiannis [20], categorize personalization into four groups. In content based filtering the recommendation is done based on the user's individual preferences. In collaborative filtering the information is sorted based on personal preferences of like-minded individuals [22]. In rule-based filtering the users are asked questions by the system. The system extracts rules from the answers and then applies these rules to deliver appropriate content to the users. At last, in Web usage mining personalized recommendation takes place by applying data mining techniques to web usage data [22,23,24,25,26]. Our methodology for personalization falls into the first category as we utilize static profiles defined by users for re-sorting search results.

Search can be personalized in two ways: query augmentation and result processing [19]. In the former method the query is compared against user preferences. If the similarity between the query and user preferences is above a threshold the query is augmented with metadata and submitted to the search engine to obtain more precise results. In the latter method the results that are returned by a search engine are re-ranked based on the user's profile. Here, we focus on personalizing search hits through result processing.

Google has recently started beta-testing a personalized Web search service based on topical user profiles.[3] It appears that user profiles are based on hierarchical topic directories (á la Open Directory Project[4]), however due to lack of documentation we are unable to discuss the similarities or differences between that work and the methodology proposed here.

"Topic-sensitive" web search, introduced by Haveliwala [10], is similar to our work. The method suggests pre-computation of topical PageRank vectors prior to query time. The idea is to minimize the jumping probability to pages that are considered as irrelevant to the topic. Topic-sensitive PageRank vectors are then combined at query time based on the similarity between topics and query. In our approach we personalize PageRank scores by assigning weights to URLs based on matched hyperlink features. At query time the user's profile is matched with the corresponding personalized PageRank vector. As in the traditional PageRank, our method does not require the content of pages since we are only interested in URLs.

We also note that Baeza-Yates and Davis [30] introduce a variant of PageRank that gives weights to link based on a) relative position in the page, b) tag where the link is contained and c) length of the anchor text. Here, we focus on personalizing PageRank scores based on hyperlink features such as Internet domain features extracted from URLs.

3   Personalized PageRank Based on Hyperlink Features

3.1   Traditional PageRank Computation

PageRank is one of the most well known algorithm that is based on global popularity of web pages. It was first introduced by Brin and Page [3]. The computation of plain PageRank vectors is done as described below.

---

[3] http://labs.google.com/personalized

[4] http://dmoz.org

$$R(p) = (1 - d) + d \cdot \sum_{\{q:q \to p\}} \frac{R(q)}{|s : q \to s|}$$

where d is the traditional jump probability (or damping factor) and the sum over pages q that link to p has each element normalized by the number of outlinks from page q.

3.2   Personalized PageRank Vectors

Personalized PageRank vectors provide a ranking mechanism which in turn creates a personalized view of the Web for individual users. The computation of personalized PageRank vectors is done prior to search time. When calculating the PageRank vectors, predefined user profiles are taken into consideration.

We use the following recursive definition for personalized PageRank computation:

$$R_U(p) = (1 - d) + d \cdot \sum_{\{q:q \to p\}} \frac{W_U(q) \cdot R_U(q)}{|s : q \to s|}$$

where U is the user profile, d is the traditional jump probability (or damping factor), the sum over pages q that link to p has each element normalized by the number of outlinks from page q, and $W_U(q)$ is the weight of page q based on profile U. The reader will immediately note that it is the weight vector that generalizes PageRank to the personalized case, and that the definition readily reverts to the traditional PageRank in the special case where $W_U(q) = 1$ irrespective of users or pages.

3.3   User Profile from Internet Domains

In this paper we study user profiles based on hyperlink features. Profiles can be based on any hyperlink features such as path keywords, protocols, host names, etc. Let us focus on Internet (DNS) domains. A user is expected to input his/her interests as a set of domain features, before query time. When a query is submitted by the user, we retrieve the personalized PageRank vector corresponding to his/her profile in order to rank the hits satisfying the query.

Alternatively, one could extend the profile by adding features associated with the protocols (say, if a user was interested mainly in FTP sites) or with keywords (say, if a user was interested in certain organizations such as webMD). Figure 1 shows the hyperlink feature space.

A domain profile is a binary feature vector. Domain features are divided into N groups or categories, such as geographic or topical features (N is a parameter). When assigning a weight to a URL based on its features we use the following algorithm, which takes a URL in input and returns a corresponding normalized weight. We first analyze the fully qualified domain name of the server host. This domain analysis creates a URL feature vector. Let n be the number of matched feature groups between the user profile vector U and the feature vector of page p's URL. The normalized weight for this URL and user profile is then defined by $W_U(p) = 2^{n-N}$.

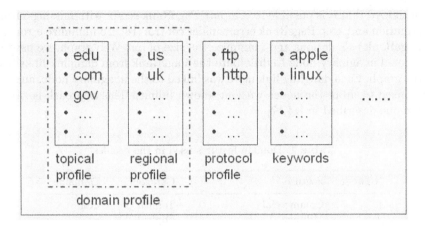

Fig. 1. Various kinds of profiles can be used on hyperlink features. Here we focus on domain-based features.

Let us illustrate the above algorithm with an example. Consider a site p that belongs to the United Kingdom's government, http://www.direct.gov.uk; and a user profile U with *geographic* domain features (America, Europe) and *topical* domain features (Educational, Commercial). Let us also assume that $N = 2$, i.e. we consider only the two groups of geographic and topical domain features. In this example the domain analysis yields a URL feature vector (Europe, Government) from the domains uk and gov. As a result $n = 1$ feature groups are matched, namely the geographic feature Europe, and therefore $W_U(p) = 0.5$.

4   Evaluation

To evaluate our methodology we carried out a Web crawl and implemented an extension of the Nutch[5] open-source search engine to combine similarity and PageRank computations. We then conducted a user study to explore the improvement in precision/recall when applying our idea of personalizing PageRank based on hyperlink features.

4.1   Design and Architecture

For our experiment we used a collection of pages obtained by crawling the Web in April 2004, starting from three seed categories ("Education," "Region," and "Government") of the Yahoo Directory[6]. The resulting crawl data consists of 107,890 URLs and 468,410 links forming a Web graph. When calculating the PageRank scores, one must deal carefully with the problem of danglink links — nodes that don't have known outlinks — as explained in [5,17]. It has also

---

[5] http://www.nutch.org
[6] http://dir.yahoo.com

been showed that it is possible to compute PageRank scores with missing outlink information and keep PageRank errors under control [18]. To minimize error rate in PageRank calculations and maximize the size of our Web graph, we used an additional imaginary node to distribute the PageRank from danglink links back to the graph. Each dangling link node was linked to the imaginary node, and this was linked to all of the nodes without known inlinks. This approach is similar to the one described in [14,17].

Table 1. Domain features used in the profiles

Number	Feature	Category	Domains
1	Commercial	Topical	com
2	Military	Topical	mil
3	Government	Topical	gov
4	Non-Profit Organizations	Topical	org
5	Network Organizations	Topical	net
6	Educational	Topical	edu
7	America	Geographic	ca,us,...
8	Asia	Geographic	jp,tw,...
9	Europe	Geographic	it,uk,...

Offline, we pre-computed $2^9 - 1 = 511$ personalized PageRank vectors including a plain PageRank vector (the case where all features are selected and the case where no features are selected are considered identical and equivalent to plain PageRank). Personalized PageRank vectors were computed based on predefined domain profiles. In our design, a domain profile may consist of 9 features: 6 topical and 3 geographic domain features as illustrated in Table 1. PageRank vectors are computed once and stored prior to query time. We used the compressed sparse row (CSR) data structure to store the adjacency matrix representation of our Web graph. The CSR data structure stores its row and column index for each entry. Entries are listed one row after another. This is simply done by a data structure which is a triplet (i,j,value). We defined a Java object to represent a triplet and a global array to store the triplet objects. This way we do not store non-zero values unnecessarily. Also, to avoid increasing the online query time, we updated the Nutch index system so that it can also accommodate PageRank scores along with the existing information such as anchor text, keywords, and similarity score. This prevents the heavy I/O overhead of reading the PageRank scores from an external database or file store. We used global parallel arrays for vertices and PageRank vectors.

For online query processing and to manage our user study, we implemented various user interfaces using Java Server Pages. When a query is submitted, we use the Nutch search mechanism to retrieve the hits. Nutch uses a TFIDF based similarity metric [1,2] to rank hits satisfying a query, returning a similarity score with each hit. We reorder the hits based on plain and personalized PageRank scores — the latter based on the profile of the user who submitted the query.

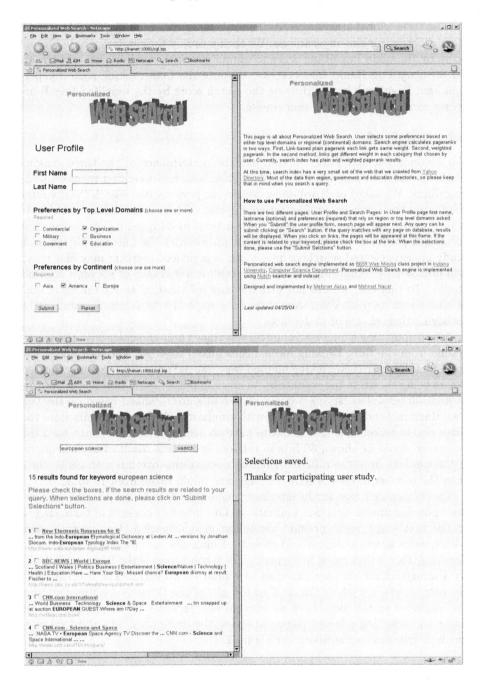

Fig. 2. Web-based interface to conduct our user study. Top: User Profile Page. The user enters his/her identification information and choices of topical and geographic domain interests to create a user profile. Bottom: Web Search Page. The user submits a query and selects any relevant results, which are saved with each query.

We use three global arrays to store the ranking scores of the hits based on these three different ranking mechanisms. We then multiply the similarity-based Nutch score by the plain PageRank score to obtain the final ranking score of each hit for ordinary PageRank. Likewise, we compute the final ranking score for personalized PageRank by multiplying the Nutch score by the weighted PageRank scores corresponding to the user profile.

4.2 User Study

We conducted a user study to compare the performance of the three ranking methods based on pure similarity, plain PageRank and weighted (personalized) PageRank. We asked each volunteer to use our personalized search facility after they input their domain profiles into our system. There were 30 human subjects who contributed to our user study with a total of 30 queries. We realize that recall and precision values are dependent on whether the human subjects in a study are experienced searchers or not. An experienced searcher may bias recall and precision by composing queries that result in very many or very few relevant results. To this end, we did not give out any information about the main goal of the search engine. Volunteers were only expected to select relevant URLs satisfying their choice of preferences.

After submitting a query, a volunteer was shown a single screen with the search results from the three ranking mechanisms mixed together. For each query, the top 10 results from each ranking method were merged and then randomly shuffled before being shown to the volunteer. As an example, suppose that Nutch returns at least 30 results satisfying a query. These hits are reranked based on the two PageRank methods (each combined with similarity). If the top 10 hits from the three ranking mechanisms turn out to have no overlap with each other, then the volunteer would be shown 30 hits in random order as a result of his/her query. If the top hits from the different ranking mechanisms overlap with each other, then the number of results shown to the user would range from 10 to 30.

The Web-based user study interface was designed to be easy to use and reduce possible mistakes in user evaluations. Our interface consists of three stages. In the first stage, users provide identification information (to associate users with queries across sessions) and choices of interests in topical and geographic domains. This is illustrated in Figure 2. The second stage is the Web search facility, through which users are expected to submit their queries. The third stage of the user interface is where the shuffled top hits of the three ranking mechanisms are displayed to the user. Here we also provide facilities for displaying the hit pages and selecting relevant pages satisfying the user query. The third stage of our user interface is also shown in Figure 2.

5   Results

Once a user submits the evaluation for the results of a query, we calculate precision/recall pairs for that query as follows. For each hit h we have the rank from each of the three ranking scores, and the user's binary (0/1) relevance assessment

u. Therefore for each ranking mechanism r and query q we compute precision and recall at rank i:

$$precision_r(i, q) = \frac{1}{i} \sum_{j=1}^{i} u(h(r, j, q))$$

$$recall_r(i, q) = \frac{1}{|h : u(h(q)) = 1|} \sum_{j=1}^{i} u(h(r, j, q))$$

where $h(r, j, q)$ is the hit ranked j by ranking mechanism r for query q.

Precision-recall plots for the three ranking mechanism and for $i = 1, \ldots, 10$ are shown in Figure 3. The measurements are averaged across the 30 queries posed by the users.

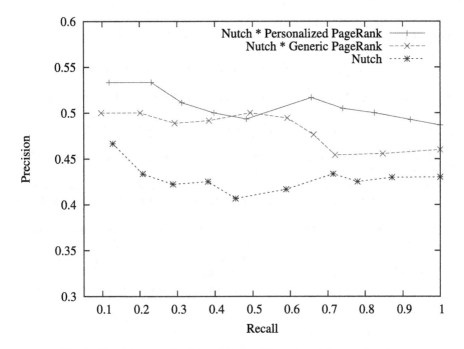

Fig. 3. Precision-recall plots of three different ranking mechanisms

Both PageRank based ranking methods outperform pure similarity based ranking; this is not surprising — it is quite established that link analysis helps to identify important pages. The more important question here is the difference between the two PageRank based methods. The plots suggest that personalized PageRank vectors can help improve the quality of results returned by a search engine. While these results are not highly significant statistically, they are promising. Domain-based personalization seems to provide us with a mechanism to adjust the estimated importance of pages based on user preferences.

6 Conclusions

In this paper we introduced a methodology for personalizing PageRank based on user profiles built from hyperlink features such as server host domains. We outlined the implementation of a simple personalized Web search engine based on these ideas, and on a small set of URL domain features. Results based on a limited Web crawl suggest that personalized PageRank vectors can improve the quality of results.

Acknowledgments

We are grateful to the 30 volunteers who helped with the user study. FM is partially supported by NSF award N. IIS-0348940.

References

1. van Rijsbergen, C.: Information Retrieval. Butterworths, London (1979) Second edition.
2. Salton, G., McGill, M.: An Introduction to Modern Information Retrieval. McGraw-Hill, New York, NY (1983)
3. Brin, S., Page, L.: The anatomy of a large-scale hypertextual Web search engine. Computer Networks **30** (1998) 107–117
4. Kleinberg, J.: Authoritative sources in a hyperlinked environment. Journal of the ACM **46** (1999) 604–632
5. Page, L., Brin, S., Motwani, R., Winograd, T.: The PageRank citation ranking: Bringing order to the Web. Technical report, Stanford University Database Group (1998)
6. Brin, S., Motwani, R., Page, L., Winograd, T.: What can you do with a Web in your pocket. IEEE Data Engineering Bulletin **21** (1998) 37–47
7. Arasu, A., Cho, J., Garcia-Molina, H., Paepcke, A., Raghavan, S.: Searching the web. ACM Trans. Inter. Tech. **1** (2001) 2–43
8. Langville, A.N., Meyer, C.D.: Deeper inside PageRank. Internet Mathematics (Forthcoming)
9. Langville, A.N., Meyer, C.D.: A survey of eigenvector methods of Web information retrieval. SIAM Review (Forthcoming)
10. Haveliwala, T.: Topic-sensitive PageRank. In Lassner, D., De Roure, D., Iyengar, A., eds.: Proc. 11th International World Wide Web Conference, ACM Press (2002)
11. Richardson, M., Domingos, P.: The intelligent surfer: Probabilistic combination of link and content information in PageRank. In: Advances in Neural Information Processing Systems 14, Cambridge, MA, MIT Press (2002) 1441–1448
12. Jeh, G., Widom, J.: Scaling personalized Web search. In: Proc. 12th International World Wide Web Conference. (2003)
13. Haveliwala, T.: Efficient computation of pagerank. Technical report, Stanford Database Group (1999)
14. Kamvar, S.D., Haveliwala, T.H., Manning, C.D., Golub, G.H.: Exploiting the block structure of the Web for computing PageRank. Technical report, Stanford University (2003)

15. Kamvar, S.D., Haveliwala, T.H., Manning, C.D., Golub, G.H.: Extrapolation methods for accelerating the computation of pagerank. In: Proc. 12th International World Wide Web Conference. (2003)
16. Kamvar, S.D., Haveliwala, T.H., Golub, G.H.: Adaptive methods for the computation of PageRank. Technical report, Stanford University (2003)
17. Eiron, N., McCurley, K., Tomlin, J.: Ranking the Web frontier. In: Proc. 13th conference on World Wide Web, ACM Press (2004) 309–318
18. Acharyya, S., Ghosh, J.: Outlink estimation for pagerank computation under missing data. In: Alt. Track Papers and Posters Proc. 13th International World Wide Web Conference. (2004) 486–487
19. Pitkow, J., Schutze, H., Cass T., Cooley R., Turnbull D., Edmonds A., Adar E., Breuel T.: Personalized Search. Vol. 42, No. 9 Communication of ACM. (2002)
20. M. Eirinaki, M. Vazirgiannis.: Web Mining for Web Personalization ACM Transactions on Internet Technologies (ACM TOIT). Vol.3. Issue 1
21. Javed Mostafa: Information Customization IEEE Intelligent Systems Vol 17.6 (2002)
22. Sung Ho Ha: Helping Online Customers Decide through Web Personalization IEEE Intelligent Systems Vol 17.6 (2002)
23. M. Jenamani, P. Mohapatra, and S. Ghose: Online Customized Index Synthesis in Commercial Web Sites IEEE Intelligent Systems Vol 17.6 (2002)
24. Nasraoui O., Petenes C.: Combining Web Usage Mining and Fuzzy Inference for Website Personalization. in Proc. of WebKDD 2003 - KDD Workshop on Web mining as a Premise to Effective and Intelligent Web Applications, Washington DC, August 2003, p. 37
25. Mobasher B., Dai H., Luo T., and Nakagawa M.: Effective personalizaton based on association rule discovery from Web usage data. ACM Workshop on Web information and data management, Atlanta, GA
26. Li J. and Zaiane O.: Using Distinctive Information Channels for a Mission-based Web-Recommender System. In Proc. of "WebKDD-2004 workshop on Web Mining and Web Usage Analysis", part of the ACM KDD: Knowledge Discovery and Data Mining Conference, Seattle, WA.
27. B.D. Davison: Topical locality in the Web. In Proceedings of the 1st International World Wide Web Conference, Geneva, 1994. www1.cern.ch/PapersWWW94/reinpost.ps
28. Shannon Bradshaw and Kristian Hammond: Automatically Indexing Research Papers Using Text Surrounding Citations. In Working Notes of the Workshop on Intelligent Information Systems, Sixteenth National Conference on Artificial Intelligence, Orlando, FL, July 18-19
29. Fang Liu, Clement Yu, Weiyi Meng: Personalized Web Search For Improving Retrieval Effectiveness. IEEE Transactions on Knowledge and Data Engineering, January 2004
30. Ricardo BaezaYates and Emilio Davis: Web Page Ranking using Link Attributes. WWW2004, May 17-22, 2004, New York, New York, USA.

Discovering Links Between Lexical and Surface Features in Questions and Answers

Soumen Chakrabarti

IIT Bombay
soumen@cse.iitb.ac.in

Abstract. Information retrieval systems, based on keyword match, are evolving to question answering systems that return short passages or direct answers to questions, rather than URLs pointing to whole pages. Most open-domain question answering systems depend on manually designed hierarchies of question types. A question is first classified to a fixed type, and then hand-engineered rules associated with the type yield keywords and/or predictive annotations that are likely to match indexed answer passages. Here we seek a more data-driven approach, assisted by machine learning. We propose a simple log-linear model over a pair of feature vectors, one derived from the question and the other derived from the a candidate passage. Features are extracted using a lexical network and surface context as in named entity extraction, except that there is no direct supervision available in the form of fixed entity types and their examples. Using the log-linear model, we filter candidate passages and see substantial improvement in the mean rank at which the first answer is found. The model parameters distill and reveal linguistic artifacts coupling questions and their answers, which can be used for better annotation and indexing.

1 Introduction

A Question Answering (QA) system responds to queries like *Who is the Greek God of the Sea?* with a precise answer like *Poseidon.* An important first step, which we focus on here, is to identify short *snippets* or passages of up to several words which contain the answer.

Traditionally, Web search engines have not rewarded queries that are grammatical and coherent. Users have adapted by translating their information need (e.g., *When was the Space Needle built?*) into telegraphic keyword queries (e.g., "Space Needle" history). However, this process remains a tentative one.

Meanwhile, the QA community, building on top of Information Retrieval (IR) systems, part-of-speech and named-entity (NE, e.g., people, place, time) taggers, and shallow parsers, has made substantial advances in building high-accuracy QA systems [2,7,8,10,4,17,26,5,15].

However, the success comes at a price: significant human effort is needed to study the corpus and typical questions and their answers, and turn that experience into elaborate pattern matching and extraction strategies. The best

B. Mobasher et al. (Eds.): WebKDD 2004, LNAI 3932, pp. 116–134, 2006.
© Springer-Verlag Berlin Heidelberg 2006

QA systems incorporate expert input based on manual analysis of large corpora and a large collection of questions (over 27600 in one case).

Expert input is coded in at least two forms. The first is a question *typology* with several hundred question types, such as location (Where is John Wayne airport?), events (When is Bastille Day?), creation-time (When did World War 1 start?), population (What is the population of Venezuela?), why-famous (Who was Galileo?) and so on. Further wisdom is embedded in routines that produce the final ranking of passages short-listed by a conventional IR engine. The best-performing ranking routines exploit well-tuned heuristic that set rewards, discounts, and penalties for exact matches, case-insensitive matches and stemmed matches between words.

Our goal: We wish to harness robust data mining and machine learning tools to ease—and ideally automate—the process of mapping ad-hoc questions to likely answer passages, without having to fashion and maintain a question taxonomy, or to tune passage ranking heuristics through manual intervention.

We draw on two kinds of resources. First, we use a database of **is-a** relations (e.g., a horse is a mammal). WordNet[1] is a source of is-a relations widely used in natural language analysis. Moreover, recent research has enabled the bootstrapping of is-a databases, largely automatically, from the Web [6]. Many focused domains have already created ontologies suited to their use, e.g., the MeSH hierarchy for medical abstracts and the UNSPSC taxonomy for e-commerce catalogs. These knowledge bases feed naturally into our system.

Second, we borrow basic feature extraction strategies from the named entity (NE) extraction and information extraction (IE) communities. Unlike IE, we do not have a fixed set of labels. Ground features on both the question and answer sides must be abstracted into "soft labels" which allow for probabilistic matching. Intuitively, if a test question is "similar" to a sufficient number of training questions, we should be able to predict the kind of features we wish to see in an answer passage directly, without first embedding the question into a type system.

Consider questions that are answered with the name of a place. There are several ways to ask such questions, starting with "Where ..." or "In which city ..." etc. Likewise, there are several ways in which the answer can be embedded in the context of a passage, where the answer

- Almost always has token/s starting with an uppercase letter and continues with lowercase letters
- Is almost always flagged as a noun or noun phrase by a POS tagger
- Tends to be preceded by *in* or *at*
- Is often a specialization ("hyponym") of the compound noun *geographical location* in WordNet.

Similar comments hold for most common types of factual questions. Note that accumulation of "soft" evidence for a match can happen at both the question and the answer end.

---

[1] http://wordnet.princeton.edu/

To be sure, machine learning is already heavily used inside many QA modules, such as part-of-speech (POS) and named entity (NE) taggers, and shallow parsers. These modules demand training data for different tasks in diverse forms, so it is no wonder that most modules are used as black boxes, pre-trained with generic data which we can only hope suffices for our application. We have often seen BBN's Identifinder[2] flag Japanese person names as *organization*; *m.p.h.* and *Gaffney, SC* as *person*; and *telephone, all in all*, and *look* as *work of art*. The gazetteer in GATE[3] regards *2000* as possibly representing a year, but not *1803*. Moreover, as described above, these modules are put together via *engineered bias* rather than learning the weight of their evidence for specific QA instances. Clearly, the black-box mode of usage can be improved upon.

Our contributions: To a first approximation, we represent questions and answers using feature vectors in the style of modern information extraction systems like MALLET[4] or Minor Third[5], and then learn high-density regions in the joint distribution of these features. More specifically, given a new query and a candidate answer, we estimate if their combined feature vector is sufficiently close to a high-density region to accept the candidate answer. We argue that many QA ranking strategies are "hard" approximations to such "soft" scoring. As we shall see, the high-density zones can also be conditioned on questions to yield eminently meaningful passage features, which can be used as predictive annotations [16].

In this paper, we start by showing that useful high-density regions are indeed recoverable from the joint distribution of question and answer features. We then propose a log-linear model to predict if there is enough evidence that a candidate passage is likely to answer a given question. We fit the model to features extracted from TREC QA data in conjunction with WordNet, with no customization whatsoever. The model reveals feature correlations which are intuitive and useful in retrospect.

Our trained model can be used to filter candidate response tokens from a passage-level IR system. Experiments with TREC 2000 and TREC 2002 show significant improvements in the earliest rank at which an answer passage is found. Owing to the simplicity of our model, applying our classifier to a passage span is very fast, allowing us to scale up the filtering step to 300 responses from the IR system in 1–2 seconds. Our results move us closer to shrink-wrapped, trainable QA systems which are as easy to deploy as a basic IR system.

2   Preliminaries and Related Work

In this section we set up our problem more formally, and review some related work.

A factual question is a sequence of **tokens**, such as *Who wrote "20,000 Leagues Under the Sea"*, possibly containing quoted strings (which are regarded

---

[2] http://www.bbn.com/speech/identifinder.html

[3] http://gate.ac.uk

[4] http://mallet.cs.umass.edu

[5] http://sourceforge.net/projects/minorthird

as single tokens). A **corpus** is a set of **documents**; each document is a sequence of **sentences**; and each sentence is a sequence of tokens. The QA system returns a ranked list of **passages**. Working definitions of a passage range from a 50- or 250-byte text window, some number of consecutive tokens, or a small number (1–3) of consecutive sentences.

In this work we address queries which seek as answer an **entity** of a **type** that is specified only indirectly, where the entity satisfies some **constraints** expressed in the question. We call the desired answer type the **atype** of the question. In the question above, the answer entity is Jules Verne, the atype is *person*, and the constraint is that the answer entity must have written the specified book.

The constraint is expressed in two parts. First, there are ground constants (like the book title) which we expect to occur essentially unchanged in an answer passage. Constants are matched reasonably easily using an IR system. But enforcing the second part, the *relation* "wrote," generally requires a parse and quite some engineering; this is where many QA systems avoid "NLP completeness" for simplicity and speed. At this stage, we will do likewise, and think of the IR probe as being derived from the template

```
FIND x NEAR GroundConstants(question)
    WHERE x IS-A Atype(question)
```

For starters, **NEAR** may mean linear proximity in text, and as we see later, this is already surprisingly effective. But the stage is wide open for introducing diverse evidence of nearness, including chunking and parsing, and this is an exciting area of future work. The focus of this paper is the predicate

```
x IS-A Atype(question).
```

Most QA systems use a two-step approach to evaluate this predicate. First, they build a *question classifier* to evaluate `Atype(question)`. This classifier is usually completely supervised, and uses a taxonomy of question types [19,24]. Second, they map the estimated atype to tokens expected to be found in an answer passage [16,18]. Notable departures from the standard paradigm include inferring paraphrases [12], predicting answer tokens from question features [1,5], and using a language model conditioned on the question type [23]. A key feature of our approach is that we do not have a small, fixed system of atypes, and we do not know how to materialize `Atype(question)` in a deterministic manner. Instead, we evaluate the soft predicate `DoesAtypeMatch(x,question)`.

As we shall see next, `DoesAtypeMatch(x,question)` is estimated as a function over a joint feature space extracted from x and question. Given a question, the results in this paper enables us to predict features of x that make it a likely answer, in a soft or probabilistic manner. These desirable features may involve lexical networks or surface patterns. Apart from regular words and phrases, the corpus is indexed under these features. E.g., wherever *Jules Verne* occurs in the corpus, we pretend that `person#n#1` and `hasCap` (has uppercase letters) also occur. As shown in Fig. 1, this helps the specially-designed IR subsystem ("IR4QA" i.e. IR for QA) score passages in terms of a two-part question: one part

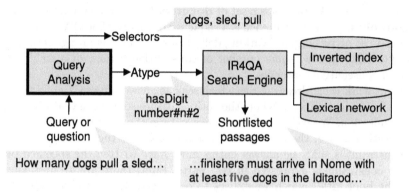

Fig. 1. This paper focuses on the "query analysis" module shown in the system diagram above

providing atype clues, the other matching words literally. The job of the IR4QA module is to return the top-scoring passages as if the whole corpus were scored with respect to `DoesAtypeMatch(.,question)`, while making few and efficient index probes. Summarizing, this paper presents a machine learning approach to implementing the module labeled "query analysis."

3   Features

Each token in a question or passage may be associated with a variety of *features*. We will use *surface* features such as orthography and specific word forms, and *taxonomy* features which help us recognize that a passage token is an instance of the atype that the question seeks. Inspired by Yarowsky and others, we will adopt the "kitchen sink" approach [22]: include as many useful-looking features as we can find, use learning techniques robust to redundant features, and exploit the ones that float to the top.

Our approach is to generalize each passage token to many levels of detail, in a redundant fashion. If a token is a noun found in WordNet, the hypernym paths (definitions are in the next section) to noun roots provides one kind of generalization. Words not found in WordNet are generalized to surface context patterns.

Individually, each feature thus derived can be unreliable. E.g., both place and person names tend to start with an uppercase letter and continue with lowercase letters. But person names are rarely preceded by a preposition. Our hope is that a robust learning algorithm can combine such noisy evidence to give high accuracy.

3.1   Lexical Network-Based Features

We start this section with a brief WordNet primer. For our purposes, WordNet [14] is a graph where nodes are concepts and edges are relations between concepts. A concept is called a **synset** because it is described by a set of synonyms, also called **lemmas**. A synset may be described by many lemmas. Conversely, a lemma (like *match*) can describe many synsets, in which case it is highly **polysemous**. A lemma, a part-of-speech, and a (standardized) sense number together defines a synset uniquely, and is written as `match#n#1` (first noun sense of *match*). We only consider **hypernym** and **hyponym** edges in WordNet, which represent IS-A relations. E.g., in this chain of generalization:

> horse, Equus caballus $\rightarrow$ equine, equid $\rightarrow \cdots \rightarrow$ ungulate, hoofed mammal $\rightarrow$ placental, placental mammal, eutherian, eutherian mammal $\rightarrow$ mammal $\rightarrow \cdots \rightarrow$ animal, animate being, beast, brute, creature, fauna $\rightarrow \cdots \rightarrow$ entity

beast and *brute* are synonyms, *equid* is a **hyponym** of *ungulate*, *horse* is a **hyponym descendant** of *mammal*, *equid* is a **hypernym** of *horse*, and *entity* is a **hypernym ancestor** of *horse*.

Each passage token is mapped to one or more synsets in the WordNet noun hierarchy. Holding extreme faith in the kitchen sink approach (and mainly because it would be computationally expensive), we perform no word sense disambiguation. From each synset we walk up the noun hypernym hierarchy and collect all hypernym ancestor synsets as features associated with the given token. We do not consider non-noun hypernym hierarchies because they are known to not be as usable as the noun hierarchy, and because most answers are nouns or noun-related entities.

WordNet is only a representative example; we can use the occurrence of a token in any precompiled dictionary, and any available sources of instance-of and part-of information as features. E.g., in a medical application, we can use the extensive MeSH hierarchy, and if wanted to support QA on product reviews, we might use the UNSPSC product taxonomy[6].

3.2   Surface Context Features

Lexical features work only for finite domains, and surface context features are one way to supplement lexical features to handle infinite domains (e.g., quantities).

Surface features for questions currently include (lowercased) token sequences of length up to **three** tokens, starting from standard wh-word question leaders: *when, what, how, where, which, who, whom, whose, why, name*, and *define*. This set is language-specific, and is designed to capture clues about the desired atype.

Surface features of passage tokens are extracted in a manner similar to information extraction systems. We flag if a token has some uppercase letter (`hasCap`), is all uppercase letters, is an abbreviation (uppercase letters and periods), has an uppercase letter followed by two or more lowercase letters (`hasXxx`), has a digit (`hasDigit`), and is entirely digits. (Later, we intend to use the part of speech of the token and its adjacent tokens; our current POS tagger is not as fast as our indexer.)

3.3   Proximity Features

Most QA systems reward linear proximity between candidate answers and matched question tokens, and some provide a reasonably formal justification [4].

---

[6] http://www.eccma.org/unspsc

In our setup, when we consider a passage token as (part of) a candidate answer, we also measure the linear distance (number of intervening tokens) between the candidate token and each matched question token. To make proximity features compatible with all other boolean features, we combine the **reciprocal** of the distances, in two ways: take their **average** or take their **maximum**.

4   Likelihood Ratio Tests

We start with some exploratory data analysis: are there indeed consistent, detectable patterns that can be extracted from the feature classes we collect? We limit our study to pairs of features, one from the question and one from the answer. Searching for larger correlated itemsets would be prohibitive in such high dimensional spaces.

Fig. 2 shows some pairs of features (only surface features from question and passage tokens) that pass the well-known likelihood ratio test with the highest scores, showing strong association between the feature pairs.

Q-feature	A-feature	Score	
whom	hasCap	159	
whom	hasXxx	162	
who_wrote	hasCap	164	
where_are	hasXxx	166	
who_wrote	hasXxx	167	
who_invented	hasXxx	181	
who_invented	hasCap	200	
what_year	hasDigit	280	
what_city	hasCap	373	
what_city	hasXxx	378	
how_many	hasDigit	449	
of	hasXxx	480	*
what	hasXxx	540	*
what	hasCap	555	*
name	hasXxx	897	
name	hasCap	911	
is	hasXxx	1110	*
is	hasCap	1115	*
where	hasXxx	1196	
where	hasCap	1205	
when	hasDigit	1367	
who	hasXxx	1594	
who	hasCap	1707	

Fig. 2. The most strongly associated pairs of surface features in questions and answer tokens are highly intuitive. The score shown is the standard $-2\log\Lambda$ score which is χ^2-distributed. (Meaningless and/or useless pairs are marked "*" and commented upon in the text.)

Can we simply retain some of the top-scoring pairs in Fig. 2 in a question-to-answer mapping table and achieve our objective? Perhaps, but any score threshold would be rather arbitrary. A χ^2 table shows almost *all* pairs as significantly associated. Even pairs which are meaningless or too general to be useful, like (who, hasDigit), (what, hasXxx), (what, hasCap), and (is, hasXxx), get significant scores (see "*"). The problems are obvious: the likelihood ratio test

Q-feature	A-feature	Score
who_painted	artist#n#1	12
how_much	definite_quantity#n#1	24
how_much	metric_unit#n#1	25
how_far	nautical_linear_unit#n#1	26
how_far	mile#n#1	26
how_much	metric_weight_unit#n#1	33
how_many	definite_quantity#n#1	37
how_many	number#n#2	55
how_many	large_integer#n#1	60
when_is	time_period#n#1	79
when_is	calendar_day#n#1	98
who_wrote	writer#n#1	103
when_is	day#n#4	135
city	state_capital#n#1	236
what_city	state_capital#n#1	236
king	sovereign#n#1	275
where_is	region#n#3	283
where	location#n#1	288
king	king#n#1	294
who	person#n#1	316
where	region#n#3	370

Fig. 3. Strong associations between surface features of questions and WordNet-derived features of answers are also intuitive. Synsets are written in the standard lemma#pos#sense format. Note that `region#n#3` is chosen naturally over other senses because many answers to where questions (like cities) are hyponyms of `region#n#3` but not other senses of region.

does not discriminate among token labels, and does not capture redundancies in correlation information across different pairs.

In other words, a measure of association does not, in itself, tell us how to combine evidence from multiple pairs, because they are often highly redundant. Apart from redundancy among surface features, there is much redundancy among IE and WordNet features. Consider Fig. 3, which shows strongly associated pairings between surface features in the question and WordNet synsets derived from the answer passage. These are also by-and-large meaningful, but it is not clear how to discount evidence from one source against evidence from another, based purely on measures of association.

5   Passage Scoring and Filtering

Current practice in mapping questions to likely answer passages amounts to the following procedure. Given a question q, extract from it a suitable feature vector q. Using precompiled mapping tables (and/or an automatic classifier) predict some properties of a feature vector p that is likely to be generated by an answer passage, and then look for passages p that generate or satisfy p.

Here we seek to avoid a fixed classification of q by inducing a two-class (yes/no) classifier on the joint distribution of q and p. I.e., we concatenate q and p into a single feature vector $x = (q, p)$, and let y be a boolean prediction. Many classifiers will output not only a boolean prediction but also a score (which may be an estimated probability of belonging to the "yes" class). We can use the score in at least two ways:

Rerank: Use the score given by the classifier to rerank passages, ignoring their
original rank as returned by the IR engine.

Eliminate: The original IR ranking is retained, but passages with scores less
than a threshold are eliminated, reducing the ranks of true answer passages.

5.1   Non-linear Learners

A linear classifier such as a linear SVM will fit a weight vector $w = (w_q, w_p)$
from the training data, and then predict $y \in \{-1, +1\}$ as $\text{sign}(w \cdot x) = \text{sign}(w_q \cdot q + w_p \cdot p)$. A linear classifier is unlikely to be suitable. Ideally, we would like
different questions to substantially modulate the kinds of features we should
seek in passages. But, in case of a linear classifier, fixing the question merely
materializes the $w_q \cdot q$ part into a constant, and the portion w_p that scores p
remains unchanged. Thus the discriminant will assign static notions of positive
or negative importance to passage features, irrespective of the question.

The study of pairwise likelihood ratio suggests that our model should directly
capture pairwise interactions between features. In kernel classifiers, this can be
done using a **quadratic** kernel $K(x_1, x_2) = (x_1 \cdot x_2 + 1)^2$, which will potentially
capture all pairwise interaction of attributes. For training instances x_i, $1 \leq i \leq n$,
the SVM will estimate dual variables α_i, $1 \leq i \leq n$, mostly zero, such that the
prediction for a new feature vector $x = (q, p)$ is $\sum_i \alpha_i y_i K(x_i, x)$.

Because the α_i's, x_i's and y_i's are known, given q (the question part of x),
we can "materialize" the discriminant $\sum_i \alpha_i y_i K(x_i, x)$ explicitly as a linear
(because q is known and fixed) function of p. E.g., if q switches on the feature
how_many, we expect the coefficient of the features hasDigit and number#n#2
to be large in a positively-labeled p, and we can use this information to look for
and score promising passages more effectively.

5.2   A Log-Linear Model

In our prototype, we retain the discriminative learning strategy, but we use a log-
linear model with our feature-pairs explicitly materialized instead of a SVM with
a quadratic kernel. In our experience, the log-linear model is faster to train given
the very large number of instances created in our QA application. Moreover, in
this application, SVM cannot really give us the benefit of kernelization, because
during query time, the kernel has to be materialized in any case.

We explicitly model pairwise feature interactions between feature vectors q
and p by assigning one model parameter for each pair of scalar features, one (q_i)
drawn from the question and the other (p_j) drawn from the passage, as shown
in Fig. 4. We express our model as

$$\Pr(Y = +1 | q, p; w) = \text{logit}\left(w_0 + \sum_{i,j} w_{i,j} q_i p_j\right),$$
$$\text{where}\quad \text{logit}(a) = e^a / (1 + e^a). \tag{1}$$

and $\Pr(Y = -1 | q, p; w) = 1 - \Pr(Y = +1 | q, p; w)$.

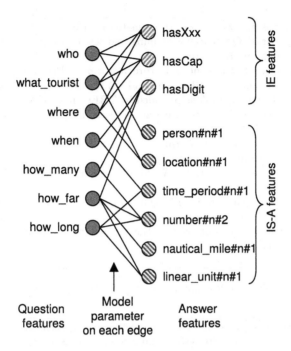

Fig. 4. Our model potentially assigns a parameter to each pair of features, one derived from the question and the other derived from the answer (Not all edges are shown)

Our overall goal is to maximize the total conditional (log) probability over all (q, p) instances over choices of parameters w, i.e.,

$$w^* = \arg\max_{w} \sum_{(q,p);y} \log \Pr(y|q, p; w). \tag{2}$$

To avoid over-fitting and improve numerical stability, we use a Gaussian prior in our optimization [3]:

$$\max_{w} \left\{ \sum_{q,p,y} \log \Pr(y|q, p; w) - \gamma \sum_{i,j} w_{i,j}^2 \right\}$$

involving a smoothing parameter γ which is chosen by cross-validation. Experimental data suggests that careful tuning of γ can help the log-linear model compete favorably with SVMs [25]. We use L-BFGS, a sparse, limited-memory, quasi-Newton numerical solver[7] to search for the best w.

Note that each parameter $w_{i,j}$ (except the offset w_0 and parameters associated with proximity features, which we avoid discussing for simplicity) is associated with one question feature and one answer feature. Therefore, inspection of these parameters can reveal interesting and possibly unexpected structures in the relationship between question and passage features.

---

[7] http://riso.sourceforge.net

1: Index sliding passage windows of three sentences using an IR system.
2: Randomly partition QA pairs for training and testing (5–10 folds were used).
3: **for** each training question q **do**
4:    Collect question features into a feature vector q as described.
5:    Send the question to the IR system and get top 300 response passages
6:    Using the regular expressions provided by TREC, mark token spans where the correct answer appears. Keep each answer span as tight as possible.
7: **end for**
8: **for** each token over all passages **do**
9:    Collect surface features from token.
10:    Map token to noun synset(s) in WordNet if possible, and collect all hypernym ancestors.
11:    Together, these features give p, the feature vector derived from the passage.
12:    q and p together define an instance.
13:    The label y for the instance is $+1$ if the passage token is inside an answer span, and -1 otherwise.
14: **end for**

Fig. 5. Collection of training instances for the log-linear classifier

1: Collect question features into a feature vector x_q as described.
2: Send the question to the IR system and get top 300 response passages
3: **for** each token over all candidate passages **do**
4:    Obtain passage features x_p and combined feature vector x as during training
5:    Using the log-linear classifier, get a boolean prediction for the token
6: **end for**
7: **if** all tokens in a passage are eliminated **then**
8:    Eliminate the passage
9: **end if**
10: Present surviving passages in the order originally provided by the IR system.

Fig. 6. Using the classifier to prune the passage list

6   Experiments

We experimented with two years of TREC QA data (2000 and 2002) and got broadly similar results. The corpus was chopped up into sentences. Three consecutive sentences[8] were defined as a passage. Passages were indexed using Lucene[8], which implements a standard TFIDF search.

The training process is shown in Fig. 5, and the testing process is shown in Fig. 6. Each token may typically trigger up to half a dozen surface features. Roughly half to two-thirds of the tokens scanned from candidate passages will connect to some WordNet noun (less if we could afford to disambiguate), and we would follow a hypernym chain of typical length 5–10. Thus each feature on average would fire roughly 5–20 features on the right hand side of Fig. 4.

---

[8] http://jakarta.apache.org/lucene/

TREC 2000 yielded a training set with 198496 instances and 674631 (largely boolean) features, where the average instance had only 42 features turned on. For TREC 2002 the corresponding numbers were 170264 instances, 540901 features and average fill of 43.6. Convergence was declared when $\|\nabla(w)\|/\|w\|$ dropped below 0.001; this happened between 500 and 2000 iterations (10–40 minutes on a 1GHz 1GB P4) depending on γ.

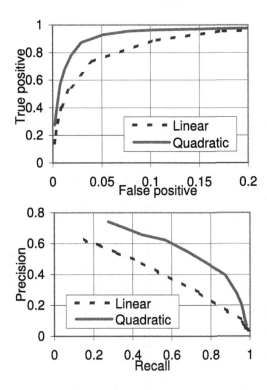

Fig. 7. The quadratic representation enables a much better fit to the data and consequent accuracy on test data. ROC and recall-precision curves are shown. The breakeven F1 value is 0.44 for the linear model and 0.61 for the quadratic model.

There are two related design choices during testing where more exploration is warranted in future work. First, we *eliminate* passages rather than *rerank* them (see §5). We also tried reranking, but the actual value of the logistic score was not reliable enough. Second, a passage survives if any of its tokens cannot be eliminated. I.e., token scores are not combined into a passage score in any sophisticated fashion.

6.1   Linear vs. Quadratic

For many applications, dependencies between features are not well-understood, and the choice of a kernel is an experimental art. In our application, however, verifying that a quadratic representation gave much greater accuracy was an important part of vindicating our model. Fig. 7 confirms our intuition. In both ROC and recall-precision measures, the quadratic model is far superior.

Our positive experience with the quadratic representation may have implications for setting up log-linear models in IE and shallow parsing. Efforts to synthesize non-linear combinations of raw features to strengthen the log-linear model in these domains are relatively recent [13].

A. where		B. who	
hasXxx	0.27	hasXxx	0.38
region#n#3	0.25	hasCap	0.31
location#n#1	0.25	entertainer#n#1	0.16
hasCap	0.18	leader#n#1	0.14
country#n#1	0.17	artist#n#1	0.14
district#n#1	0.17	performer#n#1	0.13
hasDigit	-0.1	person#n#1	0.09
artifact#n#1	-0.13	poet#n#1	0.08
measure#n#3	-0.14	location#n#1	-0.18
abstraction#n#6	-0.16	entity#n#1	-0.21
act#n#2	-0.16	hasDigit	-0.21
		abstraction#n#6	-0.31

C. when		D. how_many	
hasDigit	0.65	hasDigit	0.16
time_period#n#1	0.08	integer#n#1	0.07
holiday#noun#2	0.06	twelve#n#1	0.06
day#noun#4	0.06	number#n#2	0.06
calendar_month#n#1	0.05	definite_quantity#n#1	0.06
calendar_day#n#1	0.05	measure#n#3	0.03
hasXxx	-0.09	cognition#n#1	-0.03
hasCap	-0.12	relation#n#1	-0.03
object#n#1	-0.13	object#n#1	-0.05
entity#n#1	-0.18	act#n#2	-0.05
		entity#n#1	-0.07

E. how_far		F. linear_unit#n#1	
nautical_mile#n#2	0.02	how_far	0.02
hasDigit	0.02	where_is	0.009
linear_measure#n#1	0.02	what_speed	0.005
linear_unit#n#1	0.02	how_long	0.003
measure#n#3	0.01	whom	-0.002
hasXxx	-0.004	when	-0.004
hasCap	-0.005	what_city	-0.004
object#noun#1	-0.006	how_many	-0.005
entity#n#1	-0.007	what	-0.007

G. location#n#1		H. hasDigit	
where	0.249	when	0.65
city	0.109	what_year	.18
province	0.029	how_many	0.16
country	0.015	how_much	0.09
state	0.012	which_date	0.05
tourist	0.004	how_hot	0.02
year	-0.0230	how_far	0.02
how	-0.0314	company	-0.03
when	-0.043	city	-0.05
name	-0.113	name	-0.09
who	-0.178	where	-0.10
		who	-0.21

Fig. 8. Fixing features of questions and watching answer parameters, and vice versa

6.2   Model Parameter Anecdotes

Each component (except for w_0) of the parameter vector w estimated by the classifier corresponds to a question feature and a passage feature. We can set a feature in the question (respectively, answer), sort the model parameters, and look for the answer (respectively, question) features with the smallest and largest coefficients.

Fig. 8(A–E) shows the results. *Where* and *who* questions share hasCap and hasXxx, but differentiate answers based on WordNet features. Similarly, the sharing of hasDigit does not confound *when, how_many*, and *how_far*.

In all cases, very generic features (e.g., the noun roots) get negative coefficients. Why not zero? A little thought shows this is necessary for rejecting false positives. As a by-product, the sign may help us decide which predictive annotations to index.

In (F–H) we set *answer* features to reveal abstraction of question features. Again, we see intuitive question classes which require answers of the set type.

6.3   Rank Improvement Via Filtering

As shown in Fig. 6, passages are considered in the order returned by Lucene. We scan the top response passages, convert each token to a feature vector, and subject the token to the trained classifier. The classifier returns a score $\Pr(Y = +1|x)$ for each token. We eliminate tokens that have scores lower than a fixed threshold and eliminate a passage if all its tokens are eliminated. Surviving passages are presented in their original order. If the passage contains the TREC-specified answer as a substring, it is an answer passage.

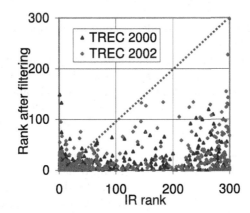

Fig. 9. Scatter plot of ranks of first correct passages before (x) and after (y) filtering. Points below the diagonal are good news.

In Fig. 9 we plot a scatter of ranks before and after filtering. We see that filtering is very effective at improving the ranks of answer passages, often dropping them from 200–300 down to less than 50. The comparison with the IR

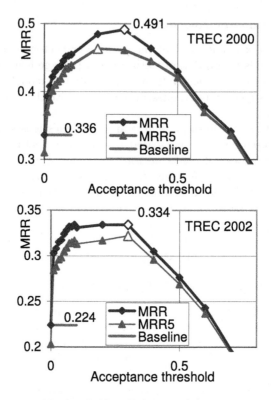

Fig. 10. By using a suitable threshold on $\Pr(Y = +1|x)$, we can prune away large number of non-answer passages and increase MRR beyond the IR baseline (threshold=0)

baseline demonstrates that our model is good at discriminating answer tokens from non-answer tokens.

It is possible that we mistakenly eliminate a correct answer token. If another correct answer token is available ranked lower in the original list, we might pick that one up. If all answer tokens are mistakenly eliminated, we regard the true answer as being reported at infinite rank. Therefore, filtering can both improve and hurt accuracy in principle, but the aggregate effect in practice is very favorable.

Why use an IR baseline which is worse than the best QA systems reported? Ideally, we should start with the best system, enhance it with our new feature representation and learning ideas, and make standard end-to-end MRR5 measurements. In practice, hardly any QA system is available for downloading, and even demos are rare. LCC[9], among the best QA systems, is an exception, but the exact corpus is not known and the results must be scraped from HTML. Unless code is available, it is impossible to replicate the myriad undocumented details of tokenization, compound word detection, chunking, POS tagging, query formulation, and so on.

---

[9] http://www.languagecomputer.com/

For all these reasons, it is very common [9,20] for researchers to use an IR baseline, change very few things at a time, and make careful assessments of the effect of each enhancement. Katz and Lin [9] claim that an extensive recent study [11] presents "substantial empirical evidence that boolean-based passage retrieval techniques are sufficient to obtain reasonable performance in question answering tasks."

In the QA literature the **mean reciprocal rank (MRR)** is commonly used as an aggregated figure of merit. Suppose $n_q \geq 1$ is the earliest rank of the passage at which the answer to question $q \in Q$ is found. Then MRR is defined as $(1/|Q|) \sum_q (1/n_q)$. MRR is between 0 and 1, and a higher MRR is better. TREC contestants are required to report MRR5, where any value of $n_q > 5$ must be regarded as ∞.

MRR and MRR5 (while perhaps reasonable as final figures of merit) offer little guidance in diagnosing the strengths and weaknesses of the many components of QA systems. MRR assigns the same penalty for dropping an answer from rank 1 to rank 2 as the penalty for dropping the answer from rank 2 to rank ∞ (i.e., not reporting it at all). MRR5 will ignore a rank reduction from 20 to 6, just as it would ignore a rank reduction from 20 to 10, even though the first system is probably better. Both MRR and MRR5 conflate many critical measurements into single end-to-end numbers.

In Fig. 10 we plot MRR and MRR5 against the posterior probability threshold at which a passage token is accepted as (part of) an answer. As we assert larger acceptance thresholds, we filter out non-answers and increase MRR beyond the IR baseline. Beyond some acceptance threshold, we get too demanding and start losing the true answer tokens. As can be seen, the peak MRR is substantially larger than the IR baseline (+46% for TREC 2000, +49% for TREC 2002). MRR and MRR5 differ only slightly; in many cases we do not get an answer because there *is* no answer in the top 300 passages, and query expansion or back-off techniques will likely help. To give an impression of where we stand relative to highly-engineered champion systems, for TREC 2001, where our MRR5 is 0.463, the top scores are 0.76, 0.46, 0.46, and 0.31 [21]. Our "clean-room" approach to QA is therefore quite promising, at least considering rank order. (We could not obtain MRR5 scores for other systems for TREC 2002.)

6.4   Ablation and Drill-Down Studies

We also did ablation experiments with features. For TREC 2002, filtering passages with the *known* BBN IdentiFinder tag gave us an MRR which was several percent lower. Clearly, the log-linear model is learning something extra from all those features. As Fig. 11 shows, features derived from WordNet turn out to be more important than surface patterns, but for one of our two data sets, surface patterns have visible marginal benefits.

Fig. 12 shows how MRR gains for specific question types compared with the average gain (scaled to 1). The most visible deviations from the mean are for *what*, *which* and *who*. Questions with *who* are doing very well by combining evidence from orthography and WordNet. Questions with *what* and *which* are doing relatively poorly (even as the absolute improvement is 30–40%).

Features	Recall	Precision	F1
	TREC 2000		
Surface	0.024	0.497	0.047
WordNet	0.427	**0.634**	0.510
Surface+WordNet	**0.447**	0.619	0.519
	TREC 2002		
Surface	0.035	0.492	0.066
WordNet	0.383	**0.662**	0.485
Surface+WordNet	**0.451**	0.653	**0.533**

Fig. 11. Effect of including/excluding feature subsets

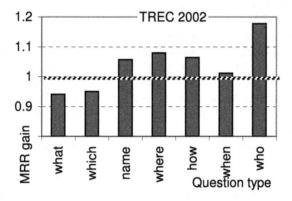

Fig. 12. MRR gain ratio of various question types relative to average overall MRR gain ratio

We found two distinct factors that explain our observation. First, sequences of 1–3 tokens starting with *what* are not enough to capture enough clues about the atype. Second, for both *what* and *which* questions, the atype space is, in principle, unbounded. In ongoing work, we are adding a synthesized "test for equality" feature for *what* and *which* questions. Summarizing, we feel that we can retain the simplicity of our basic approach and perform better with some more work on feature extraction and representation.

7   Conclusion

We have presented a very simple but promising log-linear model coupling question and passage features for the QA problem. Our results move us closer to shrink-wrapped, end-user trainable QA systems. We believe that such indirect supervision of language tasks will become increasingly important, and components must plug into a global probabilistic infrastructure rather than be engineered black boxes.

Our work opens up some obvious avenues for exploration. We should explore higher order kernels with maximum margin learners. We should improve feature extraction, especially for *what* and *which*, possibly using chunking on the question. It would be nice to integrate disambiguation naturally into the framework, rather than as a preprocessing step. Finally, it would be promising (but computationally challenging) to extend the flat feature space in our log-linear model to a more elaborate graphical model involving some salient parts of the lexical network.

References

1. E. Agichtein, S. Lawrence, and L. Gravano. Learning search engine specific query transformations for question answering. In *WWW Conference*, pages 169–178, 2001.
2. E. Breck, J. Burger, D. House, M. Light, and I. Mani, editors. *Question Answering from Large Document Collections*, AAAI Fall Symposium on Question Answering Systems, 1999.
3. S. F. Chen and R. Rosenfeld. A gaussian prior for smoothing maximum entropy models. Technical Report CMU-CS-99-108, Carnegie Mellon University, 1999.
4. C. L. A. Clarke, G. V. Cormack, and T. R. Lynam. Exploiting redundancy in question answering. In *SIGIR*, pages 358–365, 2001.
5. S. Dumais, M. Banko, E. Brill, J. Lin, and A. Ng. Web question answering: Is more always better? In *SIGIR*, pages 291–298, 2002.
6. O. Etzioni, M. Cafarella, et al. Web-scale information extraction in KnowItAll. In *WWW Conference*, New York, 2004. ACM.
7. S. Harabagiu, D. Moldovan, M. Pasca, R. Mihalcea, M. Surdeanu, R. Bunescu, R. Girju, V. Rus, and P. Morarescu. FALCON: Boosting knowledge for answer engines. In *TREC 9*, pages 479–488. NIST, 2000.
8. E. Hovy, L. Gerber, U. Hermjakob, M. Junk, and C.-Y. Lin. Question answering in Webclopedia. In *TREC 9*. NIST, 2001.
9. B. Katz and J. Lin. Selectively using relations to improve precision in question answering. In *EACL Workshop on Natural Language Processing for Question Answering*, Budapest, Hungary, 2003.
10. C. Kwok, O. Etzioni, and D. S. Weld. Scaling question answering to the Web. In *WWW Conference*, volume 10, pages 150–161, Hong Kong, 2001.
11. M. Light, G. Mann, E. Riloff, and E. Breck. Analyses for elucidating current question answering technology. *Journal of Natural Language Engineering*, 7(4):325–342, 2001.
12. D. Lin and P. Pantel. Discovery of inference rules for question answering. *Natural Language Engineering*, 7(4):343–360, 2001.
13. A. McCallum. Efficiently inducing features of conditional random fields. In *UAI*, 2003.
14. G. Miller, R. Beckwith, C. Fellbaum, D. Gross, and K. Miller. Introduction to WordNet: An online lexical database. *International Journal of Lexicography*, 1993.
15. E. Nyberg, T. Mitamura, J. Callan, J. Carbonell, R. Frederking, K. Collins-Thompson, L. Hiyakumoto, Y. Huang, C. Huttenhower, S. Judy, J. Ko, A. Kupsc, L. V. Lita, V. Pedro, D. Svoboda, and B. V. Durme. The JAVELIN question-answering system at TREC 2003: A multi-strategy approach with dynamic planning. In *TREC*, volume 12, 2003.
16. J. Prager, E. Brown, A. Coden, and D. Radev. Question-answering by predictive annotation. In *SIGIR*, pages 184–191. ACM, 2000.

17. D. Radev, W. Fan, H. Qi, H. Wu, and A. Grewal. Probabilistic question answering on the web. In *WWW Conference*, pages 408–419, 2002.
18. G. Ramakrishnan, S. Chakrabarti, D. A. Paranjpe, and P. Bhattacharyya. Is question answering an acquired skill? In *WWW Conference*, pages 111–120, New York, 2004.
19. J. Suzuki, T. Hirao, Y. Sasaki, and E. Maeda. Hierarchical directed acyclic graph kernel: Methods for structured natural language data. In *ACL*, pages 32–39, 2003.
20. S. Tellex, B. Katz, et al. Quantitative evaluation of passage retrieval algorithms for question answering. In *SIGIR*, pages 41–47, 2003.
21. E. Voorhees. Overview of the TREC 2001 question answering track. In *The Tenth Text REtrieval Conference*, volume 500-250 of *NIST Special Publication*, pages 42–51, 2001.
22. D. Yarowsky. Decision lists for lexical ambiguity resolution: Application to accent restoration in Spanish and French. In *ACL*, volume 32, pages 88–95, Las Cruces, NM, 1994.
23. D. Zhang and W. S. Lee. A language modeling approach to passage question answering. In *Text REtrieval Conference (TREC)*, volume 12. NIST, Nov. 2003.
24. D. Zhang and W. S. Lee. Question classification using support vector machines. In *SIGIR*, Toronto, Canada, 2003. ACM.
25. J. Zhang and Y. Yang. Robustness of regularized linear classification methods in text categorization. In *SIGIR*, pages 190–197. ACM, 2003.
26. Z. Zheng. AnswerBus question answering system. In *HLT*, 2002.

Integrating Web Conceptual Modeling and Web Usage Mining

Rosa Meo[1], Pier Luca Lanzi[2], Maristella Matera[2], and Roberto Esposito[1]

[1] Università di Torino, Italy
[2] Politecnico di Milano, Italy
{meo, esposito}@di.unito.it, {lanzi, matera}@elet.polimi.it

Abstract. We present a case study about the application of the inductive database approach to the analysis of Web logs. We consider rich XML Web logs – called *conceptual logs* – that are generated by Web applications designed with the WebML conceptual model and developed with the WebRatio CASE tool. Conceptual logs integrate the usual information about user requests with meta-data concerning the structure of the content and the hypertext of a Web application. We apply a data mining language (MINE RULE) to conceptual logs in order to identify different types of patterns, such as: recurrent navigation paths, most frequently visited page contents, and anomalies (e.g., intrusion attempts or harmful usages of resources). We show that the exploitation of the nuggets of information embedded in the logs and of the specialized mining constructs provided by the query languages enables the rapid customization of the mining procedures following to the Web developers' need. Given our on-field experience, we also suggest that the use of queries in advanced languages, as opposed to ad-hoc heuristics, eases the specification and the discovery of large spectrum of patterns.

Keywords: Association Rules, Inductive Databases, MINE RULE, Web Log, Web Structure Mining, Web Usage Mining.

1   Introduction

In this paper we present a case study on mining Web log files of a University Department. The analysis has been conducted over *WebML conceptual logs* [14], which are Web logs enriched with additional information with respect to standard Web logs. Indeed, they have been obtained by integrating the (ECFL) Web server logs with information on the composition of Web pages in terms of atomic units of contents, the information entities such units refer to, the entity instances they publish dynamically, and some other meta-data about the organization of the overall hypertext.

The analysis has exploited a query language for association rule mining – MINE RULE – and has used it in a fashion typical to inductive databases. Inductive databases were proposed in [15] to leverage decision support systems by applying specific mining languages to the analysis of data stored in databases.

B. Mobasher et al. (Eds.): WebKDD 2004, LNAI 3932, pp. 135–148, 2006.
© Springer-Verlag Berlin Heidelberg 2006

According to this paradigm, the user/analyst can interact with the system during the knowledge discovery process in a similar way as with a DBMS, that is, by specifying interesting data mining patterns with queries that in turn retrieve and store in the database the discovered information.

The aim of our study is manifold: (i) analyzing the Web logs and extracting interesting, usable and actionable patterns; (ii) evaluating the usability (in practical cases) and the expressive power of the mining query language, by itself and inside the context of an inductive database approach; (iii) verify and experiment the suitability of some knowledge discovery (KDD) scenarios for inductive databases. In particular, KDD scenarios have been produced as a set of characteristic queries solving some frequently asked questions (mining problems) by users/analysts (Web site administrators and/or information system designers) in order to recover from frequently occurring problems.

We have identified three main typologies of mining problems for which association rules could constitute an aid:

1. the identification of frequent crawling paths by the users (Web structure and Web usage analysis),
2. the identification of user communities, and
3. the identification of critical situations (anomalies, security attacks, high traffic) in which the information system could be placed.

The first task enables both the customization and construction of adaptive Web sites and recommender systems, as well as the quality analysis of Web applications [14,10]. The analysis of user crawling paths has been used also in [1] to model the likelihood that a page belongs to a specific topic. This is a relevant problem in the construction of crawlers' indices and in Web resources discovery. Thus, mining of collective user experiences, has been applied successfully to find resources on a certain topic, though this issue is typically related to the second task, i.e. the identification of user communities. The discovery and management of user communities is an important aim for customer relationship management and business applications (e.g, e-commerce). Finally, the third task, the identification of critical situations in an information system is essential for the management of computer security, for developing reliable and efficient information technology systems and their Web front-end.

The paper is organized as follows. Section 2 provides the rationale and the background that justify the proposed approach. Section 3 describes the process of generation of conceptual logs. Section 4 provides the KDD scenarios made of queries and for each of them describes the obtained results. Finally Section 5 draws the conclusions.

2   Rationale and Background

Current Web applications are very complex and highly sophisticated software products, whose quality can heavily determine their success or failure. A number of methods have been proposed for evaluating Web application quality. In particular, Web usage mining methods are employed to analyze how users exploit the information provided by the Web site [23,2]. For instance, showing those navigation patterns which correspond to high Web usage, or those which correspond to early leaving [16].

Web usage mining is mainly performed on the server side, and therefore is based on information found in log files, containing data about single user page access requests, represented in one of the available standard formats [5,22]. Accordingly, Web usage mining approaches rely heavily on the preprocessing of log data as a way to obtain high level information regarding user navigation patterns and ground such information into the actual data underlying the Web application [24,13,6].

Preprocessing generally includes four main steps.

- *Data cleaning*, for removing information that is useless for mining purposes (requests for graphical contents, such as banners or logos; webspiders' navigation).
- *Identification of user sessions*, for extracting full users navigation paths. This step can be very demanding [24], especially due to the adoption of proxy servers by applications, which do not allow the unique identification of users.
- *Content and structure information retrieval*, for mapping users page requests into the actual information of visited pages [3].
- *Data formatting*, for preparing data obtained through the previous three steps for being processed by the actual mining algorithms.

Notwithstanding the preprocessing efforts, in most of the cases the information extracted is usually insufficient and with much loss of the knowledge that is embedded in the application design. For example, among the previous steps, the retrieval of content structure requires the adoption of expensive methods for Web Structure Mining [12]: since any assumption can be made on how the Web application was designed, these methods consist of navigating the Web site to analyze the content and the structure of all the pages found, so as to exploit this information during the Web log mining step [7]. Even more, such approaches are ineffective on Web applications which are heavily based on dynamically created Web pages, since the navigation provides only a static view of the site. Accordingly, although these projects have demonstrated the usefulness of exploiting the knowledge about the structure and content organization of a Web application [21,8], the necessary preprocessing activities are rarely taken, as proved by the limited results reported in the literature (see [13] for a review).

The first proposals to incorporate in the Web logs implicit knowledge about the conceptual structure of a Web site used a similarity measure. The purpose is to infer an implicit content hierarchy from the URLs of most Web sites which tend to be hierarchically organized [18,19].

Some efforts have been recently undertaken for enriching Web Log files, using Semantic Web techniques. [20] exploits RDF annotations of static pages for mapping page URLs into a set of ontological entities. Within dynamic applications, the same mapping is achieved by analyzing the query strings enclosed within page URLs. [9] exploits domain ontologies with the aim of Web personalization.

It wants to automatically characterize usage profiles with a set of structured Web objects. [11] proposes the use of *concept logs*, an extended form of Web usage logs that encapsulates knowledge derived from the link semantics by means of the incorporation of keywords from an ontology.

3   Integrating Web Conceptual Modeling and Web Usage Mining

The approach we present in this paper has the advantage of integrating Web usage mining goals directly into the Web application development process. Thanks to the adoption of a conceptual modelling method for Web application design, and of its supporting case tool, the generated Web applications embed a logging mechanism able to produce semantically enriched Web log files - the *conceptual log* [14]. Therefore, no extra effort is needed during or after the application development, for the extraction of meta-data about page semantics, or even for the construction of a Web site ontology. Furthermore, additional information included in the conceptual logs refers also to the identifier of the user crawling session, the identifier of specific instances that are published within dynamic pages, as well as to some data concerning the topology of the hypertext.

In the rest of this section, we will shortly illustrate the main features of the adopted design model, WebML (Web Modeling Language), and of the rich logs that WebML-based applications are able to produce.

3.1   The WebML Model and Its Supporting CASE Tool

WebML (Web Modeling Language) is a visual language for specifying the content structure of a Web application, as well as the organization and presentation of such a content in a hypertext [4]. It mainly consists of the Data Model and the Hypertext Model.

The *WebML Data Model* adopts the Entity-Relationship primitives for representing the organization of the application data. The *WebML Hypertext Model* then offers some primitives for describing how data specified in the data model are published within the application hypertext, and consists of:

- a *composition model*, concerning the definition of pages and their internal organization in terms of elementary pieces of content being published, called *content units*. Content units offer alternative ways of arranging data dynamically extracted from entities and relationships of the data schema.
- A *navigation model*, describing links between pages and content units, which have to be provided to facilitate information location and browsing.
- A *content management model*, which consists of a set of units for specifying operations for creating and updating content.

Besides the visual representation, WebML primitives are also provided with an XML-based representation, suitable to specify those properties that would not be conveniently expressed by a graphical notation. Figure 1 reports a simplified

```
01 <PAGE id="page3" name="Research Area">
02 <CONTENTUNITS>
03      <DATAUNIT id="dau84" name="Research Area"
04          entity="ent4" entity_name="Research_Area">
05          <DISPLAYATTRIBUTE attribute="att51" name="Area Title"/>
06          <DISPLAYATTRIBUTE attribute="att57" name="Area Description/>
07          <SELECTOR>
08              <SELECTORCONDITION attributes="att58" att_name="OID"
09                  id="cond90" sel_name="Area Selection"
10                  predicate="eq" value="Selected_Area_OID"/>
11          </SELECTOR>
12      </DATAUNIT>
13      <INDEXUNIT id="inu9" name="Research Fields"
14          entity="ent19" entity_name="Res_Area_Field" >
15          <SORTATTRIBUTE attribute="att60" name="Field Title"
16              order="ascending"/>
17          <DISPLAYATTRIBUTE attribute="att60" name="Field Title"/>
18          <SELECTOR>
19              <SELECTORCONDITION relationship="rel7" rel_name="Area2Field"
20                  id="cond40" sel_name="Fields_Selection"
21                  predicate="in"/>
22          </SELECTOR>
23      </INDEXUNIT>
24      ... ...
25 </PAGE>
```

Fig. 1. Simplified XML representation of the WebML schema of a page in the DEI Web application

XML specification of a hypertext page, named *Research Area*, taken from the WebML specification of the application we analyze here (see Section 4.1).

The *Research Area* page publishes the description of a DEI research area, and the list of the current research fields covered by the area. Among others, it includes two content units. The first one is a *data unit*(lines 3-12) publishing the title (**att51**) and the textual description (**att57**) of a single instance of the **Research_Area** entity of the data schema. The instance is retrieved from the database according to a *selector condition* (lines 7-11). The second content unit is an *index unit*. It lists some instances of the entity **Res_Area_Field** (lines 14), extracted from the database according to a condition (lines 18-22) based on the data schema relationship **Area2Field** that associates each research area with a set of correlated research fields.

WebRatio is the CASE tool supporting the WebML-based development[1]. It is able to process WebML conceptual schemas, by translating their visual specification into concrete page templates. The core of WebRatio is a code generator, based on XML and XSL technologies, which is able to generate automatically the application code to be deployed on J2EE or .NET platforms. It covers all the relevant dimensions of a dynamic application: queries for data extraction from the data sources, code for managing the business logic, and page templates for the automatic generation of the front-end. The Web applications generated by WebRatio feature a three-tier architecture, whose application server enables an efficient execution of business components and the construction of dynamic pages.

---

[1] http://www.webratio.com

3.2   WebML Conceptual Logs

Conceptual logs [14] are standard log files enriched with information available in the WebML conceptual schema of the Web application, and with knowledge of accessed data. They are generated thanks to some modules, developed as extensions to the WebML/WebRatio framework, that are responsible for extracting and integrating logs from the Application Server, the WebML application runtime, and the application conceptual schema.

The use of conceptual logs introduces many advantages over the approaches usually followed in Web Usage Mining. First of all, they offer rich information that is not available with most traditional approaches. Also, they eliminate the typical Web Usage Mining preprocessing phase completely. In fact, we note that according to our approach:

- data cleaning is mainly encapsulated within the procedure that integrates the different log sources;
- the identification of user session is done by the WebML at runtime, through the management of session IDs;
- the retrieval of content and structure information is unnecessary since all these information are available from the WebML conceptual schema.

Finally, since mining methods are applied specifically to a type of rich log files, it is possible to tailor these methods to improve their effectiveness in this particular context.

4   Mining Conceptual Logs

In this Section we describe the structure of information contained in the Web logs we processed and analyzed, and the KDD scenarios, i.e., the sequences of queries in a constraint-based mining language (MINE RULE) which allowed us to obtain interesting and actionable patterns for Web administrators, application designers and analysts.

4.1   DEI Web Application Conceptual Logs

The Web logs of the DEI Web site[2] record accesses on a very large application collecting one fourth of the overall clickstream directed to Politecnico di Milano, Italy. We collected the Web logs for the first consecutive 3 months in 2003. The original Web log stored by the Web server (Apache)was 60 MBytes large and is constituted by a relation that has the following information.

RequestID: the identifier of the request made by the user of a Web page;
IPcaller: IP address from which the request is originated; very often it is a proxy IP, that masks the real identification of the user.
Date: date of the request,

---

[2] http://www.elet.polimi.it

TS: time stamp of the request,
Operation: the kind of operation request (for instance, `get` or `put`)
Page URL: URL of the page to be transfered as a consequence of the request,
Protocol: transfer protocol used (such as `TCP/IP`),
Return Code: code returned by the Web server to the user,
Dimension: dimension in bytes of the page,
Browser: name of the browser from which the request is originated,
OS Type: type of the Operating System.

The additional data deriving from the WebML application design and from the application runtime debugging module include the following items:

Jsession: identifier of the user crawling session that spams over the single page requests. User crawling sessions are identified by an enabled Java browser by the Java thread identifier of a Web crawling.
Page: identifier of the page generated by the application server. Very often a page is generated dynamically but this identifier is always the same for each page.
UnitID: identifier of an atomic piece of information contained in a page. This identifier gives information on the type of content of a page.
OID: identifier of an object (for instance, a professor, a course, a publication) whose content is shown in a page. This object identifier is used by the application server to instantiate in a different way dynamic pages according to the object itself. For instance, all professor pages conform to the same template that shows personal data, photo, description of the curriculum vitae of the person and of its research area. Instead, the real information that is shown for each person changes according to the professor, and therefore to the `OID` parameter that identifies the person.
Order: ordering number in which content units are presented in the page.

The Web Log contained almost 353 thousands user sessions for a total of more than 4.2 millions of page requests. The total number of pages (dynamic, instantiated by means of OIDs) was 38554. Each user session was constituted by an average of 12 page requests.

4.2 MINE RULE

MINE RULE is an SQL-like operator for mining association rules in relational databases. A detailed description can be found in [17]. This operator extracts a set of association rules from the database and stores them back in the database in a separate relation.

Let us explain the operator with the aid of a simple example on `WebLogTable`, containing the information of the conceptual log described in Section 4.1. The following MINE RULE statement extracts rules that aim to provide a description of the situations that generate frequently an error in the Web server (a favorite situation for attacks). *WebLogTable* has been grouped by *RequestId*; requested rules associate values of ⟨*Operation, Browser, PageURL*⟩ with values of *Returncode*. Selected rules will have a value of returned code corresponding to an error (WHERE clause). Rules will have a support and a confidence greater than the minimum requested values (respectively 0.2 and 0.4).

```
MINE RULE SituationsReturnCodes AS
SELECT DISTINCT 1..n Operation, Browser, Page Url AS BODY,
                1..n Return Code AS HEAD, SUPPORT, CONFIDENCE
WHERE HEAD.Return Code LIKE '%error%'
FROM WebLogTable
GROUP BY RequestId
EXTRACTING RULES WITH SUPPORT:0.2, CONFIDENCE:0.4
```

This statement extracts each rule as an association of attribute values occurring within single tuples. In other statement cases, rule elements are constituted by values of the same attribute (e.g., Page URL) occurring in different tuples (e.g., requests) of the same group (e.g., date).

The main features of MINE RULE are:

- *Selection of the relevant set of data* for a data mining process. This feature is applied at different granularity levels, (row level or at the group level, with the *group condition*).
- Definition of the *structure of the rules* (single or multi-dimensional association rules) and cardinality of the rule body and head.
- Definition of *constraints applied at different granularity levels*. Constraints belong to different categories: constraints applied at the rule level (*mining conditions* instantiated by a WHERE clause), constraints applied at a group level (instantiated by a HAVING predicate) and constraints applied at the *cluster* level (*cluster conditions*). For lack of space we will not make use of cluster condition in this paper.
- Definition of *rule evaluation measures*. Practically, the language allows to define support and confidence thresholds.[3] Support of a rule is computed on the total number of groups in which it occurs and satisfies the given constraints. Confidence is analogously computed (ratio between the rule support and the support of the body satisfying the given constraints).

4.3   Analysis of Conceptual Logs with MINE RULE

We have imported into a relational DBMS (MySQL) conceptual logs obtaining a table named WebLogTable. In this Section we describe in detail the KDD scenarios, composed of a sequence of pre-processing, mining and post-processing queries that we have designed for discovery of useful patterns in the Web logs. These queries can be conceived as a sort of *template* that can be used to gather descriptive patterns from Web logs useful to solve some frequent, specific or critical situations.

---

[3] Theoretically, also other measures, based on body and head support, could be used.

Analysis of Users that Visit the Same Pages. This analysis aims at discovering Web communities of users on the basis of the pages that they frequently visited.

Pre-processing Query. The mining request could be preceded by a pre-processing query selecting only those page requests that occurred frequently (above a certain threshold) thus allowing to neglect the rare page requests.

Mining Query. This query finds the associations between sets of users (IP addresses) that have all visited a certain number of same pages. In particular this number of pages is given in terms of support of the rules. (In this example, support is computed over the requested pages, since grouping is made according to the requested pages). It is an open issue whether the discovered regularities among IP addresses occur because these IP addresses have been commonly used by the same users in their pages crawling. Indeed, this phenomenon could put in evidence the existence of different IP addresses dynamically assigned to the same users.

```
MINE RULE UsersSamePages AS
SELECT DISTINCT 1..n IPcaller AS BODY,
               1..n IPcaller AS HEAD, SUPPORT, CONFIDENCE
FROM WebLogTable
GROUP BY Page Url
EXTRACTING RULES WITH SUPPORT:0.2, CONFIDENCE:0.4
```

In practice, in our experiments we discovered that the most frequently co-occurring IP addresses belong to web crawlers engines or big entities, such as universities. In the immediately lower support association rules we discovered (of course) the members of the various research groups. A similar query would occur if we wish to discover user communities which share the same user profile in terms of usage of the network resources. In this case, we would add constraints (in the mining condition, for instance) on the volume of the data transferred as a consequence of a user request. Examples of discovered patterns are the requests of frequent download of materials for courses, or documentation provided in user home pages.

Post-processing Query. As a post-processing query instead we could be interested in finding those pages that have been all visited most frequently by certain sets of users. This is a query that crosses-over extracted patterns and original data. With this request we could discard from the discovered patterns those belonging to web crawlers.

The following two query scenarios aim at performing Web structure mining.

Most Frequent Crawling Paths

Mining Query. This query returns sequences of pages (ordered by date of visit) frequently visited.

```
MINE RULE FreqSeqPages AS
SELECT DISTINCT 1..n Page Url AS BODY,
               1..n Page Url AS HEAD, SUPPORT, CONFIDENCE
WHERE BODY.Date < HEAD.Date
FROM WebLogTable
GROUP BY IPcaller
EXTRACTING RULES WITH SUPPORT:0.3, CONFIDENCE:0.4
```

You can notice that in this case we grouped by user (IPcaller) and searched for sets of pages frequently occurring in the visits of a sufficient number of users (support). Notice also that we used a mining condition to constrain the temporal ordering between pages in antecedent and consequent of rules, thus ensuring the discovery of sequential patterns. In practice, examples of resulting patterns showed that requests of a research center page, or research expertise area, were later followed by the home page of a professor. This pattern was later used by Web administrators as a hint for restructuring the Web site access paths.

Units that Occur Frequently Inside Users Crawling Sessions. The following query extracts associations between two sets of content units that appeared together in at least a certain number of crawling sessions.

```
MINE RULE UnitsSessions AS
SELECT DISTINCT 1..n UnitID AS BODY,
               1..n UnitID AS HEAD, SUPPORT, CONFIDENCE
FROM WebLogTable
GROUP BY Jsession
EXTRACTING RULES WITH SUPPORT:0.05, CONFIDENCE:0.4
```

With this query we discovered patterns that helped Web designers to redesign the Web application. In fact, we obtained that the units that most frequently co-occurred in visits are the structural components of the Web site (indexes, overview pages, and so on).

Anomaly Detection. This query tries to determine the associations between pages and users that caused a bad authentication error when making access to those pages. Therefore, this query wants to determine those pages that could be effectively used by callers as a way to enter illegally into the information system.

Pre-processing Query. The mining request was preceded by a pre-processing query selecting only those page requests that occurred a sufficient number of times. This discards those requests that have been mistakenly submitted by the user (a wrongly typed password), that if not repeated many times, cannot be considered an intrusion attempt.

```
MINE RULE BadAuthentication AS
SELECT DISTINCT 1..1 IPcaller AS BODY,
               1..n Page Url AS HEAD, SUPPORT, CONFIDENCE
WHERE BODY.IPcaller = HEAD.IPcaller
```

```
FROM WebLogTable WHERE Return Code='bad authentication'
GROUP BY Date
EXTRACTING RULES WITH SUPPORT:0.03, CONFIDENCE:0.4
```

In this query we grouped source data by date, thus identifying patterns (association of users to page requests) that are frequent in time. Notice that mining condition `WHERE BODY.IPcaller = HEAD.IPcaller` ensures that page requests (head) effectively were originated by the callers associated to them (body). Examples of most retrieved patterns are attempts to change passwords, or downloading some reserved information.

High Traffic Users

Pre-processing query. Similarly to previous queries, also this data mining query could be preceded by a pre-processing step, selecting only the frequent page requests. (Indeed, rare page requests can be neglected).

Mining query. This query returns the associations between two sets of user IP addresses from which a request of pages is characterized by a large volume of data. This constraint is enforced by means of a preprocessing predicate `WHERE dimension>=1024` that selects only those requests generating high volume of traffic on the network.

```
MINE RULE HighTrafficUsers AS
SELECT DISTINCT 1..n IPcaller AS BODY,
                1..n IPcaller AS HEAD, SUPPORT, CONFIDENCE
FROM WebLogTable
     WHERE dimension>=1024
GROUP BY date
EXTRACTING RULES WITH SUPPORT:0.03, CONFIDENCE:0.4
```

Notice that we grouped the input relation by date thus identifying the users that request high volume pages frequently in time.

Post-processing query. A cross-over query can discover those pages originating the frequently occurring page requests.

As examples of discovered patterns there are the requests of frequent download of materials for courses from remote locations, or documentation provided in user home pages.

Errors Correlated to the Usage of an Operating System. This query returns associations between the operating system and the error code frequently returned by the Web server.

```
MINE RULE OSErrors AS
SELECT DISTINCT 1..1 OStype AS BODY,
                1..n Return Code AS HEAD, SUPPORT, CONFIDENCE
```

```
WHERE BODY.OStype=HEAD.OStype
FROM WebLogTable  WHERE Return Code LIKE '%error%'
GROUP BY Date
EXTRACTING RULES WITH SUPPORT:0.01, CONFIDENCE:0.4
```

Notice the pre-processing predicate (WHERE Return Code ..) that selects only the page requests that result in some errors. This query is similar to query named BadAuthentication for the discovery of anomalies. We launched another similar query, requesting associations between a set of pages to an error and a browser. Both of them can be useful to test the reliability and robustness of a new Web application.

Users that Visit Certain Pages Frequently. This request aims at discovering if recurrent requests of a set of pages from a certain IP exist. This puts in evidence the *fidelity* of the users to the service provided by the web site.

```
MINE RULE UsersPages AS
SELECT DISTINCT 1..1 IPcaller AS BODY,
                1..2 Page Url AS HEAD, SUPPORT, CONFIDENCE
WHERE BODY.ipaddress = HEAD.ipaddress
FROM WebLogTable
GROUP BY requestId
EXTRACTING RULES WITH SUPPORT:0.01, CONFIDENCE:0.4
```

Examples of patterns we discovered are provided by the pages that allow the download of material (course slides, research reports).

One of the main advantages gained by the conceptual web logs is the knowledge of the information content of the pages. These content units can give us a more precise information on the reasons why certain pages are frequently requested by the users. For this purpose we have also considered another query (omitted here) retrieving associations between users and content units placed in pages frequently visited by those users. Patterns resulting from this request confirm that the most recurrent requests are download requests of materials from the Web site.

5   Conclusions

We presented a case study, the analysis of conceptual Web logs of the DEI Department, in which we applied and evaluated the usability and expressive power of a mining query language – MINE RULE. The Web log was a conceptual log, obtained by integration of standard (ECFL) Web server logs with information on web application design and web page content information. The adoption of this case study also aims to verify and experiment the suitability of some KDD scenarios developed for inductive databases, and proved the possibility to employ them with the mining query languages in practice to solve real case problems.

The obtained patterns can be exploited for the definition of effective navigation and composition of hypertext elements to be adopted for improving the Web site quality. We also obtained some concrete examples of interesting or suspicious event that are useful to the end-users (web and system administrators).

The query examples that we provided show that the mining language is powerful, and at the same time versatile because its operational semantics seems to be the basic one. Indeed these experiments allow us to claim that Mannila and Imielinski's initial view on inductive databases [15] was correct: "There is no such thing as real discovery, just a matter of the expressive power of the query languages".

References

1. C. C. Aggarwal. On leveraging user access patterns for topic specific crawling. *Data Mining and Knowledge Discovery*, 9(2):123–145, 2004.
2. B. Berendt. Web usage mining, site semantics, and the support of navigation. In *Proceedings of the Web Mining for E-Commerce - Challenges and Opportunities Workshop (WEBKDD'00)*, Boston, MA, USA, August 2000. Springer-Verlag.
3. B. Berendt, A. Hotho, and G. Stumme. Towards semantic Web Mining. In *Proc. of the Semantic Web Conference, ISWC 2002, Sardinia, Italy, 2002*, LNCS, pages 264–278. Springer Verlag, June 2002.
4. S. Ceri, P. Fraternali, A. Bongio, M. Brambilla, S. Comai, and M. Matera. *Designing Data-Intensive Web Applications*. Morgan Kauffmann, 2002.
5. A. Cocoon. Cocoon. http://xml.apache.org/cocoon/.
6. R. Cooley. *Web Usage Mining: Discovery and Application of Interesting Patterns from Web Data*. PhD thesis, University of Minnesota, 2000.
7. R. Cooley, B. Mobasher, and J. Srivastava. Data preparation for mining world wide web browsing patterns. *Knowledge and Information Systems*, 1(1):5–32, 1999.
8. R. Cooley, P. Tan, and J. Srivastava. *Discovery of Interesting Usage Patterns from Web Data*. LNCS/LNAI. Springer Verlag, 2000.
9. H. Dai and B. Mobasher. Using ontologies to discover domain-level web usage profiles. In *Proceedings of the Second Semantic Web Mining Workshop at ECML/PKDD-2002*, Helsinki, Finland, August 2002.
10. A. Demiriz. Enhancing product recommender systems on sparse binary data. *Data Mining and Knowledge Discovery*, 9(2):147–170, 2004.
11. M. Eirinaki, H. Lampos, M. Vazirgiannis, and I. Varlamis. Sewep: Using site semantics and a taxonomy to enhance the web personalization process. In *Proceedings of the Ninth ACM SIGKDD International Conference on Knowledge Discovery and Data Mining*, Washington, DC, USA, August 2003. Springer-Verlag.
12. O. Etzioni. The world-wide web: Quagmire or gold mine? *Communications of the ACM*, 39(11):65–68, 1996.
13. F. M. Facca and P. L. Lanzi. Mining interesting knowledge from weblogs: A survey. Technical Report 2003.15, Dipartimento di Elettronica e Informazione. Politecnico di Milano., Apr. 2003.
14. P. Fraternali, M. Matera, and A. Maurino. Conceptual-level log analysis for the evaluation of web application quality. In *Proceedings of LA-Web'03, Santiago, Chile, November 2003*. IEEE Computer Society, 2003.
15. T. Imielinski and H. Mannila. A database perspective on knowledge discovery. *Coomunications of the ACM*, 39(11):58–64, November 1996.

16. R. Kohavi and R. Parekh. Ten supplementary analyses to improve e-commerce web sites. In *Proceedings of the Fifth WEBKDD Workshop: Webmining as a premise to effective and intelligent Web Applications*, ACM SIGKDD, Washington, DC, USA, 2003. Springer-Verlag.

17. R. Meo, G. Psaila, and S. Ceri. An extension to SQL for mining association rules. *Journal of Data Mining and Knowledge Discovery*, 2(2), 1998.

18. O. Nasraoui, H. Frigui, A. Joshi, and R. Krishnapuram. Mining web access logs using a fuzzy relational clustering algorithm based on a robust estimator. In *Proceedings of the 8th International World Wide Web Conference (WWW8)*, Toronto, Canada, May 1999.

19. O. Nasraoui, H. Frigui, A. Joshi, and R. Krishnapuram. Mining web access logs using relational competitive fuzzy clustering. In *Proceedings of the 8th International Fuzzy Systems Association Congress*, Hsinchu, Taiwan, August 1999.

20. D. Oberle, B. Berendt, A. Hotho, and J. Gonzales. Conceptual User Tracking. In *Proc. of the First International Atlantic Web Intelligence Conference, AWIC 2003, Madrid, Spain, 2003*, LNAI 2663, pages 142–154. Springer Verlag, May 2003.

21. P. Pirolli, J. Pitkow, and R. Rao. Silk from a sow's ear: Extracting usable structures form the web. In *Proc. of CHI 96 Conference*. ACM Press, April 1996.

22. J. R. Punin, M. S. Krishnamoorthy, and M. J. Zaki. Logml: Log markup language for web usage mining. In R. Kohavi, B. Masand, M. Spiliopoulou, and J. Srivastava, editors, *WEBKDD 2001 - Mining Web Log Data Across All Customers Touch Points, Third International Workshop, San Francisco, CA, USA, August 26, 2001. Revised Papers*, volume 2356 of *Lecture Notes in Computer Science*, pages 88–112. Springer, 2002.

23. M. Spiliopoulou and L. Faulstich. Wum: A web utilization miner. In *Proceedings of the International Workshop on the Web and Databases*, Valencia, Spain, March 1998.

24. J. Srivastava, R. Cooley, M. Deshpande, and P.-N. Tan. Web usage mining: Discovery and applications of usage patterns from web data. *SIGKDD Explorations*, 1(2):12–23, 2000.

Boosting for Text Classification with Semantic Features

Stephan Bloehdorn[1] and Andreas Hotho[2]

[1] University of Karlsruhe, Germany
Institute AIFB, Knowledge Management Research Group
sbl@aifb.uni-karlsruhe.de
[2] University of Kassel, Germany
Knowledge and Data Engineering Group
hotho@cs.uni-kassel.de

Abstract. Current text classification systems typically use term stems for representing document content. Semantic Web technologies allow the usage of features on a higher semantic level than single words for text classification purposes. In this paper we propose such an enhancement of the classical document representation through concepts extracted from background knowledge. Boosting, a successful machine learning technique is used for classification. Comparative experimental evaluations in three different settings support our approach through consistent improvement of the results. An analysis of the results shows that this improvement is due to two separate effects.

1 Introduction

Most of the explicit knowledge assets of today's organizations consist of unstructured textual information in electronic form. Here, users are facing the challenge of organizing, analyzing and searching the ever growing amounts of documents. Systems that automatically classify text documents into predefined thematic classes and thereby contextualize information offer a promising approach to tackle this complexity [17]. During the last decades, a large number of machine learning methods have been proposed for text classification tasks. Recently, especially Support Vector Machines [9] and Boosting Algorithms [16] have produced promising results.

So far, however, existing text classification systems have typically used the *Bag-of-Words model* known from information retrieval, where single words or word stems are used as features for representing document content. In this approach, words or word stems are used as features and indicator variables, word frequencies or more elaborated weighting schemes like TFIDF are used as feature values [15]. By doing so, the chosen learning algorithms are restricted to detecting patterns in the used *terminology* only, while *conceptual* patterns remain ignored. Specifically, systems using only words as features exhibit a number of inherent deficiencies:

1. *Multi-Word Expressions* with an own meaning like *"European Union"* are chunked into pieces with possibly very different meanings like *"union"*.
2. *Synonymous Words* like *"tungsten"* and *"wolfram"* are mapped into different features.

B. Mobasher et al. (Eds.): WebKDD 2004, LNAI 3932, pp. 149–166, 2006.

3. *Polysemous Words* are treated as one single feature while they may actually have multiple distinct meanings.
4. *Lack of Generalization*: there is no way to generalize similar terms like "beef" and "pork" to their common hypernym "meat".

While items 1 – 3 directly address issues that arise on the lexical level, items 4 rather addresses an issue that is situated on a conceptual level.

In this paper, we show how *background knowledge* in form of simple ontologies can improve text classification results by directly addressing these problems. We propose a hybrid approach for document representation based on the common term stem representation which is enhanced with concepts extracted from the used ontologies. For actual classification we suggest to use the AdaBoost algorithm which has proven to produce accurate classification results in many experimental evaluations and seems to be well suited to integrate different types of features. Evaluation experiments on three different text corpora, namely the Reuters-21578, OHSUMED and FAODOC collections show that our approach leads to consistent improvements of the results. We also show that in most cases the improvement can be traced to two distinct effects, one being situated mainly on the lexical level and the generalization on the conceptual level.

This paper is organized as follows. We introduce some preliminaries, namely the classical bag-of-words document representation and ontologies in section 2. A detailed process for compiling conceptual features into an enhanced document representation is presented in section 3. In section 4 we review the AdaBoost algorithm and its inner workings. Evaluation Measures for text classification are reviewed in section 5. In the following, experimental evaluation results of our approach are presented for the Reuters-21578, OHSUMED, and FAODOC corpora under varying parameter combinations. It turns out that combined feature representations perform consistently better than the pure term-based approach. We review related work in section 7 and conclude with a summary and outlook in section 8.

2   Preliminaries

The Bag-Of-Words Paradigm In the common term-based representation, documents are considered to be bags of terms, each term being an independent feature of its own. Let D be the set of documents and $T = \{t_1, \ldots, t_m\}$ the set of all different terms occurring in D. For each term $t \in T$ in document $d \in D$ one can define feature values functions like binary indicator variables, absolute frequencies or more elaborated measures like TFIDF [15].

Typically, not the whole words are used as features. Instead, documents are processed with stemming algorithms, e.g. the Porter stemmer for English [14], first. In addition, *stopwords*, i.e. words which are considered as non–descriptive within a bag–of–words approach, are typically removed. In our experiments later on, we removed stopwords from T, using a standard list with 571 stopwords.

Ontologies. The background knowledge we have exploited is given through simple ontologies. We first describe the structure of these ontologies and then discuss their usage for the extraction of conceptual feature representations for text documents. The background knowledge we will exploit further on is encoded in a *core ontology*. For the purpose of this paper, we present only those parts of our more extensive ontology definition [2] that we need within this paper.

Definition 1 (Core Ontology). *A core ontology is a structure $\mathcal{O} := (C, <_C)$ consisting of a set C, whose elements are called concept identifiers, and a partial order $<_C$ on C, called concept hierarchy or taxonomy.*

Definition 2 (Subconcepts and Superconcepts). *If $c_1 <_C c_2$ for any $c_1, c_2 \in C$, then c_1 is a subconcept (specialization) of c_2 and c_2 is a superconcept (generalization) of c_1. If $c_1 <_C c_2$ and there exists no $c_3 \in C$ with $c_1 <_C c_3 <_C c_2$, then c_1 is a direct subconcept of c_2, and c_2 is a direct superconcept of c_1, denoted by $c_1 \prec c_2$.*

These specialization/generalization relationships correspond to what we know as is-a vs. is-a-special-kind-of, resulting in a hierarchical arrangement of concepts[1]. In ontologies that are more loosely defined, the hierarchy may, however, not be as explicit as is-a relationships but rather correspond to the notion of narrower-than vs. broader-than[2]

According to the international standard ISO 704, we provide names for the concepts which we will call 'sign' or 'lexical entries' to better describe the functions for which they are used.

Definition 3 (Lexicon for an Ontology). *A lexicon for an ontology $\mathcal{O}$ is a tuple $Lex := (S_C, Ref_C)$ consisting of a set S_C, whose elements are called signs for concepts (symbols), and a relation $Ref_C \subseteq S_C \times C$ called lexical reference for concepts, where $(c, c) \in Ref_C$ holds for all $c \in C \cap S_C$. Based on Ref_C, for $s \in S_C$ we define $Ref_C(s) := \{c \in C | (s, c) \in Ref_C\}$. Analogously, for $c \in C$ it is $Ref_C^{-1}(c) := \{s \in S_C | (s, c) \in Ref_C\}$. An ontology with lexicon is a pair $(\mathcal{O}, Lex)$ where $\mathcal{O}$ is an ontology and Lex is a lexicon for $\mathcal{O}$.*

Ontologies for the experimental evaluation. For the purpose of actual evaluation in the experiments, we have used three different resources, namely WordNet and the MeSH Tree Structures Ontology and the AGROVOC ontology.

Although not explicitly designed as an ontology, *WordNet* [13] largely fits into the ontology definitions given above. The WordNet database organizes simple words and multi-word expressions of different syntactic categories into so called *synonym sets (synsets)*, each of which represents an underlying concept and links these through semantic relations. The current version 2.0 of WordNet comprises a total of 115,424 synsets and 144,309 lexical index terms. The noun category, which was the main focus of our attention[3], contains nearly 70 % of the total synsets, links from 114,648 index

---

[1] Note that this hierarchical structure is not necessarily a tree structure. It may also be a *directed acyclic graph* possibly linking concepts to multiple superconcepts at the same time.

[2] In many settings this view is considered as bad practice as naturally leads to inconsistencies and/or errors when actually reasoning with ontologies. Obviously, this problem does not arise in the context of this work.

[3] Beside the noun category, we have also exploited verb synsets, however, without making use of any semantic links.

terms to 79,689 synsets in a total of 141,690 mappings. The collection of index terms in WordNet comprises base forms of terms and their exceptional derivations. The retrieval of base forms for inflected forms is guided by a set of category-specific morphological transformations, which ensure a high precision in the mapping of word forms to index words.

The MeSH Tree Structures Ontology is an ontology that has been compiled out of the Medical Subject Headings (MeSH) controlled vocabulary thesaurus of the United States National Library of Medicine (NLM). The ontology contains more than 22,000 concepts, each enriched with synonymous and quasi-synonymous language expressions. The underlying hierarchical structure is in large parts consistent with real hypernym relations but also comprises other forms of hierarchical arrangements. The ontology itself was ported into and accessed through the Karlsruhe Ontology and Semantic Web Infrastructure (KAON) infrastructure[4].

The third ontology that has been used is the AGROVOC ontology [11], based on AGROVOC, a multilingual agricultural thesaurus[5] developed by the United Nations Food and Agricultural Organization (FAO). In total, the ontology comprises 17,506 concepts from the agricultural domain. The lexicon contains label and synonym entries for each concept in English and six additional languages. The concept hierarchy in the AGROVOC ontology is based on **broader-term** relationships thus not necessarily on strict superconcept relations in some cases.

3   Conceptual Document Representation

To extract concepts from texts, we have developed a detailed process, that can be used with any ontology with lexicon. The overall process comprises five processing steps that are described in this section.

Candidate Term Detection.   Due to the existence of multi-word expressions, the mapping of terms to concepts cannot be accomplished by querying the lexicon directly for the single words in the document. We have addressed this issue by defining a candidate term detection strategy that builds on the basic assumption that finding the longest multi-word expressions that appear in the text and the lexicon will lead to a mapping to the most specific concepts. The candidate expression detection algorithm we have applied for this lookup procedure is given in algorithm 1[6].The algorithm works by moving a window over the input text, analyze the window content and either decrease the window size if unsuccessful or move the window further. For English, a window size of 4 is sufficient to detect virtually all multi-word expressions.

Syntactical Patterns.   Querying the lexicon directly for any expression in the window will result in many unnecessary searches and thereby in high computational requirements. Luckily, unnecessary search queries can be identified and avoided through an analysis of the part-of-speech (POS) tags of the words contained in the current window. Concepts are typically symbolized in texts within *noun phrases*. By defining appropriate

---

[4] see http://kaon.semanticweb.org/

[5] see http://www.fao.org/agrovoc/

[6] The algorithm here is an improved version of one proposed in [18].

Algorithm 1 The candidate expression detection algorithm

Input: document $d = \{w_1, w_2, \ldots, w_n\}$,
    $Lex = (S_C, Ref_C)$ and window size $k \geq 1$.
    $i \leftarrow 1$
    list L_s
    index-term s
    while $i \leq n$ **do**
      for $j = min(k, n - i + 1)$ to 1 **do**
        $s \leftarrow \{w_i \ldots w_{i+j-1}\})$
        if $s \in S_C$ **then**
          save s in L_s
          $i \leftarrow i + j$
          break
        else if $j = 1$ **then**
          $i \leftarrow i + j$
        end if
      end for
    end while
    return L_s

POS patterns and matching the window content against these, multi-word combinations that will surely not symbolize concepts can be excluded in the first hand and different syntactic categories can be disambiguated. Also, such patterns help to filter out expressions of another syntactical arrangement that might match a lexical entry but do not refer to a concept.

Morphological Transformations. Typically the lexicon will not contain all inflected forms of its entries. If the lexicon interface or separate software modules are capable of performing base form reduction on the submitted query string, queries can be processed directly. For example, this is the case with WordNet. If the lexicon, as in most cases, does not contain such functionalities, a simple fallback strategy can be applied. Here, a separate index of stemmed forms is maintained. If a first query for the inflected forms on the original lexicon turned out unsuccessful, a second query for the stemmed expression is performed.

Word Sense Disambiguation. Having detected a lexical entry for an expression, this does not necessarily imply a one-to-one mapping to a concept in the ontology. Although multi-word-expression support and pos pattern matching reduce ambiguity, there may arise the need to disambiguate an expression versus multiple possible concepts. The *word sense disambiguation (WSD)* task is a problem in its own right [8] and was not the focus of our work. In our experiments, we have used three simple strategies proposed in [7] to process polysemous lexical entries:

- The "all" strategy leaves actual disambiguation aside and uses all possible concepts.
- The "first" strategy exploits WordNet's capability to return synsets ordered with respect to usage frequency. This strategy chooses the most frequent concept in case of ambiguities.

- The "context" strategy performs disambiguation based on the degree of overlap of lexical entries for the semantic vicinity of candidate concepts and the document content as proposed in [7].

Generalization. The last step in the process is about going from the specific concepts found in the text to more general concept representations. Its principal idea is that if a term like 'arrythmia' appears, one does not only represent the document by the concept corresponding to 'arrythmia', but also by the concepts corresponding to 'heart disease' and 'cardiovascular Diseases' etc. up to a certain level of generality. This is realized by compiling, for every concept, all superconcept up to a maximal distance h into the concept representation. Note that the parameter h needs to be chosen carefully as climbing up the taxonomy too far is likely to obfuscating the concept representation.

4   Boosting

Boosting is a relatively young, yet extremely powerful machine learning technique. The main idea behind boosting algorithms is to combine multiple *weak learners* – classification algorithms that perform only slightly better than random guessing – into a powerful composite classifier.

Although being refined subsequently, the main idea of all boosting algorithms can be traced to the first practical boosting algorithm, AdaBoost [4], which we will concentrate on in this paper. AdaBoost and related algorithms have proved to produce extremely competitive results in many settings, most notably for text classification [16]. At the beginning, the inner workings of boosting algorithms were not well understood. Subsequent research in boosting algorithms made them rest on a well developed theoretical framework and has recently provided interesting links to other successful learning algorithms, most notably to Support Vector Machines, and to linear optimization techniques [12].

AdaBoost. The idea behind "boosting" weak learners stems from the observation that it is usually much easier to build many simple "rules of thumb" than a single highly complex decision rule. Very precise overall decisions can be achieved if these weak learners are appropriately combined.

This idea is reflected in the output of the boosting procedure: for AdaBoost the aggregate decisions are formed in an *additive model* of the form: $\hat{f}(x) = \text{sign}(\sum_{t=1}^{T} \alpha_t h_t(x))$ with $h_t : \mathbb{X} \to \{-1, 1\}$, $\alpha_t \in \mathbb{R}$, where α_t denotes the weight of the ensemble member h_t in the aggregate decision and where the output values $\hat{f}(x) \in \{1, -1\}$ denote positive and negative predictions respectively. In such a model, AdaBoost has to solve two questions: How should the set of base hypotheses h_t be determined ? How should the weights α_t determined, i.e. which base hypotheses should contribute more than others and how much ? The AdaBoost algorithm, described in algorithm 2 aims at coming up with an optimal parameter assignment for h_t and α_t.

AdaBoost maintains a set of weights D_t over the training instances $x_1 \ldots x_i \ldots x_n$. At each iteration step t, a base classifier is chosen that performs best on the *weighted* training instances. Based on the performance of this base classifier, the final weight

Algorithm 2 The AdaBoost algorithm.

Input: training sample $\mathcal{S}_{train} = \{(x_1, y_1), \ldots, (x_n, y_n)\}$
  with $(x_i, y_i) \in \mathbb{X} \times \{-1, 1\}$ and $y_i = f(x_i)$,
  number of iterations T.
Initialize: $D_1(i) = \frac{1}{n}$ for all $i = 1, \ldots, n$.
  for $t = 1$ to T **do**
    train base classifier h_t on weighted training set
    calculate the weighted training error:

$$\epsilon_t \leftarrow \sum_{i=1}^{n} D_t(i) \, I_{y_i \neq h_t(x_i)} \tag{1}$$

compute the optimal update step as:

$$\alpha_t \leftarrow \frac{1}{2} \ln \frac{1 - \epsilon_t}{\epsilon_t} \tag{2}$$

update the distribution as:

$$D_{t+1}(i) \leftarrow \frac{D_t(i) \, e^{-\alpha_t \, y_i \, h_t(x_i)}}{Z_t} \tag{3}$$

where Z_t is a normalization factor to ensure that $\sum_{i=1}^{n} D_{t+1}(i) = 1$
    if $\epsilon_t = 0$ or $\epsilon_t = \frac{1}{2}$ **then**
      break
    end if
  end for
Result: composite classifier given by:

$$\hat{f}(x) = \text{sign}\left(\hat{f}_{soft}(x)\right) = \text{sign}\left(\sum_{t=1}^{T} \alpha_t h_t(x)\right) \tag{4}$$

parameter α_t is calculated in equation (2) and the distribution weights D_{t+1} for the next iteration are updated. The weight update in equation (3) assigns higher weights to training instances that have been misclassified, while correctly classified instances will receive smaller weights in the next iteration. Thereby, AdaBoost kind of "focusing in" on those examples that are more difficult while the weight each base classifier receives in the final additive model depends on its performance on the weighted training set at the respective iteration step.

Weak Lerners for AdaBoost. In theory, AdaBoost can be used with *any* base learner capable of handling weighted training instances. Although the base classifiers are not restricted to belong to a certain classifier family, virtually all work with boosting algorithms has used the very simple class of *decision stumps* as base learners. In this presentation, we focus on simple indicator function decision stumps of the form

$$h(x) = \begin{cases} c & \text{if } x^j = 1 \\ -c & \text{else.} \end{cases} \tag{5}$$

with $c \in \{-1, 1\}$. A decision stump of this form takes binary features (e.g. word or concept occurrences) as inputs. The index j identifies a specific binary feature whose presence either supports a positive classification decision, i.e. $c = 1$ or a negative decision, i.e. $c = -1$.

5   Evaluation Metrics

A standard set of performance metrics is commonly used to assess classifier performance which we will review shortly in this section.

Classification Metrics. Given a set of test documents $S = \{x_1, \ldots, x_n\}$ with binary labels $\{y_1, \ldots, y_n\}$ where $y_i \in \{-1, 1\}$ codes the membership in a class in question. Given further a classifier $\hat{f}$ trained on an independent training set with $\hat{f}(x) \in \{-1, 1\}$ indicating the binary decisions of the classifier. Then the test sample can be partitioned into sets $S = S^+ \cup S^-$, i.e. the set of positive and negative test documents. These partitions can be decomposed further into $S^+ = TP \cup FN$ and $S^+ = FP \cup TN$ with: $TP = \{x_i \in S | \hat{f}(x_i) = 1 \land y_i = 1\}$, $FP := \{x_i \in S | \hat{f}(x_i) = 1 \land y_i = -1\}$, $TN := \{x_i \in S | \hat{f}(x_i) = -1 \land y_i = -1\}$ and $FN := \{x_i \in S | \hat{f}(x_i) = -1 \land y_i = 1\}$ called the sets of documents classified *true positive, false positive, true negative* and *false negative,* often referred to as the classification contingency table.

Based on these definitions, different evaluation measures have been defined [19]. Commonly used classification measures in text classification and information retrieval are the *classification error, precision, recall* and the F_β *measure*:

1. Classification Error

$$err(\hat{f}, S) := \frac{|FP| + |FN|}{|TP| + |FP| + |TN| + |FN|} . \tag{6}$$

2. Precision

$$prec(\hat{f}, S) := \frac{|TP|}{|TP| + |FP|} . \tag{7}$$

3. Recall

$$rec(\hat{f}, S) := \frac{|TP|}{|TP| + |FN|} . \tag{8}$$

4. F_1 measure

$$F_1(\hat{f}, S) := \frac{2 \, prec(\hat{f}, S) \, rec(\hat{f}, S)}{prec(\hat{f}, S) + rec(\hat{f}, S)} . \tag{9}$$

Ranking Metrics. The ensemble classifiers produced by AdaBoost are capable of returning a real-valued output $\hat{f}_{soft}(x) \in [-1, 1]$. The magnitude $|\hat{f}_{soft}(x)|$ reflects the "confidence" of the classifier in a decision and allows to rank documents. In such a scenario, a ranking metric has to evaluate how close the ordered list defined by $\hat{f}_{soft}(x)$ is to an ideal ordering which should put every positive document in front of every negative document. Consequently, a parameterized classifier $\hat{f}_k$ can be defined that returns

$\hat{f}_k(x) = 1$ if $\hat{f}_{soft}(x)$ ranks among the first k documents and $\hat{f}_k(x) = -1$ otherwise. On this basis, values for precision and recall can be calculated and tuned with respect to different values of k. When precision and recall coincide at some k, this value is called the break-even point (BEP). It can be shown that this is necessarily the case at $k = |\mathcal{S}^+|$[7].

Micro- and Macro Averaging. To average evaluation results over binary classifications on the per-class level, two conventional methods exist. The *macro-averaged* figures are meant to be averages on the class level and are calculated as simple averages of the scores achieved for the different classes. In contrast, *micro-averaged* figures are computed by summing the cells of per-class contingency tables together and then computing performance scores based on these global figures. These can consequently be seen as averages on the document level.

Statistical Significance Tests. Statistical significance tests are useful in order to verify to which extent the claim of an improvement can be backed by the observations on the test set. For the experiments we report in this paper, we focused on two statistical significance tests, a sign test ("S-test") and a paired t-test ("T-test") on an improvement of individual F_1 scores for the different classes that have been evaluated in each experiment described in detail in [20]. Note that neither of these two tests is "perfect" as both are based on different hypotheses. As a sign-test, the S-test is considered to be more robust against the influence of outliers, but may not be sufficiently sensitive as it ignores the absolute differences among the individual F_1 values. The T-test is much more sensitive but could be overly sensitive when facing highly unstable F_1 scores. Also note that both tests evaluate only improvements on F_1 values and on the macro level. Following common statistical practice, we have required a significance level $\alpha = 0.05$ is required for claiming an improvement to be *significant*. The significance level of $\alpha = 0.01$ was used for the claim that an improvement was *very significant*.

6 Experiments

The focus of our evaluation experiments was directed towards comparing whether AdaBoost using the enhanced document representation would outperform the classical term representation.

6.1 Evaluation on the Reuters-21578 Corpus

A first set of evaluation experiments was conducted on the well-known Reuters-21578 collection. We used the "ModApte" split which divides the collection into 9,603 training documents, 3,299 test documents and 8,676 unused documents.

---

[7] This follows from the fact that if there are m negative documents among the first $|\mathcal{S}^+|$ documents in the ranked list, there must also be exactly m positive examples in the remainder of the list, thus: $FP_k = FN_k = m$, which guarantees precision and recall to be equal according to the formulas given above.

Experimental Setup. In the first stage of the experiment, terms and concepts were extracted as features from the documents in the training and test corpus. For terms, the feature extraction stage consisted of the stages described in section 2, namely chunking, removal of the standard stopwords for English defined in the SMART stopword list and stemming using the porter stemming algorithm, resulting in a total number of 17,525 distinct term features. Conceptual features were then extracted for noun and verb phrases using WordNet as background ontology. Different sets of concept features were extracted based on varying parameters for disambiguation strategy and maximal hypernym distance ranging from 10,259 to 27,236 distinct concept features.

In the next stage of the experiment, classification was performed using AdaBoost. We performed binary classification on the top 50 categories containing the highest number of positive training documents. The number of boosting iterations for training was fixed at 200 rounds for all feature combinations.

Results. As a general finding, the results obtained in the experiments suggest that AdaBoost typically achieves better classification for both macro- and micro-averaged results when used with a combination of term-based and concept-based features. Table 1 summarizes the results of the experiments for different feature types with the best values being highlighted. The relative gains on the F_1 value, which is influenced both by precision and recall, compared to the baseline show that in all but one cases the performance can be improved by including conceptual features, peaking at an relative improvement of 3.29 % for macro-averaged values and 2.00 % for micro-averaged values. Moderate improvements are achieved through simple concept integration, while larger improvements are achieved in most cases through additional integration of more general concepts.

The results of the significance tests allow us to conclude that these improvements are significant in at least half of the cases. In general, the improvements of macro-averaged F_1 are higher than with micro-averaging which seems to suggest that the additional concepts are particularly helpful for smaller classes.

6.2   Evaluation on the OHSUMED Corpus

A second series of experiments was conducted using the OHSUMED collection, initially compiled by Hersh et al. [6]. It consists of titles and abstracts from medical journals, each being indexed with multiple MeSH descriptors. We have used the 1987 portion of the collection containing a total of 54,708 entries. Two thirds of the entries were randomly selected as training documents while the remainder was used as test set, resulting in a training corpus containing 36,369 documents and a test corpus containing 18,341 documents.

Experimental Setup. Term stems were extracted as with Reuters-21578 resulting in a total number of 38,047 distinct features. WordNet and the MeSH Tree Structures Ontology were used to extract conceptual features. For WordNet, noun and verb phrases were considered while for the MeSH Tree Structures Ontology, only noun phrases were considered. For WordNet, the same disambiguation strategies were used as in the Reuters-21578 experiments. For the MeSH Tree Structures Ontology, only the "all" strategy

Table 1. Experimental Results on the top 50 Reuters-21578 Categories. All numbers are percentages. The three best values per column are highlighted.

Feature Type	Error	macro-averaged (in percentages)			
		Prec	Rec	F_1	BEP
term	00.65	80.59	66.30	72.75	74.29
term & synset.first	00.64	80.66	67.39	73.43	75.08
term & synset.first.hyp5	00.60	80.67	**69.57**	74.71	74.84
term & synset.first.hyp10	00.62	80.43	68.40	73.93	**75.58**
term & synset.context	00.63	79.96	68.51	73.79	74.46
term & synset.context.hyp5	00.62	79.48	68.34	73.49	74.71
term & synset.all	00.64	80.02	66.44	72.60	73.62
term & synset.all.hyp5	**00.59**	**83.76**	68.12	**75.14**	75.55

Feature Type	Error	micro-averaged (in percentages)			
		Prec	Rec	F_1	BEP
term	00.65	89.12	79.82	84.21	85.77
term & synset.first	00.64	88.75	80.79	84.58	85.97
term & synset.first.hyp5	00.60	89.16	**82.46**	85.68	85.91
term & synset.first.hyp10	00.62	88.78	81.74	85.11	86.14
term & synset.context	00.63	88.86	81.46	85.00	85.91
term & synset.context.hyp5	00.62	89.09	81.40	85.07	85.97
term & synset.all	00.64	88.82	80.99	84.72	85.69
term & synset.all.hyp5	**00.59**	**89.92**	82.21	**85.89**	**86.44**

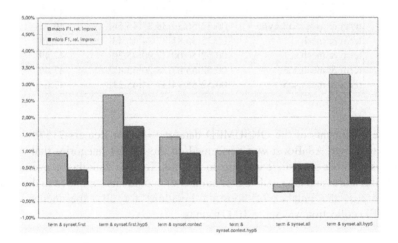

Fig. 1. Bar Chart Illustration of the Relative Improvements of F_1 Scores on the top 50 Reuters-21578 Categories for combined Term-Synset Features vs. 'term'. All numbers are percentages.

was used due to the observation that polysemy problems occur extremely rarely with this ontology as descriptor terms are most naturally unique. For both ontologies, different degrees of depth were used for hypernym or superconcept integration, resulting in a total of 16,442 to 34,529 synset features and 11,572 to 13,663 MeSH concept features.

Table 2. Experimental Results on the top 50 OHSUMED Categories with WordNet and MeSH as Background Knowledge Resources. All numbers are percentages. The three best values per column are highlighted.

Feature Type	Error	macro-averaged (in percentages)			
		Prec	Rec	F_1	BEP
term	00.53	52.60	35.74	42.56	45.68
term & synset.first	00.52	53.08	36.98	43.59	46.46
term & synset.first.hyp5	00.52	53.82	38.66	45.00	48.01
term & synset.context	00.52	52.83	37.09	43.58	46.88
term & synset.context.hyp5	**00.51**	**54.55**	**39.06**	**45.53**	**48.10**
term & synset.all	00.52	52.89	37.09	43.60	46.82
term & synset.all.hyp5	00.52	53.33	38.24	44.42	46.73
term & mesh	00.52	53.65	37.56	44.19	47.31
term & mesh.sc1	00.52	52.91	37.59	43.95	46.93
term & mesh.sc3	00.52	52.77	38.06	44.22	46.90
term & mesh.sc5	00.52	52.72	37.57	43.87	47.16

Feature Type	Error	micro-averaged (in percentages)			
		Prec	Rec	F_1	BEP
term	00.53	55.77	36.25	43.94	46.17
term & synset.first	00.52	56.07	37.30	44.80	47.01
term & synset.first.hyp5	00.52	56.84	38.76	46.09	48.31
term & synset.context	00.52	56.30	37.46	44.99	47.34
term & synset.context.hyp5	**00.51**	**58.10**	**39.18**	**46.81**	**48.45**
term & synset.all	00.52	56.19	37.44	44.94	47.32
term & synset.all.hyp5	00.52	56.29	38.24	45.54	46.73
term & mesh	00.52	56.81	37.84	45.43	47.78
term & mesh.sc1	00.52	56.00	37.90	45.20	47.49
term & mesh.sc3	00.52	55.87	38.26	45.42	47.45
term & mesh.sc5	00.52	55.94	37.94	45.21	47.63

On the documents of the OHSUMED dataset — as on Reuters-21578 — binary classification with AdaBoost was performed on the top 50 categories that contained the highest number of positive training documents. To cope with the on average larger number of features and the much higher number of documents compared to the Reuters-21578 corpus, the number of boosting iterations for all experiments with the OHSUMED collection was set to 1000 rounds.

Results. Different runs of the classification stage were performed based on the different features, leading to often substantially different results. Again, the general finding is that complementing the term stem representation with conceptual features significantly improves classification performance.

Table 2 summarizes the macro- and micro-averaged results. The relative improvements for the F_1 scores compared to the term stem baseline are depicted in figure 6.2 for WordNet as background knowledge resource. These range from about 2% to a maximum of about 7 %. The relative F_1 improvements when using the MeSH Tree Structure Ontology, were on the 3% to 5% level in all cases. The statistical significance tests revealed that in virtually all cases, these improvements can be claimed to be significant and actually even very significant in most cases.

Again, the integration of conceptual features improved text classification results. The relative improvements achieved on OHSUMED are generally higher than those achieved on the Reuters-21578 corpus. This makes intuitively sense as the documents in the OHSUMED corpus are taken from the medical domain. Documents from this domain typically suffer heavily from the problems described in section 2, especially synonymous terms and multi-word expressions. But this is only a first effect. The even better results achieved through hypernym integration with WordNet indicate that also the highly specialized language is a problem that can be remedied through integration of more general concepts.

A comparison between WordNet and the MeSH Descriptor Ontology is hard. On the one hand, without generalization, the domain specific MeSH Tree Structures Ontology is able to achieve slightly better results. Taking into account that the extraction was here bases solely on noun phrases and that WordNet's coverage is much broader, this is a positive surprise. On the other hand, WordNet achieves much better results when generalization comes into play. In contrast to WordNet, superconcept integration for MeSH does not really improve the results and varying levels of superconcept integration lead to similar or even worse results. Apparently, the broader-term relation of the MeSH thesaurus is indeed not well suited to improve the results. Also note that in contrast to the Reuters-21578 experiments, "context" word sense disambiguation strategy performs best in combination with hypernym integration. Apparently, it is easier to disambiguate polysemous words in the medical context.

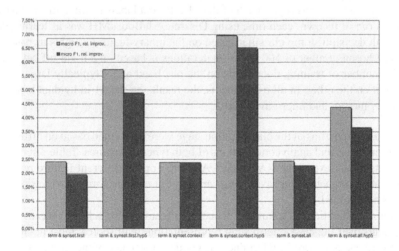

Fig. 2. Relative Improvements of F_1 Scores on OHSUMED for combined Term-Synset Features vs. Term Stems

6.3   Evaluation on the FAODOC Corpus

The third and last series of experiments uses a collection of documents from the FAO Document Online Catalogue (FAODOC)[8], managed by the United Nations Food and Agricultural Organization. The FAODOC database houses articles and other publications from the agricultural domain together with metadata information, including subject and category elements.

Experimental Setup. The FAODOC collection contains English, French and Spanish HTML documents. All documents are indexed with one or multiple category codes, each of which refers to one of 115 FAODOC subject categories (details in [11]). In the experiments, only the subset of English documents has been used where each of the categories has at least 50 positive documents. In total, this document set contains 1 501 HTML documents each indexed with one to three labels from 21 distinct subject categories. From the total number of 1 501 documents, the first 1 000 documents were used for training while the remainder of 501 documents were held out as test set.

The FAODOC dataset is very different from the other datasets encountered so far. Besides being taken from a different domain, the total number of documents is much smaller. The documents in the FAODOC dataset are typically much larger in size, ranging from 1.5 kilobytes to over 600 kilobytes, which is also reflected in the resulting feature representations with 68 608 word stems. Besides the extraction of term stems as usual, conceptual features were extracted again, this time using the AGROVOC ontology as background knowledge resource. For both types of features, the documents were first converted from HTML to plain text, then proceeding in the same way as with the documents in the other corpora. Again as by the OHSUMED corpus only the all strategy was apply to disambiguate word stems if necessary.

As in the other experiments, each of the 21 different labels resulted in a binary classification run of its own, each time using DiscreteAdaBoost.MH was as learning algorithm with decision stump classifier based on the binary feature weights as base learners. The chosen number of 500 boosting iterations is based on a trade-off between the smaller number of training documents on the one hand and a typically larger size per document on the other. In all experiments, the results on the 21 individual labels were eventually macro- and micro-averaged.

Results. Different runs of the classification stage were performed based on different features: term stems and again combinations of both types of features. Table 3 summarizes the results of the experiments with the FAODOC for the different feature representations, evaluation metrics and averaging variants. For each performance metric, the best result is highlighted.

Again, combinations of terms and concepts as features also achieve considerable improvements over the classic term stem representation in all scores, most notably in respect to precision. Figure 3 undermines the good performance of the term and 'agrovoc' concept representation achieving a maximum relative improvement of 10.54 % on the macro-averaged F_1 value compared to the 'term' representation. The maximum relative improvement on the micro-averaged F_1 lies at 4.33 %. Again, one observes a heavy

---

[8] See http://www4.fao.org/faobib/index.html

Table 3. Experimental Results on all 21 FAODOC Categories. All numbers are percentages. Only the best values per column are highlighted.

| Feature Type | Error | macro-averaged | | | |
		Prec	Rec	F_1	BEP
term	06.87	45.47	27.11	33.97	36.93
term & agrovoc	**06.66**	**50.96**	28.63	36.66	39.84
term & agrovoc.sc1	06.76	49.26	27.48	35.28	39.40
term & agrovoc.sc3	06.79	49.08	**30.41**	**37.55**	**41.69**

| Feature Type | Error | micro-averaged | | | |
		Prec	Rec	F_1	BEP
term	06.87	50.44	31.22	38.57	44.29
term & agrovoc	**06.66**	**52.91**	32.46	**40.24**	**48.01**
term & agrovoc.sc1	06.76	51.75	**32.60**	40.00	46.77
term & agrovoc.sc3	06.79	51.47	31.36	38.97	47.73

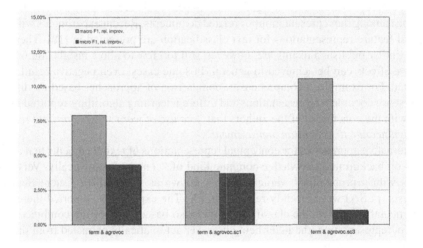

Fig. 3. Bar Chart Illustration of the Relative Improvements of F_1 Scores on all 21 FAODOC Categories for combined Term-Concept Representations vs. 'term'. All numbers are percentages.

discrepancy between the macro- and micro-averaged scores. Again, macro-averaged performance gains are higher than those for micro-averaging, which makes sense taking into account the fairly unequal category sizes. In contrast to the other experiments, the amount of deviation however varies considerably among the different feature representations. Furthermore, the question which superconcept integration depth leads to the best improvement cannot be answered easily because the effects vary considerably between micro- and macro-averaging.

The inconsistent results on the FAODOC collection could be attributed to the fact that random effects are much likelier compared to the other experiments as the number of training and test documents is considerably smaller. This is one reason that significance testing has not been conducted for the set of experiments with the FAODOC collection.

Another reason is that the smaller number of categories would also lead to a worse reliability of the tests.

7   Related Work

Representing document content through metadata descriptions is a well-known task in the semantic web context, also known as annotation[5]. Typically, however, this is a semi-automatic task that aims at precise metadata descriptions and not at creating features for machine learning algorithms.

To date, the work on integrating semantic background knowledge into text classification or other related tasks is quite scattered. Much of the early work with semantic background knowledge in information retrieval was done in the context of *query expansion* techniques [1]. Feature representations based on concepts from ontological background knowledge were also used in text clustering settings [7] where it could be shown that conceptual representations can significantly improve text cluster purity and reduce the variance among the representations of related documents. Recent experiments with conceptual feature representations for text classification are presented in [18]. These and other similar published results are, however, still too few to allow insights on whether positive effects can be achieved in general. In some cases, even negative results were reported. For example, a comprehensive comparison of approaches based on different word-sense document representations and different learning algorithms reported in [10] ends with the conclusion of the authors that *"the use of word senses does not result in any significant categorization improvement"*.

Alternative approaches for conceptual representations of text documents that are not based on background knowledge compute kind of "concepts" statistically. Very good results with a probabilistic variant of LSA known as Probabilistic Latent Semantic Analysis (pLSA) were recently reported in [3]. The experiments reported therein are of particular interest as the classification was also based on boosting combined term-concept representation, the latter being however automatically extracted from the document corpus using pLSA.

8   Conclusions

In this paper, we have proposed an approach to incorporate concepts from background knowledge into document representations for text document classification. A very successful ensemble learning algorithm, AdaBoost, was proposed to perform the final classifications based on the classical word vector representations and the conceptual features. Boosting Algorithms, when used with binary feature representations, scale well to a large number of dimensions that typically occur when superconcepts are used as well. At the same time, AdaBoost is capable of integrating heterogenous features that are based on different paradigms without having to adjust any parameters in the feature space representation.

Experiments on three different datasets clearly showed that the integration of concepts into the feature representation clearly improves classification results. The absolute scores achieved on Reuters and OHSUMED are highly competitive with other published results and the reported relative improvements appear to be statistically significant in most cases. A comparative analysis of the improvements for different concept integration strategies revealed that two separate effects lead to these improvements. A first effect that can be mainly attributed to multi-word expression detection and synonym conflation is achieved through the basic concept integration. A second effect building on this initial improvement is attributed to the use of the ontology structures for generalization through hypernym retrieval and integration.

Outlook. The experiments that have been conducted show that the presented approach appears to be promising in most settings. However it has also become obvious that the results depend on the specific constellation of parameters. These include — most importantly — the choice of the appropriate ontology. Further research and experiments should investigate how the specific choice and setup of the used ontologies can lead to even better results and wether other concept extraction strategies lead to a further improvement in classification performance.

At the same time the focus of our approach can be extended towards including other groups of ontological entities like relations and instances. It has been mentioned that feature extraction for machine learning and metadata annotation[5] have many things in common. Future work will also analyze, how results for documents that are already enriched with metadata will evolve in the classification context. Future work will also pay attention to the setup of the classification algorithm as the general nature of AdaBoost would allow to integrate more advanced weak learners which might also exploit background knowledge even more directly.

Acknowledgements

This research was partially supported by the European Commission under contracts FP6-001765 aceMedia and IST-2003-506826 SEKT. The expressed content is the view of the authors but not necessarily the view of the project consortia.

References

1. R. C. Bodner and F. Song. Knowledge-Based Approaches to Query Expansion in Information Retrieval. In *Advances in Artificial Intelligence*. Springer, New York, NY, USA, 1996.
2. E. Bozsak et al. KAON – Towards a Large Scale Semantic Web. In *Proc. of the 3rd International Conference on E-Commerce and Web Technologies (EC-Web 2002)*, pages 304–313, Aix-en-Provence, France, 2002. LNCS 2455 Springer.
3. L. Cai and T. Hofmann. Text Categorization by Boosting Automatically Extracted Concepts. In *Proc. of the 26th Annual Int. ACM SIGIR Conference on Research and Development in Informaion Retrieval*, Toronto, Canada, 2003. ACM Press.
4. Y. Freund and R. E. Schapire. A Decision Theoretic Generalization of On-Line Learning and an Application to Boosting. In *Second European Conference on Computational Learning Theory (EuroCOLT-95)*, pages 23–37, 1995.
5. S. Handschuh and S. Staab, editors. *Annotation for the Semantic Web*. IOS Press, 2003.

6. W. R. Hersh, C. Buckley, T. J. Leone, and D. H. Hickam. Ohsumed: An Interactive Retrieval Evealuation and new large Test Collection for Research. In *Proceedings of the 17th Annual International ACM SIGIR Conference on Research and Development in Informaion Retrieval*. ACM Press, 1994.

7. A. Hotho, S. Staab, and G. Stumme. Wordnet improves Text Document Clustering. In *Proc. of the Semantic Web Workshop of the 26th Annual International ACM SIGIR Conference*, Toronto, Canada, 2003.

8. N. Ide and J. Véronis. Introduction to the Special Issue on Word Sense Disambiguation: The State of the Art. *Computational Linguistics*, 24(1):1–40, 1998.

9. T. Joachims. Text Categorization with Support Vector Machines: Learning With Many Relevant Features. In *Proceedings of ECML-98*, 1998.

10. A. Kehagias, V. Petridis, V. G. Kaburlasos, and P. Fragkou. A Comparison of Word- and Sense-Based Text Categorization Using Several Classification Algorithms. *Journal of Intelligent Information Systems*, 21(3):227–247, 2000.

11. B. Lauser. Semi-Automatic Ontology Engineering and Ontology Supported Document Indexing in a Multilingual Environment. Master's thesis, University of Karlsruhe, 2003.

12. R. Meir and G. Rätsch. An Introduction to Boosting and Leveraging. In *Advanced Lectures on Machine Learning*, LNCS. Springer, Heidelberg, DE, 2003.

13. G. A. Miller, C. Fellbaum, D. Gross, and K. J. Miller. Introduction to WordNet: an On-Line Lexical Database. *International Journal of Lexicography*, 3(4):235–244, 1990.

14. M. F. Porter. An algorithm for suffix stripping. *Program*, 14(3):130–137, 1980.

15. G. Salton. *Automatic Text Processing*. Addison-Wesley Publishing Inc, Boston, MA, USA, 1989.

16. R. E. Schapire and Y. Singer. BoosTexter: A Boosting-based System for Text Categorization. *Machine Learning*, 39(2/3):135–168, 2000.

17. F. Sebastiani. Machine Learning in Automated Text Categorization. *ACM Computing Surveys*, 34(1):1–47, 2002.

18. B. B. Wang, R. I. Mckay, H. A. Abbass, and M. Barlow. A comparative study for domain ontology guided feature extraction. In *Proceedings of the 26th Australian Computer Science Conference (ACSC-2003)*, pages 69–78. Australian Computer Society, 2003.

19. Y. Yang. An Evaluation of Statistical Approaches to Text Categorization. *Information Retrieval*, 1(1-2):69–90, 1999.

20. Y. Yang and X. Liu. A re-examination of text categorization methods. In *Proceedings of SIGIR-99, 22nd ACM International Conference on Research and Development in Information Retrieval*, Berkeley, CA, 1999.

Markov Blankets and Meta-heuristics Search: Sentiment Extraction from Unstructured Texts

Edoardo Airoldi[1], Xue Bai[1,2,*], and Rema Padman[2]

[1] School of Computer Science
Carnegie Mellon University, Pittsburgh, PA USA, 15213
eairoldi@cs.cmu.edu
[2] The John Heinz III School of Public Policy and Management
Carnegie Mellon University, Pittsburgh, PA USA 15213
{xbai, rpadman}@andrew.cmu.edu

Abstract. Extracting sentiments from unstructured text has emerged as an important problem in many disciplines. An accurate method would enable us, for example, to mine online opinions from the Internet and learn customers' preferences for economic or marketing research, or for leveraging a strategic advantage. In this paper, we propose a two-stage Bayesian algorithm that is able to capture the dependencies among words, and, at the same time, finds a vocabulary that is efficient for the purpose of extracting sentiments. Experimental results on online movie reviews and online news show that our algorithm is able to select a parsimonious feature set with substantially fewer predictor variables than in the full data set and leads to better predictions about sentiment orientations than several state-of-the-art machine learning methods. Our findings suggest that sentiments are captured by conditional dependence relations among words, rather than by keywords or high-frequency words.

1 Introduction

Traditionally, researchers have used surveys to collect limited amounts of data in a structured form for their analyses. In recent years, the advent of the Internet, and the widespread use of advanced information technologies in general, have resulted in a surge of information that is freely available online in an *unstructured format*. For example, many discussion groups and review sites exist where people post their opinions about a product. The automatic understanding of *sentiments* expressed within the texts of such posts could lead to a number of new applications in the fields of marketing and information retrieval, and could enable the automated learning of elements of ontologies from online data, e.g., the "trustable level" of the trust ontology [1].

Researchers have been investigating the problem of automatic text categorization for the past two decades. Satisfactory solutions have been found for the cases of topic categorization and of authorship attribution; briefly, topics are captured

---

* Corresponding author.

B. Mobasher et al. (Eds.): WebKDD 2004, LNAI 3932, pp. 167–187, 2006.

by sets of keywords, whereas authors are identified by their choices about the use of non-contextual, high-frequency words [2]. Pang et al [3] showed that such solutions, or extensions of them, underperform when ported to sentiment extraction, yielding cross-validated accuracies and areas under the curve (AUC) in the high 70%s to low 80%s. Even more worrisome is the fact that these performances are obtained using large vocabularies, whose words' discriminatory power is likely to be due to chance for many of the words. We conjecture that one reason for the failure of such approaches maybe attributed to the fact that the words used in the classification are *selected independently* of one another, whereas we argue that their very interactions lead to the emergence of sentiments in the text. The goal of this paper is to present a machine learning technique for learning predominant sentiments of online texts, available in unstructured format, that:

- is capable of selecting words that are related to one another and to the sentiment embedded in the texts significantly, i.e., beyond pure chance, and
- is capable of finding a minimal vocabulary that leads to good performance in categorization and prediction tasks.

Our two-stage Markov Blanket Classifier (MBC) learns conditional dependencies among the words and encodes them into a *Markov Blanket Directed Acyclic Graph* (MB DAG) for the sentiment variable (first stage), and then uses a *Tabu Search* (TS) meta-heuristic strategy to fine tune the MB DAG (second stage) in order to yield a higher cross-validated accuracy. Learning dependencies allows us to capture semantic relations and dependent patterns among the words, which help us approximate the meaning of sentences with respect to the sentiment they encode. Further, performing the classification task using a Markov Blanket (MB) for the sentiment variable (in a Bayesian network) has important properties: (a) it specifies a statistically efficient prediction of the probability distribution of the sentiment variable from the smallest subset of predictors, and (b) it provides accuracy while avoiding over-fitting due to redundant predictors. We test our algorithm on the publicly available "movie reviews" data set [4] and on three proprietary corpora of online news with different degrees of topicality [5], and achieve a cross-validated accuracy and AUC comparable to the best performances of competing state-of-the-art classifiers, with an extremely parsimonious vocabulary.

This paper is organized as follows: Section 2 surveys related work. Section 3 provides some background about Bayesian networks, Markov Blankets, and Tabu Search. Section 4 contains details about our proposed methodology. Section 5 describes the data and presents the experimental results. Last, Section 6 discusses of our findings and Section 7 concludes.

2   Related Work on Sentiments

The problem of sentiment extraction is also referred to as opinion extraction or semantic classification in the literature. A related problem is that of studying the semantic orientation, or polarity, of words as defined by Osgood et al. [6].

Hatzivassiloglou and McKeown [7] built a log-linear model to predict the semantic orientation of conjoined adjectives using the conjunctions between them. Huettner and Subasic [8] hand-crafted a cognitive linguistic model for *affection* sentiments based on fuzzy logic. Das and Chen [9] used domain knowledge to manually construct lexicon and grammar rules that aim at capturing the "pulse" of financial markets as expressed by online news about traded stocks. They categorized news as *buy, sell* or *neutral* using five classifiers and various voting schemes to achieve an accuracy of 62% (random guesses would top 33%). Turney and Littman [10] proposed a compelling semi-supervised method to learn the polarity of adjectives starting from a small set of adjectives of known polarity, and Turney [11] used this method to predict the opinions of consumers about various objects (movies, cars, banks) and achieved accuracies between 66% and 84%. Pang et al. [3] used off-the-shelf classification methods on frequent, non-contextual words in combination with various heuristics and annotators, and achieved a maximum cross-validated accuracy of 82.9% on data from IMDB. Dave et al. [12] categorized positive versus negative movie reviews using support vector machines on various types of semantic features based on substitutions and proximity, and achieved an accuracy of at most 88.9% on data from Amazon and Cnn.Net. Liu et al. [13] proposed a framework to categorize emotions based on a large dictionary of common sense knowledge and on linguistic models.

3   Problem - Background

We introduce the problem and briefly discuss its scope in Section 3.1. We review concepts relevant to our methodology in Sections 3.2 and 3.3; specifically we review Bayesian networks, Markov blankets, and Tabu search.

3.1   Problem Definition

Our problem can be formally stated as a typical classification problem. Briefly, our data consists of a collection of N documents, $\{y_d, x_{d1}, ...x_{dV}\}_{d=1}^{N}$, that is, of N examples of the corresponding random variables, $\{Y, X_1, ...X_V\}$. The overall sentiment of each document d is encoded by the variable $Y = y_d$, which can take one of a finite number of sentiment values ($y_d = s$, $s = 0, ..., S$). The index w identifies a unique word in the vocabulary, and V denotes the size of the vocabulary observed in the collection of N documents. Each of the variables $\{X_w\}_{w=1}^{V}$ encodes the presence or absence of word w in document d, i.e., $x_{dw} \in \{0, 1\}$ for $d = 1, ..., N$.

Problem (Sentiment Classification). Given a collection of N documents, $\{x_{d1}, ...x_{dV}\}_{d=1}^{N} \in \{0, 1\}^V$, along with an indication of the corresponding sentiments they encode, $\{y_d\}_{d=1}^{N} \in [0, S]$, we want to learn a classifier that predicts the overall sentiments of new documents, $f : \{0, 1\}^V \to [0, S]$, with high accuracy. Documents may show different degrees of topicality.

Note that, although the mathematical formulation of the problem is that of a typical (supervised) classification problem, its most interesting characteristic is

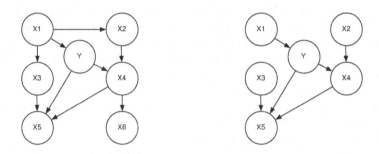

Fig. 1. (left) A sample Bayesian Network (S, P), and (right) the Markov Blanket for the variable encoding the overall sentiment of a document, Y

not expressed by the Xs and Ys alone: that is, sentiments are complex semantic elements hardly expressible by mere *independent* presence/absence of words. We develop a methodology to capture *dependent* word presence/absence patterns.

3.2   Bayesian Networks and Markov Blankets

A *Bayesian Network* is a graphical representation of the joint probability distribution of a set of random variables. A Bayesian Network for a set of variables $X = \{X_1, ..., X_V\}$ consists of: (i) a directed acyclic graph (DAG) S that encodes a set of conditional independence assertions among variables in X; (ii) a set $P = \{p_1, ..., p_V\}$ of local conditional probability distributions associated with each node and its parents. A Bayesian Network also has a causal interpretation: a directed edge from one variable to another, $X \to Y$, represents the claim that X is a direct cause of Y with respect to other variables in the DAG [14,15].

Definition 1. *P satisfies the Markov Condition for S if every node X_i in S is independent of its non-descendants and non-parents in S, conditional on its parents.*

The Markov Condition implies that the joint distribution p can be factorized as a product of conditional probabilities, by specifying the distribution of each node conditional on its parents [15]. In particular, for a given structure S, the joint probability distribution for X can be written as

$$P(X) = \prod_{i=1}^{V} P_i(X_i | pa_i),   \tag{1}$$

where pa_i denotes the set of parents of X_i; this is called a Markov factorization of P according to S.

Definition 2. *Given the set of variables X and target variable Y, a Markov Blanket (MB) for Y is the smallest subset Q of variables in X such that Y is independent of $X \backslash Q$, conditional on the variables in Q.*

Assuming that there are no conditional independence relations in P other than those entailed by the Markov condition for S, then for a given Bayesian Network (S, P), there is a unique Markov Blanket for Y consisting of pa_Y, the set of parents of Y; ch_Y, the set of children of Y; and $pa\,ch_Y$, the set of parents of children of Y.

For example, consider the two DAGs in Figure 1. The factorization of p entailed by the Bayesian Network (S, P) is the following,

$$P(Y, X_1, ..., X_6) = P_Y(Y|X_1)\, P_4(X_4|X_2, Y)\, P_5(X_5|X_3, X_4, Y)\, P_2(X_2|X_1) \times \atop \times P_3(X_3|X_1)\, P_6(X_6|X_4)\, P_1(X_1). \tag{2}$$

Instead, the factorization of the conditional probability entailed by the Markov Blanket for Y, $P(Y|X_1, ..., X_6)$, corresponds to the product of those (local) factors in equation 2 that contain the term Y,

$$P(Y|X_1, ..., X_6) = C'\, P_Y(Y|X_1)\, P_4(X_4|X_2, Y)\, P_5(X_5|X_3, X_4, Y), \tag{3}$$

where C' is a normalizing constant independent of Y.

Definition 3. *MB$_{DAG}$s that entail the same set of conditional independence relations are said to be Markov equivalent; and the set of all MB$_{DAG}$s that are Markov equivalent form a Markov equivalence class.*

3.3   Tabu Search Heuristic

Tabu Search is a meta-heuristic search strategy that is able to guide traditional local search methods to escape the trap of local optimality with the assistance of *adaptive memory* [16]. Tabu search is viewed as "intelligent" search because it makes use of adaptive memory. The adaptive memory feature of TS allows the implementation of procedures that are capable of searching the solution space economically and effectively. In its simplest form, Tabu Search starts with a feasible solution and chooses the *best move* according to an evaluation function while taking steps to ensure that the method does not revisit a solution previously generated. This is accomplished by introducing *tabu restrictions* on possible moves to discourage the reversal and in some cases repetition of selected moves. The *tabu list* that contains these forbidden move attributes is known as the short term memory function. It operates by modifying the search trajectory to exclude moves leading to new solutions that contain attributes (or attribute mixes) belonging to solutions previously visited within a time horizon governed by the short term memory. Intermediate and long-term memory functions may also be incorporated to intensify and diversify the search.

4   Methods: A Markov Blanket for Word Patterns

In this section we describe our methodology and the intuitions behind it. A sketch of the various algorithms described here can be found in Appendix A.

LrnTSMBC $(\{x_{d1}, ..., x_{dV}\}, \{y_d\}, \delta, \alpha)$

1. $L_Y = $ **Adj** $(\{y_d\}, \{x_{d1}, ..., x_{dV}\}, \delta, \alpha)$
2. **for** $X_i \in L_Y$
   2.1. $L_{X_i} = $ **Adj** $(\{x_{di}\}, \{x_{d1}, ..., x_{dV}\}\backslash x_{di}, \delta, \alpha)$
3. $G = $ **Ornt** $(Y \cup L_Y \cup_i L_{X_i})$
4. $\{MB_{DAG}(Y), L\} = $ **Trsfm** (G)
5. **TabuSrch** $(MB_{DAG}(Y), L, Max_{Iter})$

Fig. 2. Overview of the algorithm underlying the Tabu-Search-enhanced Markov Blanket Classifier. The relevant parameters are: a data set with V words and N documents; Y, the sentiment variable; δ, the maximum size of separating sets of words considered for the conditional independence tests; α, the significance level for the G^2 statistical independence tests. See the text for more details.

4.1 Markov Blanket Classifier at a Glance

The goal of the *Markov blanket classifier* (MBC) is two-fold: (1) to find a parsimonious vocabulary that is expressive enough to capture the overall sentiment of a document, and (2) to find a dependency structure among words in the vocabulary and the sentiment variable that leads to good predictions of the overall sentiment of a new document. Figure 2 presents an overview of the algorithm that we employ to learn the Tabu-Search-enhanced Markov Blanket Classifier.

The learning algorithm can be divided into two stages. In the **first stage** (steps 1. to 4.), the collection of training documents, D, is used to generate an *initial* Markov blanket for the sentiment variable, Y. The first stage aims at finding a parsimonious, yet expressive vocabulary, and the search for the "right" vocabulary takes into account dependency patterns amongst words. The first stage ends at step 4. with a subset of the words that is meant to be expressive enough to describe word patterns that lead to the emergence of the overall sentiment in the text (the MB_{DAG} for Y), as well as a list of words that are not part of the Markov Blanket (L), but which the algorithm cannot exclude (in step 3.) from being useful in expressing sentiments.

However, the initial MB_{DAG} may be highly suboptimal due to the application of repeated conditional independence tests [14], in steps 1. and 2., and propagation of errors in causal orientation [17]. Hence, Tabu Search is applied in the **second stage** (step 5.) to improve the predictive power of the structure of the initial Markov blanket. The algorithm stops after a fixed number of iterations or a fixed number of non-improving iterations.

These two steps are detailed in the rest of this section.

4.2 Description of the Algorithms

In the descriptions of the algorithms that follow, the relevant parameters are: a data set with V words and N documents; Y, the sentiment variable; δ, the maximum size of the separating sets (sets of words) considered for the conditional independence tests; α, the significance level for the G^2 statistical independence tests.[1]

Note that both the G^2 test of independence and the use of binary variables to encode presence/absence of words are choices dictated by our endeavor for a parsimonious, topic-independent vocabulary. Intuitively, we can divide the words into three groups: common words that are highly frequent in most documents of a collection, topical words that are highly frequent in a few documents, and rare words. Using presence/absence of words, rather than their frequency of occurrence, dampens the discriminative power of topical words, while selecting words with a statistically significant G^2 statistic favors words that are highly frequent overall. The composite effect is that words that are strongly associated with sentiment are retained. In fact, we can think of sentiments as behaving like "widespread topics" in terms of the frequency pattern of the words that lead to their emergence. Our methodology aims at removing "topical" words associated with narrow topics, while promoting those associated with sentiment, that is, widespread topics. This intuition can be formalized by placing each word on the "frequency spectrum" proposed in [18].

Search for an Initial Markov Blanket DAG. The first stage of $LrnTSMBC$ consists of the steps from 1. to 4. in Figure 2. It generates an initial MB_{DAG} for Y from the data that reflects dependency patterns among words in the collection of training documents [17].

Searching for Adjacent Nodes. The core of the search for a parsimonious vocabulary that is expressive enough to capture the overall sentiments of documents consists of the steps 1. and 2. There, independence and conditional independence G^2 tests are carried out according to a breadth first heuristic. In step 1. the function Adj is used to identify a list of words (corresponding to nodes of a Bayesian network) related to the sentiment variable, L_Y, and then in step 2. the function Adj is used to identify lists of words related to each word X_i in the list L_Y.

Following the intuition of a Bayesian network, the algorithm starts with a singleton graph containing the target node Y only. Then it selects those variables among $X_1, ..., X_V$ that are associated with Y within a path of length two in the graphical representation, that is, it finds potential parents and children (L_Y) of Y, and potential parents and children $(\cup_i L_{X_i})$ of nodes $X_i \in L_Y$, using conditional independence tests.

Through steps 1. and 2., the adjacencies are represented by undirected edges. At the end of step 2. we are left with an undirected graph over the words $Y \cup L_Y \cup_i L_{X_i}$, which contains the MB_{DAG} for Y in terms of pa_Y, ch_Y, and $pa\,ch_Y$—see Section 3.2 for the precise definition.

Orienting Edges. The algorithm $Ornt$ in step 3. is responsible for the orientation of the edges. The edges are oriented by repeatedly applying a set of four edge

---

[1] Intuitively, G^2 is a variation of the χ^2 test for independence of random variables. For a formal definition see [14].

TabuSrch $(MB_{DAG}, L, Max_{Iter})$

1. **init**: $best_{MB} = curr_{MB} = MB_{DAG}$, $best_{Score} = 0$
2. **repeat until** ($best_{Score}$ does not improve for k consecutive iterations)
   2.1. **form** $candidate_{Moves}$ for $curr_{MB}$
   2.2. **find** $best_{Move}$ among $candidate_{Moves}$ according to function **score**
   2.3. **if** ($best_{Score} <$ **score** ($best_{Move}$))
      2.3.1. **update** $best_{MB}$, by applying $best_{Move}$, and $best_{Score}$
      2.3.2. **add** $best_{Move}$ to $TabuList$ // not re-considered in the next m iterations
   2.4. **update** $current_{MB}$ by applying $best_{Move}$
3. **return** $best_{MB}$ // an MB_{DAG}

Fig. 3. Tabu search enhancement

orientation rules [14,19] described in detail in appendix A.2. These rules are meant to recover the true, unobservable directed acyclic graph (DAG) over the selected words. This algorithm provably guarantees to find the correct DAG in the limit (of infinite documents) [17]. The assumption underlying the asymptotic correctness argument is that every conditional independence statement that we can derive from the data also holds in the true graph, which is a typical assumption underlying methods for statistical learning of causal relations [15].

The edge orientation algorithm returns a (possibly) partially oriented DAG. In fact, while the *Ornt* algorithm guarantees the correctness of the result in the limit, it does not guarantee that all edges will be assigned a unique direction in a finite sample.

Forcing a Markov Blanket DAG. The algorithm *Trsfm* at step 4. transforms the output of step 3. into a proper MB_{DAG} by simply removing the undirected and bi-directed edges, along with the corresponding nodes, that is, words. These words are not thrown away, but are stored in the list L; these are words which were not removed from the battery of conditional independence tests, but for which there is uncertainty as to what role they may have in the MB_{DAG}.

Tabu Search Heuristic. In the final step the algorithm *TabuSrch* is applied to improve the initial MB_{DAG} and L in order to boost the predictive structure of the DAG amongst the words in the selected vocabulary. Our algorithm searches for solutions in the space of logical Markov Blankets, e.g., moves that result in cyclic graphs are not valid. In particular, four kinds of moves are allowed in *TabuSrch*: edge addition, edge deletion, edge reversal, and edge reversal with node pruning, as illustrated in Figure 4.

The algorithm runs for a fixed number of iterations, or until there is no improvement in the scoring criterion for a predetermined number of iterations. At each step, and for each allowed move, the corresponding MB_{DAG} is computed, its conditional probability factored, its predictions scored, and the best move

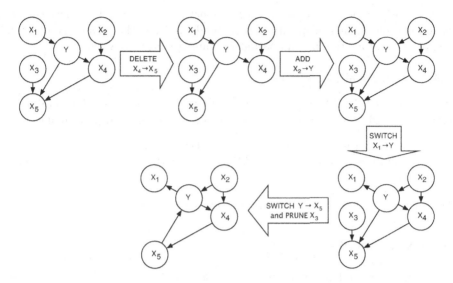

Fig. 4. An example of the moves allowed in Tabu Search

is then selected and applied. The best solution and best score at each step are tracked. The *Tabu list* keeps a record of m previous moves, so that moves in the Tabu list will not be repeated until their corresponding *Tabu tenure* expires. The value of m, called the Tabu tenure, is varied according to the complexity of the MB_{DAG}s in different problems. When the dependency structure of the Markov Blanket is very dense, the number of neighboring states that need to be considered may grow exponentially, so a larger Tabu tenure is preferred.

Implementations of simple versions of *TabuSrch* based on Tabu tenures between 7 and 12 have been found to work well in several settings where Tabu restrictions rule out a non-trivial portion of the otherwise available moves [16]. Our setting appears to be of this nature since the structure of the expected MB_{DAG}s is not complex; in our experiments we use a static Tabu tenure of 7.

4.3   Performing the Classification

Once the *LrnTSMBC* algorithm learns the classifier on the training documents, we need to perform the classification of all the documents in the testing set. We approach the classification as a multiple-class classification problem directly, i.e., we do not divide the problem into a series of binary classification problems. The overall sentiment of a new document is assigned according to its posterior probability given the words present in it. Formally, for each new document, $\{x_1, \ldots, x_V\}$, we compute: $\ell_i = \log \left[\frac{P(Y=y_i | \{x_1, \ldots, x_V\})}{P(Y=y_0 | \{x_1, \ldots, x_V\})} \right], \forall i = 1, \ldots, I$, where the y_is represent the possible values of the sentiment variable, $\{y_i\}_{i=0}^I$. We choose the sentiment that maximizes the log-odds, $i^* = \arg\max \ell_i$.

The classification is carried out using logistic regression, whose performance is comparable to more sophisticated methods and has the advantage of being completely automated, i.e., no parameter tuning is necessary [20].

4.4 Theoretical Properties

The proposed Tabu Search Markov Blanket Classifier has two fundamental properties that add "theoretical guarantees" to its good empirical performance.

1. TS-MBC learns the correct Markov blanket in the limit.
2. The complexity of training an TS-MBC is $O(N)$, i.e., linear in the number of documents N.

For an in depth analysis of these properties we refer to [17].

5   Experiments

We tested our method on the data set used in Pang et al [3], and on three proprietary collections of online news [5].

5.1   Movie Reviews Data

This data set contains approximately 29,000 posts to the rec.arts.movies.reviews newsgroup archived at the Internet Movie Database (IMDb). The original posts are available in the form of HTML pages. Some pre-processing was performed to produce the version of the data we used. Specifically, only reviews where authors' ratings were expressed explicitly (either by stars or by numerical values) were selected. Then explicit ratings were removed and converted into one of three categories: positive, negative, or neutral. Finally, 700 positive reviews and 700 negative reviews, which the authors of the corpus judged to be more extreme, were selected for our study. Various versions of the data are available online [4].

Pre-Processing. For the purpose of our study, *words* are strings of letters enclosed by non-letters to the left and to the right. Note that our definition excludes punctuation, even though exclamation signs and question marks may be helpful for the task of classifying sentiments. Intuitively the task of sentiment extraction is a hybrid task between authorship attribution and topic categorization; we look for frequent words, possibly not related to the context, that help express lexical patterns, as well as low frequency words which may be specific to few review styles, but very indicative of an opinion. We considered all the words that appeared in more than 8 documents as our input features, whereas words with lower counts were discarded since they are too rare to be helpful in the classification of many reviews. We were left with a total number of 7,716 words, as input features. In our experiments, we represented each document as a vector, $X := [X_1, ..., X_{7716}]$, of the size of the initial vocabulary, where each X_i is a binary random variable that takes the value of 1 if the ith word in the vocabulary is present in the document and the value of 0 otherwise.

5.2   Online News Data

This collection consists of three sets of 600 news articles each on the following topics: mergers and acquisitions (M&A, 600 documents), finance (600 documents), and mixed news (600 documents). These three corpora have been designed to exhibit increasing levels of specificity; M&A is the most specific corpus, Mixed News is the least specific one, and the news in the Finance corpus falls somewhere in between. Furthermore, the sentiments we consider are three: positive, neutral and negative. Each corpus contains 200 articles of each sentiment category. Articles were manually labeled with a document-level sentiment by three independent annotators from a pool of seven trained annotators; all documents in the corpus have at least a two-way consensus for their sentiment rating. The agreement rate between annotators was found to be consistently above 78%.

Online news aggregators[2] and specialist news sites[3] were used to identify suitable articles for inclusion. Articles were selected to ensure that they were not sarcastic and that they expressed sentiment concerning only one clearly identifiable entity. Articles in the M&A corpus concern only real or speculated mergers, acquisitions, take-overs or joint-ventures. The Finance corpus includes articles concerning all other corporate financial matters, except those that would merit inclusion in the M&A. Finally, the Mixed News corpus contains news and editorial content concerning a broad range of topics. A number of manual inspections of the corpora were conducted to ensure that all the above criteria were met, and to remove any duplicate items.

More in detail, six sentiment categories were initially available for annotation, as follows: (1,2) very positive or very negative: unreservedly or overwhelmingly positive or negative; (3,4) positive or negative: unreservedly, but only mildly positive or negative, or containing mixed sentiment which on balance was positive or negative; (5) neutral: entirely objective, expressing no sentiment; (6) balanced: containing both positive and negative sentiment with no clear bias towards either. All articles that did not have at least a two-way consensus, and those that had a consensus of balanced, were removed. The resulting corpora each contained 200 items of each of the remaining five sentiment categories. To obtain the data used in this paper, the two positive and negative categories were collapsed into a single positive and negative category, by randomly selecting 100 articles in each corpus from each of the four non-neutral sentiment categories.

Pre-Processing. For the purpose of our study, *words* are strings of letters enclosed by non-letters to the left and to the right. Note that our definition excludes punctuation, even though exclamation signs and question marks may be helpful for the task of classifying sentiments. We performed within-topic classification experiments for which we considered all the words in each corpus as the starting pool from which to extract the final vocabulary. This led to starting

---

[2] E.g. Google News (http://news.google.com).

[3] E.g. Reuters (www.reuters.com), This is Money (www.thisismoney.co.uk),The Motley Fool (www.fool.co.uk) and The Register (www.theregister.com).

Table 1. Characteristics of Online News Data

Data set	Problem	# Words	Examples	Variable Types
Movie Reviews	Positive/Negative	7,716	1,400	Binary
Online News	Positive/Neutral/Negative	8,492	600 × 3	Binary

vocabularies of sizes 11220, 10531, and 15685, for the Finance, M&A and Mixed News corpora respectively.

5.3   Experimental Setup

As mentioned in section 4, the parameters relevant to our experiments were: δ, the maximum size of the separating sets to consider for conditional independence tests in Adj; and α, the significance level of the tests used to decide whether to accept or reject each of these tests. In Table 2 we show the specific values for δ and α which we considered in our experimental design.

In order to estimate the predictive accuracy of our classifier on new documents, we used a five-fold cross-validation scheme for the sentiment classification experiments. In particular, we used a nested cross-validation scheme. That is, we divided each of the five training sets of documents (one for each cross-validation fold, consisting of 4/5 of the documents respectively) into a sub-training and a sub-testing set of documents, at random, using 70% and 30% of the training documents respectively. Steps 1. to 4. would then make use of the sub-training set of documents, whereas step 5. would refine the MB_{DAG} on the sub-testing set of documents, with the objective of avoiding over-fitting. This process would then be repeated for each pair (δ, α) of the configuration parameters in Table 2.

Table 2. Experimental Parameter Configurations

Performance Measures	Depth of Search δ	Significance Level α
AUC, Accuracy	1, 2, 3	0.001, 0.005, 0.01, 0.05

The dominant configuration of parameters (in terms of accuracy on the sub-testing set of documents) would then be chosen as *the best configuration*. Then, the best configuration MB_{DAG} for the sentiment variable for a given cross-validation fold, is used to measure the performance on the testing data for that fold.

5.4   Results and Analysis

We compared the performances of our two-stage MB classifier with those of four widely used classifiers: a naïve Bayes classifier based on the multivariate Bernoulli distribution with Laplace prior for unseen words, discussed in Nigam et al. [21], a support vector machine (SVM) classifier, discussed by Joachims [22], an implementation of the voted Perceptron, discussed in Freund and Schapire [23], and a maximum entropy conditional random field learner, introduced by Lafferty et al. [24].

The first two columns of Table 3 compare the two-stage MBC with the performance of the other classifiers using the *whole feature set* as input. More features did not necessarily lead to better performance, as the classifiers were not able to distinguish discriminating words from noise. In such a situation it is reasonable to expect a good performance of the SVM with respect to the other classifiers. As shown in table 3, the two-Stage MB classifier selects 32 relevant words out of 7,716 words in the vocabulary. The feature reduction ratio is 99.58%; the cross-validated AUC based on the 32 words and their dependencies is 87.52%, which is about 5% higher than the best of the other four methods; the corresponding cross-validated accuracy is 78.07%, which is comparable to maximum entropy but less accurate than SVM.[4] The first stage of the MB classifier is able to automatically identify a very discriminating subset of features (or words) that are relevant to the target variable (Y, the label of the review). Specifically, the selected features are those that form the Markov Blanket for Y. Other methods need to be paired with a variable selection strategy.

Table 3. Average performances of various classifiers on all words, on the same number of words selected by information gain, and on the same exact words selected by the Markov blanket classifier. These are the results for the movie reviews data. Notes: ** The cross-validated AUC corresponding to the MBC is obtained performing the classification on the subset of 32 selected words, rather than using all the input words.

Input	All Words		32 Words by Information Gain		32 Words by Markov Blanket		
Method	AUC (%)	Accuracy (%)	AUC (%)	Accuracy (%)	AUC (%)	Accuracy (%)	# Words Selected
MBC	**87.52****	78.08			**87.52**	**78.08**	**32**
Naïve Bayes	82.61	66.22	**81.46**	72.43	81.81	73.36	
SVM	81.32	**84.07**	67.88	72.21	69.47	73.00	
Voted perc.	77.09	70.00	78.68	71.71	80.61	73.93	
Max. entropy	75.79	79.43	69.11	**72.86**	69.81	73.44	

At this point, however, the source of the differential in the observed accuracies and AUC is not clear. A possibility could be that the competing methods perform better on an optimized subset of words as it is the case for the two stages of MBC classifier—we expect this to be not true for the SVM though, which typically benefits from a large amount of predictors. To investigate this point, we conducted two additional sets of experiments for the competing classifiers. The corresponding results are reported in columns three to six. Both sets of the experiments optimize the vocabulary that is used to perform predictions

---

[4] Current SVM implementations are very sensitive to the capacity parameter.

Table 4. Average performances of various classifiers on all words, on the same number of words selected by information gain, and on the same exact words selected by the Markov blanket classifier. These are the results for the financial, mergers & acquisitions and mixed online news data, from top to bottom respectively. Notes: ** The cross-validated accuracy corresponding to the MBC is obtained performing the classification on the subset of 36 (43) selected words, rather than using all the input words.

Input	All Words		36(43) Words by Information Gain		36(43) Words by Markov Blanket		
Method	Kappa (%)	Accuracy (%)	Kappa (%)	Accuracy (%)	Kappa (%)	Accuracy (%)	# Selected Words
MBC	N/A	73.21**			N/A	**73.21**	**36**
Naïve Bayes	41.99	61.33	10.00	40.00	23.75	49.16	
Poisson	55.25	70.16	38.00	58.66	44.99	63.33	
Voted perc.	0.75	33.83	19.75	46.50	22.25	48.16	
Max. entropy	**59.99**	**73.33**	**54.50**	**69.66**	**59.00**	72.66	
MBC	N/A	75.32**			N/A	**75.32**	**43**
Naïve Bayes	44.00	62.66	9.50	39.70	27.50	51.66	
Poisson	59.75	73.16	46.75	64.50	48.75	65.84	
Voted perc.	7.00	38.00	7.75	38.50	16.75	44.50	
Max. entropy	**66.25**	**77.50**	**58.25**	**72.16**	**58.25**	72.16	
MBC	N/A	76.68**			N/A	**76.68**	**43**
Naïve Bayes	47.75	65.16	12.25	41.50	28.50	52.33	
Poisson	57.75	71.84	39.00	59.33	44.99	63.33	
Voted perc.	1.50	34.33	9.25	39.50	10.50	40.33	
Max. entropy	**71.25**	**80.84**	**53.49**	**69.00**	**62.50**	75.00	

about sentiments using a feature selection criterion first, then feed optimized vocabulary into the competing classifiers as predictor variables. In particular, the first set of results is obtained by making predictions on words selected by information gain. The second set of results is obtained by making predictions using the words selected by MBC. A comparison between performances of competing classifiers on vocabularies by information gain selection criterion versus those by MBC tells us about the differential effect of MBC as a word selection criterion. A comparison between performances of MBC and those of competing classifiers, both on the full set of words and on two version of optimized vocabularies tells us about the differential effect of MBC as a classifier.

Columns three and four in Table 3 compare the performance of the two-stage MBC with others classifiers using the *same number of features* selected by information gain. In fact, information gain allows us to rank the features from most to least discriminating but gives no indication of how many words are correlated with the sentiment variable, significantly beyond chance. In this second comparison the two-Stage MB classifier dominates the other methods both in terms of AUC and accuracy, though it is not clear (yet) whether the extra performance comes form the different feature selection strategies, or from the dependencies encoded by the MB. To investigate this point, columns five and six in Table 3 compare the performance of the two-stage MBC with others classifiers using the *same exact features*. We find that the set of words selected as part of the Markov blanket for the sentiment variable contains better discriminative words, in fact all the four competing classifiers performed better on the set of features in the Markov blanket. Further, these words are also significantly discriminative beyond pure chance.

We repeated the same battery of experiments on the online news corpora and obtained similar results. Notice that AUC is for binary class problems only thus we report the Kappa statistics instead, which intuitively measures the incremental performance of a classifier with respect to the baseline accuracy[5]. The baseline accuracy is the accuracy of randomly guessing the sentiment class, and in the three class problem the expected accuracy is 33.33%. We did not report the results for the SVM because a multi-class implementation was not readily available to us, we reported instead the accuracy of a Poisson classifier [26,18].

These experiments are in line with more results we have obtained on several medical data sets [27]. Further, according to the empirical findings of Pang et al [3], the baseline accuracy for human-selected vocabularies can be set at about 70%. Comparing the human intuition to our fully automated machine learning technique (two-stage MBC), we observe a non-negligible improvement.

6   Discussion

The main findings that emerge from our experiments are as follows.

1. The problem of learning sentiments is essentially a word selection problem.

Pairwise dependencies amongst words, and dependent patterns, play a crucial role in finding a parsimonious, yet expressive vocabulary. The two-stage MB classifier leads to more robust predictions by: (i) selecting statistically discriminating words with respect to the sentiment variable, and (ii) learning those dependencies among the words that lead to the emergence of sentiments in the texts. Although the Tabu heuristic search in the second stage may return a final MB_{DAG} where few dependencies are present amongst words, the initial MB_{DAG} always includes a rich dependency structure.

2. The accuracy of alternative methods can be improved by using the parsimonious vocabulary selected in the first stage of TS-MBC.

Tables 3 and 4 present the performance of several widely used classifiers in extracting sentiments from movie reviews (two sentiments) and online news (three

---

[5] The kappa statistic was introduced by Carletta [25] to assess the quality of a classifier in terms of accuracy above a random baseline. It is defined as $\kappa = \frac{A-R}{1-R}$, where A is the empirical probability of agreement on a category, and R is the probability of agreement for two annotators that label documents at random (with the empirically observed frequency of each label). Hence kappa ranges from -1 to $+1$; positive values indicate a performance better than the random baseline, whereas negative values indicate a worse performance.

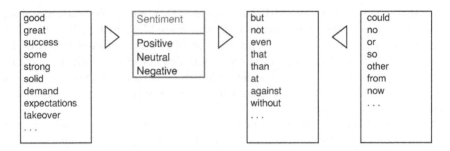

Fig. 5. An example of the words in the final vocabulary and their connections

sentiments). Using the words selected by the TS-MBC as predictors improves both cross-validated accuracy and AUC for all classifiers. See [28] for more details.

3. Words that are indicative of sentiments are not "rare."

The starting pools of words corresponding to online news data contained ten to 15 thousand words. A sample of the words we used to perform the experiments in Tables 3 and 4 is shown in Figure 5. Most of the words appear more than eight times every ten thousand words, and several of them are non-contextual, high-frequency words.

4. TS-MBC tends to select words that are relevant and "exportable."

Words that are intuitively important in predicting sentiments, e.g. *important, success, positive, solid, expected, strong*, as well as pair of non-contextual words, e.g., *no-but, or-not, POS-but, NEG-but* and others (e.g., see Figure 5), were selected in the final vocabulary by the TS-MBC procedure. These same words were not deemed as important for predicting sentiments according to their information gain score, which may be one of the reasons behind the poorer performance entailed by the words selected according to it.

Furthermore, as we discussed in 4.2 in more detail, both the G^2 test of independence and the use of binary variables to encode presence/absence of words are choices suited to creating a parsimonious, "topic-independent" vocabulary. For example, words that capture linguistic issues such as negation, ifs, buts, however, and comparisons appear in the selected vocabularies. Our methodology aims at removing words associated with latent concepts that span few documents, i.e., topics, while promoting those words associated with latent concepts that span a large number of documents, i.e., sentiments.[6].

In our experiments, however, we observed only a modest overlap between the selected vocabularies for the three data sets. Given the small number of texts in our data sets, it is possible that several different subsets of a small number of words may lead to very good classification results (i.e., presence of several local

---

[6] This intuition can be formalized by placing each word on the "frequency spectrum" proposed in [18].

optima), and that the TS-MBC may be finding a few of them, but different ones for different collections. More experiments on a larger number of corpora, and on more documents, are needed in order to draw stronger conclusions.

5. Tabu search improves the prediction performance.

6. The prediction performance is consistent on two and three class problems.

We note that our investigations generalize previous attempts particularly because we are working with both two-class and three-class problems, whereas previous works have explored two-class problems. Further, our results are consistent on both problem settings.

7   Conclusions

In this paper we have proposed the Tabu-search-enhanced Markov blanket classifier (TS-MBC) and we have shown that: (1) it is a fully automated system able to select a parsimonious vocabulary, customized for the classification task at hand in terms of size and relevant features; (2) it is able to capture and take advantage of dependencies among words while selecting the vocabulary; (3) it learns the correct Markov blanket in the limit and its complexity is linear in the number of training documents.

Our experiments show that the problem of sentiment classification is essentially a word selection problem, and our findings suggest that words that occur often, along with their statistical dependencies and few strong adjectives, include most of the vocabulary needed to express sentiments and perform reasonable predictions. As a feature selection method, our TS-MBC leads to vocabularies that enhance the predictive performance of several popular classifiers with respect to vocabularies selected with information gain. When paired with logistic regression to perform classification, our TS-MBC leads to predictive performance comparable to that of state-of-the-art classification methods. Most importantly, the limited size of the vocabulary allows for interpretability and re-usability.

In conclusion, we believe that in order to capture sentiments we have to move beyond the search for richer feature sets and the independence assumption. Rather it is crucial to capture those dependencies amongst words that lead to the emergence of context and meaning.

7.1   Future Work

In future work we plan to investigate: (1) strategies that allow TS-MBC to reach close local optima starting from corpora with different degree of topicality, i.e., strategies to select overlapping, more consistent vocabularies for predicting sentiments; (2) the performance with larger data sets, more sentiment categories, and on shorter texts, e.g., sentences; (3) cross-genre transferability; (4) the effect of pre-processing the starting pool of words, e.g., through the use of stemming, POS tagging, lemmatization or thesauri, as well as the use of generalized features for non-word, e.g., numbers, dates and punctuation; (5) how performance varies when reducing the size of the initial vocabulary, selected by frequency in corpus.

Acknowledgments

The authors wish to thank William Cohen, Clark Glymour, and Peter Spirtes, at the School of Computer Science of Carnegie Mellon University, for helpful discussions and insights; Joseph Ramsey, for helpful discussions and support during the implementation of the algorithms; Lillian Lee and Bo Pang at Cornell University for helpful discussions and suggestions; Roy Lipski for helpful suggestions and for the sharing the online news data, prepared by Infonic Ltd.; and the ACM SIGKDD anonymous reviewers for helpful comments.

References

1. Golbeck, J., Hendler, J.: Accuracy of metrics for inferring trust and reputation. In: Proceedings of 14th International Conference on Knowledge Engineering and Knowledge Management. (2004)
2. Airoldi, E.M., Anderson, A.G., Fienberg, S.E., Skinner, K.K.: Who wrote Ronald Reagan radio addresses? Bayesian Analysis 1 (2006) 289–320
3. Pang, B., Lee, L., Vaithyanathan, S.: Thumbs up? sentiment classification using machine learning techniques. In: Proceedings of the 2002 Conference on Empirical Methods in Natural Language Processing. (2002) 79–86
4. Online movie reviews data. http://www.cs.cornell.edu/people/pabo/movie-review-data/.
5. Online news data. http://www.infonic.com/.
6. Osgood, C., Suci, G., Tannenbaum, P.: The Measurement of Meaning. University of Illinois Press, Chicago, Illinois (1957)
7. Hatzivassiloglou, V., McKeown, K.: Predicting the semantic orientation of adjectives. In: Proceedings of the Eighth Conference on European Chapter of the Association for Computational Linguistics, ACL (1997) 174–181
8. Huettner, A., Subasic, P.: Fuzzy typing for document management. In: Association for Computational Linguistics 2000 Companion Volume: Tutorial Abstracts and Demonstration Notes. (2000) 26–27
9. Das, S., Chen, M.: Yahoo! for amazon: Sentiment parsing from small talk on the web. In: Proceedings of the Eighth Asia Pacific Finance Association Annual Conference, APFA (2001)
10. Turney, P., Littman, M.: Unsupervised learning of semantic orientation from a hundred-billion-word corpus. Technical Report EGB-1094, National Research Council, Canada (2002)
11. Turney, P.: Thumbs up or thumbs down? semantic orientation applied to unsupervised classification of reviews. In: Proceedings Fortieth Annual Meeting of the Association for Computational Linguistics. (2002) 417–424
12. Dave, K., Lawrence, S., Pennock, D.: Mining the peanut gallery: Opinion extraction and semantic classification of product reviews. In: roceedings of the Twelfth International Conference on World Wide Web. (2003) 519–528

13. Liu, H., Lieberman, H., Selker, T.: A model of textual affect sensing using real-world knowledge. In: Proceedings of the Eighth International Conference on Intelligent User Interfaces. (2003) 125–132
14. Spirtes, P., Glymour, C., Scheines, R.: Causation, Prediction, and Search. MIT Press (2000)
15. Pearl, J.: Causality: Models, Reasoning, and Inference. Cambridge University Press (2000)
16. Glover, F.: Tabu Search. Kluwer Academic Publishers (1997)
17. Bai, X.: Tabu search enhanced graphical models for classification of high dimensional data. Technical Report CMU-CALD-05-101, School of Computer Science, Carnegie Mellon University (2005)
18. Airoldi, E., Cohen, W., Fienberg, S.: Bayesian models for frequent terms in text. Manuscript (2005)
19. Spirtes, P., Meek, C.: Learning bayesian networks with discrete variables from data. In: Proceedings of the First International Conference on Knowledge Discovery and Data Mining, AAAI Press (1995) 294–299
20. Komarek, P., Moore, A.: Making logistic regression a core data mining tool (2005) Manuscript.
21. Nigam, K., McCallum, A., Thrun, S., Mitchell, T.: Text classification from labeled and unlabeled documents using em. Machine Learning **39** (2000) 103–134
22. Joachims, T.: A statistical learning model of text classification with support vector machines. In: Proceedings of the Conference on Research and Development in Information Retrieval, ACM (2001) 128–136
23. Freund, Y., Schapire, R.: Large margin classification using the perceptron algorithm. Machine Learning **37** (1999) 277–296
24. Lafferty, J., McCallum, A., Pereira, F.: Conditional random fields: Probabilistic models for segmenting and labeling sequence data. In: Proceedings of the Eighteenth International Conference on Machine Learning. (2001) 282–289
25. Carletta, J.: Assessing agreement on classification tasks: The kappa statistic. Computational Linguistics **22** (1996) 249–254
26. Airoldi, E., Anderson, A., Fienberg, S., Skinner, K.: Who wrote Ronald Reagan radio addresses? Journal of Bayesian Analysis (2005) to appear.
27. Ramsey, J., Bai, X., Glymour, C., Padman, R., Spirtis, P.: Mb fan search classifier for large data sets with few cases. Working paper, Department of Philosophy, Carnegie Mellon University (2004)
28. Bai, X., Padman, R., Airoldi, E.: Sentiment extraction from unstructured text using tabu search-enhanced markov blanket. In: Proceedings of KDD Workshop on Mining for and from the Semantic Web (MSWKDD). (2004)
29. Cohen, W.: Minor-third: Methods for identi-fying names and ontological relations in text using heuristics for inducing regularities from data. http://minorthird.sourceforge.net (2004)
30. Bishop, Y., Fienberg, S., Holland, P.: Discrete Multivariate Analysis. Theory and practice. MIT Press (1975)
31. Chickering, D., Meek, C., Heckerman, D.: Large-sample learning of bayesian networks is np-hard. In: Proceedings of Nineteenth Conference on Uncertainty in Artificial Intelligence, Morgan Kaufmann (2003) 124–133
32. Engstrom, C.: Topic dependence in sentiment classification. Technical Report 07-22-2004, St Edmunds College, University of Cambridge (2004)
33. Finn, A., Kushmerick, N.: Learning to classify documents according to genre. In: IJCAI-03 Workshop on Computational Approaches to Style Analysis and Synthesis. (2003)

34. Koller, D., Sahami, M.: Towards optimal feature selection. In: Proceedings of the Thirteenth International Conference on Machine Learning, Morgan Kaufmann (1996) 284–292
35. Lewis, D.D.: Evaluating Text Categorization. In: Proceedings of Speech and Natural Language Workshop, Morgan Kaufmann (1991) 312–318
36. Margaritis, D., Thrun, S.: Bayesian network induction via local neighborhoods. In: Advances in Neural Information Processing System. (1999)
37. Mitchell, T.: Machine Learning. McGraw-Hill (1997)
38. Montgomery, A., Kannan, S.: Learning about customers without asking. GSIA Working Paper,Carnegie Mellon University (2002)
39. Piatetsky-Shapiro, G., Steingold, S.: Measuring lift quality in database marketing. SIGKDD Explorations, **2** (2000) 7680
40. Provost, F., Fawcett, T., Kohavi, R.: The case against accuracy estimation for comparing induction algorithms. In: Proceedings of the Fifteenth International Conference on Machine Learning. (1998) 445–453
41. E.P. Xing, M.J., Karp, R.: Feature selection for high-dimensional genomic microarray data. In: Proceedings 18th International Conf. on Machine Learning, Morgan Kaufmann, San Francisco, CA (2001)

A   Sketch of the Algorithms

Below we present a sketch of the algorithms used in 4.2.

A.1   Searching for Adjacent Nodes

Adj (Node Y, Node List L, Depth δ, Significance α)

1. $A_Y := \{X_i \in L: X_i \text{ is dependent of } Y \text{ at level } \alpha\}$
2. **for** $X_i \in A_Y$ and **for** all distinct subsets $S \subset \{A_Y \backslash X_i\}^d$
    2.1. **if** X_i is independent of Y given S at level α
    2.2. **then** remove X_i from A_Y
3. **for** $X_i \in A_Y$
    3.1. $A_{X_i} := \{X_j \in L: X_j \text{ is dependent of } X_i \text{ at level } \alpha, j \neq i\}$
    3.2. **for** all distinct subsets $S \subset \{A_{X_i}\}^d$
        3.2.1. **if** X_i is independent of Y given S at level α
        3.2.2. **then** remove X_i from A_Y
4. **return** A_Y

The conditional independence tests are meant to test whether a pair of words is independent conditionally on a set of words. The set of words in the conditional statement is called the separating set, denoted as $sepSet(X, Z)$, and formally defined as a mapping of a set of nodes s.t. $(X \perp Z \mid sepSet(X, Z))$.

A.2   Orienting Edges

Ornt (Graph G)

Apply the following 4 rules iteratively wherever it applies:

1. **Rule 1 (Collider Orientation Rule): for** each triple of vertices (X, V, Z) in G, **if** pair (X, V) and (V, Z) are adjacent, pair (X, Z) are not adjacent (i.e. a pattern: $X - V - Z$), and **if** $V \notin sepSet(X, Z)$, **then** orient $X - V - Z$ as $X \to V \leftarrow Z$.
2. **Rule 2: for** each triple of vertices (X, V, Z) in G, **if** $X \to V$ and V, Z are adjacent, X, Z are not adjacent (i.e. a pattern $X \to V - Z$), **and** there is no arrow into V, **then** orient $V - Z$ as $V \to Z$.
3. **Rule 3: if** $(X \to Z \to V)$, **and** $\exists$ (undirected edge between X and V, i.e. pattern $X - V$), **then** orient $X - V$ as $X \to V$
4. **Rule 4: for** any undirected edge connected to X (i.e. $X - V$), **if** $\exists$ (Z, W) s.t. Z adjacent to X, W is adjacent to X, Z is not adjacent to W, and there is a pattern $W \to V \leftarrow Z$, **then** orient $X - V$ as $X \leftarrow V$

A.3   Forcing a Markov Blanket DAG

Trsfm (Graph G, Target Y)

1. **for** any X in G s. t. $X \leftrightarrow Y$ or $X - Y$, reorient this edge as $X \to Y$
2. **for** any X, Z in G s. t. $Z - X \to Y$ ($Z \notin \{Y\} \cup ParentChild(Y)$), remove the edge $Z - X$
3. **for** any X , $X \notin \{Y\} \cup ParentChild(Y) \cup ParentChild(ParentChild(Y))$
   1.1. remove X and all the associated edges
4. **return** G

Author Index

Lecture Notes in Artificial Intelligence (LNAI)

Vol. 4087: F. Schwenker, S. Marinai (Eds.), Artificial Neural Networks in Pattern Recognition. IX, 299 pages. 2006.

Vol. 4068: H. Schärfe, P. Hitzler, P. Øhrstrøm (Eds.), Conceptual Structures: Inspiration and Application. XI, 455 pages. 2006.

Vol. 4065: P. Perner (Ed.), Advances in Data Mining. XI, 592 pages. 2006.

Vol. 4062: G. Wang, J.F. Peters, A. Skowron, Y. Yao (Eds.), Rough Sets and Knowledge Technology. XX, 810 pages. 2006.

Vol. 4049: S. Parsons, N. Maudet, P. Moraitis, I. Rahwan (Eds.), Argumentation in Multi-Agent Systems. XIV, 313 pages. 2006.

Vol. 4048: L. Goble, J.-J.C.. Meyer (Eds.), Deontic Logic and Artificial Normative Systems. X, 273 pages. 2006.

Vol. 4045: D. Barker-Plummer, R. Cox, N. Swoboda (Eds.), Diagrammatic Representation and Inference. XII, 301 pages. 2006.

Vol. 4031: M. Ali, R. Dapoigny (Eds.), Advances in Applied Artificial Intelligence. XXIII, 1353 pages. 2006.

Vol. 4029: L. Rutkowski, R. Tadeusiewicz, L.A. Zadeh, J.M. Zurada (Eds.), Artificial Intelligence and Soft Computing – ICAISC 2006. XXI, 1235 pages. 2006.

Vol. 4027: H.L. Larsen, G. Pasi, D. Ortiz-Arroyo, T. Andreasen, H. Christiansen (Eds.), Flexible Query Answering Systems. XVIII, 714 pages. 2006.

Vol. 4021: E. André, L. Dybkjær, W. Minker, H. Neumann, M. Weber (Eds.), Perception and Interactive Technologies. XI, 217 pages. 2006.

Vol. 4020: A. Bredenfeld, A. Jacoff, I. Noda, Y. Takahashi (Eds.), RoboCup 2005: Robot Soccer World Cup IX. XVII, 727 pages. 2006.

Vol. 4013: L. Lamontagne, M. Marchand (Eds.), Advances in Artificial Intelligence. XIII, 564 pages. 2006.

Vol. 4012: T. Washio, A. Sakurai, K. Nakajima, H. Takeda, S. Tojo, M. Yokoo (Eds.), New Frontiers in Artificial Intelligence. XIII, 484 pages. 2006.

Vol. 4008: J.C. Augusto, C.D. Nugent (Eds.), Designing Smart Homes. XI, 183 pages. 2006.

Vol. 4005: G. Lugosi, H.U. Simon (Eds.), Learning Theory. XI, 656 pages. 2006.

Vol. 3978: B. Hnich, M. Carlsson, F. Fages, F. Rossi (Eds.), Recent Advances in Constraints. VIII, 179 pages. 2006.

Vol. 3963: O. Dikenelli, M.-P. Gleizes, A. Ricci (Eds.), Engineering Societies in the Agents World VI. XII, 303 pages. 2006.

Vol. 3960: R. Vieira, P. Quaresma, M.d.G.V. Nunes, N.J. Mamede, C. Oliveira, M.C. Dias (Eds.), Computational Processing of the Portuguese Language. XII, 274 pages. 2006.

Vol. 3955: G. Antoniou, G. Potamias, C. Spyropoulos, D. Plexousakis (Eds.), Advances in Artificial Intelligence. XVII, 611 pages. 2006.

Vol. 3949: F. A. Savacı (Ed.), Artificial Intelligence and Neural Networks. IX, 227 pages. 2006.

Vol. 3946: T.R. Roth-Berghofer, S. Schulz, D.B. Leake (Eds.), Modeling and Retrieval of Context. XI, 149 pages. 2006.

Vol. 3944: J. Quiñonero-Candela, I. Dagan, B. Magnini, F. d'Alché-Buc (Eds.), Machine Learning Challenges. XIII, 462 pages. 2006.

Vol. 3937: H. La Poutré, N.M. Sadeh, S. Janson (Eds.), Agent-Mediated Electronic Commerce. X, 227 pages. 2006.

Vol. 3932: B. Mobasher, O. Nasraoui, B. Liu, B. Masand, Advances in Web Mining and Web Usage Analysis. X, 189 pages. 2006.

Vol. 3930: D.S. Yeung, Z.-Q. Liu, X.-Z. Wang, H. Yan (Eds.), Advances in Machine Learning and Cybernetics. XXI, 1110 pages. 2006.

Vol. 3918: W.K. Ng, M. Kitsuregawa, J. Li, K. Chang (Eds.), Advances in Knowledge Discovery and Data Mining. XXIV, 879 pages. 2006.

Vol. 3913: O. Boissier, J. Padget, V. Dignum, G. Lindemann, E. Matson, S. Ossowski, J.S. Sichman, J. Vázquez-Salceda (Eds.), Coordination, Organizations, Institutions, and Norms in Multi-Agent Systems. XII, 259 pages. 2006.

Vol. 3910: S.A. Brueckner, G.D.M. Serugendo, D. Hales, F. Zambonelli (Eds.), Engineering Self-Organising Systems. XII, 245 pages. 2006.

Vol. 3904: M. Baldoni, U. Endriss, A. Omicini, P. Torroni (Eds.), Declarative Agent Languages and Technologies III. XII, 245 pages. 2006.

Vol. 3900: F. Toni, P. Torroni (Eds.), Computational Logic in Multi-Agent Systems. XVII, 427 pages. 2006.

Vol. 3899: S. Frintrop, VOCUS: A Visual Attention System for Object Detection and Goal-Directed Search. XIV, 216 pages. 2006.

Vol. 3898: K. Tuyls, P.J. 't Hoen, K. Verbeeck, S. Sen (Eds.), Learning and Adaption in Multi-Agent Systems. X, 217 pages. 2006.

Vol. 3891: J.S. Sichman, L. Antunes (Eds.), Multi-Agent-Based Simulation VI. X, 191 pages. 2006.

Vol. 3890: S.G. Thompson, R. Ghanea-Hercock (Eds.), Defence Applications of Multi-Agent Systems. XII, 141 pages. 2006.

Vol. 3885: V. Torra, Y. Narukawa, A. Valls, J. Domingo-Ferrer (Eds.), Modeling Decisions for Artificial Intelligence. XII, 374 pages. 2006.

Vol. 3881: S. Gibet, N. Courty, J.-F. Kamp (Eds.), Gesture in Human-Computer Interaction and Simulation. XIII, 344 pages. 2006.

Vol. 3874: R. Missaoui, J. Schmidt (Eds.), Formal Concept Analysis. X, 309 pages. 2006.

Vol. 3873: L. Maicher, J. Park (Eds.), Charting the Topic Maps Research and Applications Landscape. VIII, 281 pages. 2006.

Vol. 3864: Y. Cai, J. Abascal (Eds.), Ambient Intelligence in Everyday Life. XII, 323 pages. 2006.

Vol. 3863: M. Kohlhase (Ed.), Mathematical Knowledge Management. XI, 405 pages. 2006.